# TONGA ISLANDS

Niuafo'ou

Niuatoputapu

S O U T H   P A C I F I C   O C E A

Fonualei

Late

**VAVA'U GROUP**

Kao

Tofua

**HA'APAI GROUP**

Nomuka

Tongatapu

'Eua

Ata

N
W — E
S

0      50      100      150
KILOMETERS

# IN THE EYE OF
# THE STORM

# IN THE EYE OF THE STORM

## John H. Groberg

BOOKCRAFT
Salt Lake City, Utah

Library of Congress Catalog Card Number: 93-72856
ISBN 0-88494-900-1

First Printing, 1993

Printed in the United States of America

# Contents

# *Acknowledgments*

I wish to thank my wife, Jean, for her personal encouragement, support, and wisdom in helping develop this book, as well as the support and help of my parents, D. V. and Jennie H. Groberg, and our children, Nancy, Elizabeth, Marilyn, Jane, Gayle, John E., Susan, Thomas, Jennie, Viki, and Emily. Susan, Viki, and Emily have been particularly helpful in typing and proofreading.

I also acknowledge the wonderful people of Tonga, many of whom have moved beyond the veil but have left a legacy of faith that is difficult to describe.

My special thanks go to Richard Romney and Jennifer Scott, who have donated many hours in reading, editing, typing, retyping, and polishing the manuscript. I also thank the many others who have helped so much in many different ways.

I acknowledge the support and encouragement of several of my colleagues. Without their encouragement, this book would not be written. They know who they are, so without naming them I simply say thanks!

This is not an official publication of the Church. Although I have been helped in its preparation, I alone am responsible for the views it expresses.

# Introduction

Nearly forty years have passed since I began my first mission to Tonga. At the urging of many people whom I admire, I have attempted to describe some of the experiences and feelings I encountered those many years ago. The main purpose of this book is to emphasize the overwhelming need for faith in our lives.

I realize that in some ways I am describing a time and a place and circumstances that no longer exist. Yet in other ways, I am describing feelings and challenges that are as old as time and as fresh as the morning sun. I am convinced that regardless of the physical background or the decade our life's experiences are cast against, the need for love and faith to bring meaning to our lives and reason for our decisions remains unchanged.

I do not apologize for the time, the place, or the circumstances described, as that was the way it was. I suppose most people who have passed through this planet earth have lived and died closer to the type of life described herein than the hectic one we live in America today. We all need more faith, and I know we can learn from others.

In looking back and reading letters and other items written at the time, I have tried to describe how I felt then. I had no feeling that I was going into a particularly hard situation or that things were going to be tough. I had no thought of doing anything unusual, but rather simply wanted to do my best to get through each day doing as much good and as little damage as possible.

I have not attempted to analyze carefully what was going on in other people's minds or to make a sociological or psychological study, but have tried to relate things as I felt them from a twenty-year-old point of view. I suppose to a small child a horse may appear as big and fearsome as a huge monster to a grown-up. We all see and feel things based on our background and upbringing and the perceptions we have of places and people and motives at the time. I realize that some of the things I felt could be oversized or undersized and differ from how someone else might perceive them, but to me at the time, this is how things were.

I have heard people say, "Well, those people lived such a simple life and had such simple faith, it doesn't really apply to us today." I disagree.

First, their life was not so simple. At first I thought their life-style was simple, but I soon realized it was as complex as ours—not in a physical "rush here and scurry there" context, but in the context of interpersonal relationships, in finding one's place in society, and in coming to peace with God and with one's role in life. In these ways their life was no different from ours—neither more simple nor more complex—just set against a different background. Certain physical inventions may make parts of living more convenient today, but the need for faith and love has never changed—nor will it.

Second, I would not characterize their faith by the English word *simple,* but rather the word *profound.* If we say there is a "simple faith," then by extension we need to say there is a more complex or sophisticated faith and that one faith may be superior to the other. I do not believe this. I do not believe there are various types of faith, such as simple or advanced or complex or sophisticated. I believe there is just faith or lack of faith. We either have faith or we don't. Of course, some have stronger faith than others.

To me faith is like a flame; it may be as small as a tiny candle or as great as a roaring fire. A small candle can become a roaring fire or a roaring fire can be reduced to a small candle, depending on what we feed it. Both are natural flames with the power to grow or reduce; to die or consume, as opposed to a flashlight or other mechanical device that may give temporary light but cannot grow beyond its original power source.

In this world, not everyone can afford mechanical lights, but all people over all time—rich or poor, young or old, male or female—can afford fires. The growth of our personal flame depends on our faith, not on our wealth or other worldly factors.

A flame is a great refiner. I am intrigued by Malachi's words of purging and refining through fire: "But who may abide the day of his coming? and who shall stand when he appeareth? for he is like a refiner's fire, and like fullers' soap: And he shall sit as a refiner and purifier of silver. . . . For, behold, the day cometh, that shall burn as an oven; and all the proud, yea, and all that do wickedly, shall be stubble: and the day that cometh shall burn them up, saith the Lord of hosts, that it shall leave them neither root nor branch." (Malachi 3:2, 3; 4:1.)

Those who rely only on intellect can mechanically illuminate various subjects and do so quite well, but only the flame of faith, which is available to all men and women and which taps into God's power, can grow in unlimited amounts and shed enough light that we can eventually comprehend all things. Two verses in the Doctrine and Covenants state this principle well: "That which is of God is light; and he that receiveth light, and continueth in God, receiveth more light; and that light groweth brighter and brighter until the perfect day" (D&C 50:24). "And if your eye be single to my glory, your whole bodies shall be filled with light, and there shall be no darkness in you; and that body which is filled with light comprehendeth all things" (D&C 88:67).

Could increasing our faith in the Lord Jesus Christ, who is the light and life of the world, be the process of increasing the intensity of light within us so we can eventually comprehend all things?

We are all born with some light. The Lord said, "I am the true light that lighteth every man that cometh into the world" (D&C 93:2). We all have the opportunity to develop strong faith or have bright light in our lives. I hope we don't rely on temporary mechanical sources as a substitute for the eternal light of faith!

In this book, I have chosen to use the phrase *faith in God* to include faith in our Father in Heaven, faith in the Lord Jesus Christ, and faith in all Deity and their commandments and their representatives.

On my mission I learned that faith is a real power, even a substance, and that God deals with men according to their faith, as expressed in the Book of Mormon: "For behold, I am God; and I am a God of miracles; and I will show unto the world that I am the same yesterday, today, and forever; and I work not among the children of men save it be according to their faith" (2 Nephi 27:23); "For he hath answered the ends of the law, and he claimeth all those who have faith in him; and they who have faith in him will cleave unto every good thing; wherefore he advocateth the cause of the children of men; and he dwelleth eternally in the heavens" (Moroni 7:28).

I did not feel that I had much faith, in fact, as stated on page 53, "I felt more like a bystander than an active participant. I felt like I was standing on the shore of a mighty river while watching the powerful flow of faith go by. That river of faith was like an unfathomable current that I could see and feel, but not fully understand from where it came or to where it was going, yet every part of me felt its force and beauty and power. It was marvelous!"

The central role of faith in God is summarized well in Ether 12:4: "Wherefore, whoso believeth in God might with surety hope for a better world, yea, even a place at the right hand of God, which hope cometh of faith, maketh an anchor to the souls of men, which would make them sure and steadfast, always abounding in good works, being led to glorify God."

Many have asked, "How do you develop faith?" My answer is, "You develop faith by doing things that require faith." I realize that faith is a gift from God, but like many of His gifts, it requires effort on our part to receive. I have learned that some of life's sweetest experiences come from doing things that may not seem logical but that by faith you know are right, and then over time watching the justifications and blessings come rolling in.

I have had the privilege of serving as a missionary, a bishop, a mission president, in all kinds of ward and stake callings, as a Regional Representative, and as a General Authority. I have learned much from each calling, but even today I feel that possibly I learned more of real importance on my first mission to Tonga than all the rest put together. It became the foundation of almost everything else, and I still call upon experiences and feelings from those days to guide me in many of my decisions today. What a great experience a mission can be!

I learned that you can live the gospel just as well speaking a different language and using different eating methods as you can in the culture I grew up in. I learned that the gospel is truly universal and that you never need to compromise principles because of another language or culture.

At times I look back with great longing to those carefree days, when the only things I worried about were dangerous seas or broken ropes or ripped sails or being drowned or crushed against sharp coral or beaten by angry people or being seasick or learning a language or finding a place to sleep or getting enough to eat, and so forth.

But these were mostly physical concerns and really not much of a problem when your attention is focused on spiritual things and you can see clearly your duty to preach "Christ and Him crucified" (1 Corinthians 2:2) and Him resurrected and Him as the head of His church on earth and Him as the One soon to come and judge all the earth according to His laws and lead the faithful back to the joy of their Father's presence.

I hope you enjoy the spirit of the message and feel comforted as I have felt as I have reread and remembered and written those experiences of many years ago.

I know that God lives and loves and helps us, and that this knowledge is accessible to all men through faith in Him. Enjoy.

# 1

## Abandon Ship!

Three of us were returning to our home port of Pangai from ten days of preaching on some distant islands. It had been a successful trip. The people had been more receptive than usual, and we had baptized one person with promises of a few more. Testimonies had been borne and truth taught, and the three of us were feeling wonderful.

Normally we would have been in our mission sailboat, but this time we had the use of a motor launch, which, while not much faster than our sailboat, seemed more certain as to time schedule. The combination engineer-captain was very alert and knowledgeable, and throughout the journey we had experienced no major problems.

While we had enjoyed the preaching tour, we always felt a sweet nostalgia as we finally headed home. We were now but six or eight hours from Pangai.

The weather had been stormy and threatening, but it presented nothing unusual, at least not to me. We had just passed a small island and were moving into the final stretch of open sea before our home island.

The captain expressed concern as he noted the heavy storm clouds ahead. I told him not to worry, as we were on the Lord's errand. I reminded him that many people had heard and believed our testimonies. We were now on our way home, and He would surely protect us the rest of the way. The captain said that the storm was directly in our path and seemed to be coming toward us; he even suggested that we turn back to the last island. I again told him not to worry, but something deep inside me kept me uncomfortable. We continued on.

The sea got heavier and the wind more boisterous. The waves became rougher and the swells deeper; before long we were in the midst of a furious tropical squall. I still had confidence that all would be well. After all, we were on the Lord's errand, and He did protect those who served Him—I was sure of that—so why did I feel uneasy?

The boat labored up the giant waves, then dipped over the top. The propeller raced when it briefly came out of the water. I wished we were in our faithful old sailboat. Sailboats rarely overturn, since they can go with the waves, whereas motorboats tend to fight the waves.

Up, up, up we went on increasingly menacing waves. Then down, down, down into ever deeper valleys. As we got to the bottom of one of these valleys, I looked up and saw another huge wave bearing down on us. This was getting scary. The captain turned the boat to try to go along the side of the wave rather than hitting it head on.

The motor struggled with all its might to climb the monstrous wave. I still felt we would be safe but realized we were in for a rough time. This was worse than any roller coaster ride, and the stakes were much higher.

We were just approaching the top of this huge wave when immediately behind it appeared another one even larger. The boat turned crazily as we reached the top of the wave and started down. Suddenly, almost without warning, the second wave came roaring through and caught the front of our boat, flipping us into the air like a lion discarding a dead mouse.

There was no question about what was happening. We all fell over each other and grabbed for anything we could hold onto. The last thing I remember was the insane squealing of the racing propeller and the captain yelling, "Abandon ship!"

As I flew through the air, I remember thinking, "This can't be happening! This isn't right! Where's our protection?" My whole life seemed to flash before me in that instant. It was not a pleasant—or unpleasant—sensation, just factual. Somewhere between my bruised confidence and temporary complaining, I felt a distant assurance that gave me an element of peace.

I remember the sensation of falling, falling, falling through hissing winds and stinging salt spray into the boiling cauldron of an angry sea. As I hit the water, I remember wondering where the others were, and where the boat was, and hoping it wouldn't land on top of me. I thought I could still hear the uncontrolled whining of that frantic, racing propeller.

As I sank below the water, I still seemed to be falling down, down, deeper and deeper. The pressure was almost unbearable; my lungs seemed ready to burst. *When would it end? And how?* I wondered about my scriptures and the tracts and what few other things we had on the boat. I wondered about the most recent baptismal certificate I was carefully carrying in my scriptures. It's strange what you think of at times like that.

Then I was on the surface again, out of the grasp of that terrible pressure but still in the center of a universe in unbelievable commotion. I could see no one and hear nothing but the confused sounds of a swirling sea of madness.

For a moment I thought again, "This can't be! This isn't true! I'm a missionary; this isn't supposed to happen! I'm not supposed to swim!" But it *was* true and I *was* there, and I knew I had better quit complaining and start swimming.

Even as those thoughts filled my mind, another giant wave roared over me and I sank again. As the pressure built up, I realized that I could not spare one ounce of effort in complaining or wondering. I needed to conserve all my energy to swim, and breathe, and keep my head above water. I realized that my sandals had been ripped off my feet, that my shirt was torn, but that my tie and belt were still there, for which I was grateful.

As I rose above the surface the second time, I began to swim. It seemed almost useless as the unbridled fury of the sea threw me here and there and pulled and tugged me in every direction and appeared unsatisfied with anything short of tearing me to pieces.

I began to despair a little and found myself once again underwater. Then that hint of assurance I had briefly felt before found its way into my consciousness. I seemed to sense the Savior calming the troubled sea, and I cried out in my heart, "Master, help me! Oh, please help me!"

The tiny light of peace started to widen and deepen. As I came to the surface the third time, swimming and actually staying above the water seemed more plausible. There was extra help and I was feeling it. I sensed that if I put forth all the effort I could, things would be all right. I began to swim once more.

It was midafternoon, and I remembered we had passed a small island not more than an hour before. As I rode the crest of a large wave, I looked in all directions. Just before I started down the back of the wave, I saw the outline of the island. It was a long way off, but it was there. I headed in that direction.

Nothing mattered now but to get out of the stormy sea and onto the shore, where I could put my feet on solid ground. I looked for the others but could see or hear no one. As I rose to the top of another large wave, I thought I saw the broken shape of our poor motorboat, but I was not sure.

I swam steadily. I knew I must not panic or swim too hard. Land was far away, and I needed to float as much as possible and swim hard only to keep above the surface. The squall was moving on, and I sensed that the waves were gradually lessening in intensity and that the wind was not quite as strong.

I swam, floated, and looked. Finally, over a wave, I saw one of my shipmates. He seemed to be all right, and I motioned in the direction of the island. He also motioned to the other side of me. When I looked, I saw our other shipmate. He was a little less confident. We continued moving toward the island and trying to get closer to each other.

It is hard to tell how long we were in the water—probably a few hours. The storm moved on, but the seas were still rough. It was getting late in the afternoon. We were now close enough to keep track of one another. I was starting to get tired but felt comforted knowing that if I got a cramp or started to go down, the other two were close enough to help.

As time moved on and we got closer to shore, the waves and the wind became less boisterous. I heard the shipmate on my right yell and then saw him stand unsteadily and wave his hands. He was standing on a rock that was mostly below the surface! Up to that time, I had been mainly concerned about keeping my head above the water, but when I saw him, I thought how nice it would be to stand on a rock, even if for only a moment. I made my way to him, and, sure enough, I also was able to stand with at least my head above water. It felt so good. We were still far from shore, but that brief moment of standing, like a kind word of encouragement, had the effect of assuring me that things would be all right.

As we started swimming again, I thought, "We all need assurances from time to time, such as a word of encouragement, an expression of love and confidence, or a rock to stand on in the midst of a sea of trouble. All of these things, if heard or felt even for a moment, give us courage to go on, to move forward." I was grateful for that submerged but solid rock and felt I should do better in giving encouragement and love to others more frequently.

We were closer together now and even managed to smile a little. We continued to swim slowly for a long time. Just before the sun went down, we were able to touch the sand and rocks and half swim, half walk to shore. What a beautiful feeling it was to have firm sand under our feet! As we got close enough to kneel and still be above water, we joined in a heartfelt prayer of thanksgiving.

Some of the folks from the island saw us as we came ashore and invited us to stay with them. We explained what had happened, and they offered to help any way they could. They were very hospitable. We stayed with them for several days. Eventually we located what was left of our boat, and with lots of help and much more favorable weather, we salvaged most of it. We eventually made it back to our home port in calmer seas.

I have thought a lot about that experience. God was with us. He saved us. He could have brought us through the storm unscathed and landed us safely in our home port of Pangai. But for some reason, He chose otherwise. I have heard it said that sometimes the Lord calms the storm, and sometimes He lets the storm rage and calms His child.

I don't know why the storm came, why we got caught in it, or why things went the way they did, but I do know we eventually arrived home safely. No matter the trouble, we were safe and alive and had experienced firsthand His saving grace.

So often in life we think that because we have done things in a certain way, certain results should follow. But life is like the ocean. Sometimes we get caught in squalls and storms and things don't go the way we think they should, even when we think we have done right. But God can find us in the eye of a storm and give us courage to swim in rough water. We learn lessons from storms that we cannot learn from calm seas.

I felt on a more personal basis than before that I could relate to the Lord's words to all of us: "If thou be cast into the deep; if the billowing surge conspire against thee; if fierce winds become thine enemy; if the heavens gather blackness, and all the elements combine to hedge up the way; and above all, if the very jaws of hell shall gape open the mouth wide after thee, know thou, my son, that all these things shall give thee experience, and shall be for thy good" (D&C 122:7).

I thought of Joseph in prison in Egypt and Joseph Smith in prison in Missouri and remembered the Lord telling Joseph to bear all things with patience. I thought of Job and of modern people with great afflictions, which are seemingly and probably unmerited by their actions. I thought of people crippled by accidents or diseases and of good families who hold home evening and do all they should and still have family members do wrong things. I realized that the storms and squalls of life come to us all.

I understood better than ever that the Lord's promise to us personally is that if we do what is right, He will give us peace no matter what the environment. I know that to be true. That peace may not come in the way we think or how, where, or when we think, but in the eternal scheme of things, it will come in the way best for us and we will yet praise His name for things we do not now understand.

Those many years ago in the islands, I reminded myself that there would be other squalls to pass through, but I now knew perfectly that we could make it so I preached to myself, "When we find ourselves in these squalls or storms, we should remember we don't have enough energy to complain and still keep our head above water. Our duty is to swim, not wonder or complain. We need to get to shore and must leave the reasons for the storm with the Lord. If all the effort we put into asking 'why' were used in swimming, a lot more of us, with His help, would reach shore."

This single episode is somewhat typical of the many wonderful learning experiences I remember from my first mission to Tonga.

I suppose if I learned anything on my mission, it was that if we sincerely try to do our duty, and work hard and are patient and prayerful, and, above all, have unrelenting faith in God, we can accomplish whatever He desires, for God *always* comes through.

But let me start at the beginning.

# 2

## *In the Beginning*

I was born and reared in Idaho Falls, Idaho. I thought I knew everyone in town. I was sure everyone knew my father. I grew up in the middle of the Great Depression, so I guess we were poor like everyone else, but we didn't think or talk about it.

Idaho Falls was largely a farm-based community. Everyone worked hard, and everyone seemed to have enough to eat. No one told us to work hard or to not waste—that was just what we did because that was what everyone did. We wore the same clothes almost every day and had some form of potatoes nearly every meal. We went to school and played Kick the Can, Red Rover, and other such games and enjoyed our family and friends immensely.

When World War II began, things started to change. When I was about five, I remember pulling the covers over my head one evening and trying to hide deep in the blankets as the newsboys yelled, "Extra! Extra! War in Europe! German planes are bombing Poland!" I didn't know exactly what it meant but sensed something bad was going on.

I was in the second grade when Pearl Harbor was bombed. We went to an uncle's home that Sunday. He had sons in the Navy in Hawaii. Everyone was glued to the radio, and some were crying. I didn't understand much but again sensed that something was very wrong.

I went through the war with memories of patriotism and rationing. I remember Dad announcing one evening, "Guess what? We're going to have real butter for supper tonight!" I remember the heavy black headlines, the wailing sirens, and the air-raid drills at school. I remember the movies and radio pushing us to hate the Japanese and the Germans. I could never quite do that as so many of our neighbors were Japanese. They were good farmers, and I knew their children at school and at church. They were good people. Later, there were some German prisoners of war working on the roads near town. They seemed like fine young men to me.

As children we fought the war by playing soldier, pilot, or navy commander. One of the trees in our backyard had a perfect branch for a pilot and a copilot, one for a gunner, another for a bombardier, and so on. We always got hit on our bombing runs but always barely made it back to base.

It was the era of Captain Midnight, Tom Mix, Gene Autry, the Lone Ranger, and many other stars of popular radio serials. I was fascinated by The Shadow ("Who knows what evil lurks in the hearts of men?" I was sure he did!) I could hardly wait to get home and hear the next episode on the radio. There was no TV.

I remember watching the heat waves rise from the radiators and slightly blur my view out of the window on the third floor of the old East Side grade school. I often stared through those waves and wondered what might be beyond them.

Dad was the bishop of our ward, and Mom played the organ every Sunday. We all went to church together.

It was a good time and place to grow up. Everyone worked hard, everyone was patriotic, and everyone loved their family. No one had much, but everyone enjoyed what they had. I remember coming home from school one day wearing my favorite corduroy pants (which I wore almost every day) and hearing two ladies whisper that the "poor little Groberg boy only has one pair of pants to wear." When I was beyond them, I turned and yelled, "I wear them because I like them! My mom made them!" I was telling the truth. It never occurred to me that it may have been my only pair.

When I was six, I went to the cornerstone-laying ceremony of the Idaho Falls Temple and held President McKay's hat while Dad took a picture. I was wearing my corduroy pants!

I was in the fifth grade when our principal, Miss Bunker, had the whole school come outside and stand at attention while she lowered the flag to half-mast. We had done this once before when United States President Franklin D. Roosevelt died, but this day was even more solemn. She made us all bow our heads as she explained something about an atomic bomb, thousands of people dying, and a new era beginning. It was confusing, but I had the definite feeling that things were going to change.

The war ended, only to be followed by the Cold War, the Iron Curtain, and the Korean Conflict. There were new victories and new enemies.

Junior high and high school were exciting with drive-ins, tests, ball games, dances, dates, band trips, working, and driving, which you could legally do at age fourteen in Idaho. I played the piano, the trumpet, and the French horn. I'm not sure how much I enjoyed them or how much I did it because my folks wanted me to, but I'm glad they saw that I persevered.

I remember once putting a frog in my pocket when I didn't want to go to piano lesson. When the frog croaked, my piano teacher made me take it outside and let it go. I thought she would send me home, but she made me come back and continue the lesson after I washed my hands.

I had a variety of jobs, such as clerking in a hardware store, surveying, farming, doing yard work, picking potatoes, hoeing, and topping sugar beets. We worked on the Church welfare farm, collected fast offerings, and delivered orders to "the poor people."

I was the oldest of seven boys with two older and two younger sisters. Music was a big part of our life, as was school, church, play, work, and summer trips to visit relatives. We took vacations to Utah, California, Yellowstone, and other areas. I graduated from Idaho Falls High School in 1952.

College was the next step, and the old army dorms at Brigham Young University and an ROTC class gave me a tiny taste of military life. On my first date, a blind date set up by my sister and Jean's sister, I met a girl from California named Jean Sabin, who intrigued me no end. She was beautiful, yet not affected. She was nice, evasive, mysterious, yet familiar. I had a feeling I would marry her someday. We both dated others but tended to come back to dating each other for the two years of college before I received my call to serve a mission.

At that time you had to wait your turn, as the draft board would allow only two per ward per year to serve a mission. Even though the Korean War had ended when I was sixteen and the draft was winding down, I was almost twenty before I received approval from the draft board to go on a mission.

I sent my papers in and was told I would receive my mission call in two or three weeks. At the end of that time, no call had arrived. I waited and waited. More weeks went by. I finally called Church head-quarters in Salt Lake City and was told to be patient. I wondered what problems there were, but about two months later, I received a call signed by President David O. McKay to serve a mission in Tonga.

I was excited! I had never heard of Tonga and thought it might be in Africa. An atlas and some encyclopedias soon showed it to be in the South Pacific. I anxiously informed an older relative whom I admired about my call to Tonga. He looked at me and said, "Oh, no! A smart young boy like you! Why can't they send you someplace civilized, like England?" I was crestfallen by his attitude. However, I recovered and replied, "I'm going to Tonga, and it will be the right place for me be-cause that is where the Lord wants me to go. I know the call is right."

A flurry of activity took place before I left on 17 August 1954. I wrote to Jean and told her about my call. The only agreement we had was that we would write occasionally and "see what happens." One of my sisters got married the day before I left. We all went to the temple and had a full day before I caught the midnight train to Salt Lake City to start my mission.

There was a three-day orientation in Salt Lake City for new mis-sionaries, and then we boarded a train to Los Angeles. I left with six other Elders—three going to Australia, three to New Zealand, and my-self to Tonga.

The California mission president met us at the train station in Los Angeles and took us to the mission home next to the nearly completed Los Angeles Temple. We had a meal and rested for a while. He then took us to Wilmington Harbor, where we put our bags on board the SS *Ventura* for the voyage to Pago Pago, American Samoa.

The ship was to leave at 2:00 A.M., but at midnight there was a wildcat strike over some labor dispute. The mission president told us we would have to wait a few days until things were settled.

Things didn't get settled and the sailing was postponed indefi-nitely, so the mission president assigned us to work in various parts of southern California with missionaries already there. I was assigned to the Orange District and lived in Whittier. We covered all of Orange County. There were still lots of orange groves and the towns were dis-tinct from one another. I was given a great companion who saw that we worked hard.

During the few weeks we were together, we were able to tract out and baptize several families and individuals and had many great expe-riences. I will mention only two.

One day we received a call from a funeral home asking if we would conduct a service for a man "who used to be a Mormon." My companion agreed, and we were directed to the sister of the dead man to get a little more information on him. His sister also "used to be a Mormon." She was older and in poor health. She told us she and her brother had moved to California from Utah many years ago. Her brother married, but soon divorced and had no children. She never married. They eventually moved into the same house while they each pursued separate careers.

She told us that they were the only children of their parents, who had now passed away. She gave us a little history on her brother and then asked if we would also conduct her funeral when she died. We gave her the mission home telephone number and assured her someone from the Church would.

She then looked off into the distance and sighed. "I guess this is the end of the line. My folks were good people. I don't know why we rebelled. I'm sorry now we left the Church. When you get to my age, you realize how important the Church is, but the world and its money, its glamour and power have great appeal. I wish I would have listened more to my parents. This is the end of the line. I guess our family is finished. It's sad."

We tried to encourage her to come back to the Church, but she changed the subject and said we needed to get to the funeral home. We conducted the funeral the best we knew how. There were six people there, besides the dead man: two missionaries, two funeral home workers, the sister, and one of the ladies she had known at work.

When we finished, I went down and shook hands with her. She thanked me, then said, "Please obey your parents. They know more than you think. Good-bye." It made a deep and lasting impression on me.

The other experience happened as we were tracting. It was my turn to speak. A middle-aged man opened his door and asked what we wanted.

I said, "We're ministers of the gospel, and we have a message for you."

He replied, "Come on in. I'm Reverend Miller. I've just been selected as the minister for a new church to be built in Beverly Hills. A group of investors are building a beautiful chapel, and they have been listening to various preachers in the area, and they picked me! They'll give me a certain percentage of the collections. If I say the things those people want to hear, I'm sure I can do pretty well. Isn't that great? By the way, how much do you fellows make?"

This was the first time I had personally talked to someone who had chosen preaching as a good way to make money, and I was shocked. The thought of altering teachings to bring in more money had never occurred to me. I thought how grateful we should be to have correct doctrines for people to measure up to rather than measuring our doctrine to the whims of people!

I asked, "What is the name of your church?"

"Oh, they haven't decided that yet, but I'm sure they'll come up with a good one. They're sharp men, smart investors."

I was fascinated, as the concept was new to me. "And they pay you for preaching?" I blurted out.

"Of course," he said incredulously. "Why else would you preach? You've got to make a living. By the way, you never answered my question. How much do you get paid, and what church do you work for?"

I told him we didn't get paid and we were members of The Church of Jesus Christ of Latter-day Saints. "Never heard of such a thing," he said. "Where are you located?"

I said, "Maybe you have heard us called 'Mormons'."

"Oh, you're *Mormon* missionaries?"

I saw a gleam come over his face like a cat ready to devour two hapless mice. For the next half hour that's just about what happened. He opened the scriptures and took us up one road and down another. We could hardly answer anything.

He finally closed his book, stood up, and said, "Oh, fellas, this is no fun; you don't know anything."

I nearly agreed with him. Then suddenly a feeling came over me, and I said, "Mr. Miller, I admit we don't know the Bible very well compared to you, but there's one thing I know that you don't."

He looked at me with a somewhat contemptuous smile and said, "What do you know that I don't?"

"I know the church I belong to, The Church of Jesus Christ of Latter-day Saints, is the true church of God on earth and that it has the authority of His priesthood. I know Joseph Smith was a true prophet of God. And I know we have a living prophet today. You don't know that."

"Joseph Smith was a false prophet," he retorted.

"You don't *know* that," I said.

He replied, "I just told you."

I responded, "You said it in words, but you don't know it. I know he was a true prophet, and you can't deny it." The only way I could have said this was by the Spirit of the Lord, because I didn't have the courage to do it on my own. I continued, "I bear my testimony that I know the church I belong to is true and that Joseph Smith is a true prophet of God. Now, I challenge you to bear testimony that you know your church is true and that the founder of your church is a true prophet of God."

He stood there for a little while and looked at us. He still had his Bible in his hand. He looked at it, looked at the floor, and looked back at us, sort of shaking his head. He looked at the Bible again and then said, "Ah, c'mon, fellas, this is no fun. Good-bye."

As we went out of the door, I said gently, "See, you can't do it, can you? You can't testify that you know your church is true." I don't suppose we made many points as far as he was concerned, but it was a great testimony to me.

I should mention that some of the best people I know are preachers in other churches. Most of them are very sincere and give their all to teach the truth. I have deep respect for them, but this man's attitude was new to me and his philosophy struck me as very strange.

I learned that one of the things that brings strength to a missionary is bearing testimony of the divine mission of Joseph Smith. When we find ourselves in places and situations in which we're not sure what to do, we can bear testimony of Joseph Smith. The very act of sincerely bearing that testimony seems to set in motion eternal processes that allow us to come up with the right words, the right feelings, and the right actions appropriate for the occasion.

We continued working in our area from Santa Fe Springs to Laguna Beach and everywhere in between. I was starting to get used to California and enjoyed the work greatly. I knew I was close to Jean, who lived in North Hollywood, but I never called her, because it was against mission rules. Days stretched into weeks. We checked with the mission home every day; finally, after seven weeks we were told, "The boat sails tomorrow." I said farewell to the Orange District, packed a few things, and went to the mission home in Los Angeles.

The mission president took me and the six other missionaries to the boat the next afternoon. We finally boarded the SS *Ventura* and were ready to set sail from California for the South Pacific.

# 3

## The Trip Down

The SS *Ventura* was a freighter carrying a load of lumber. It was scheduled to stop in American Samoa, where I was to get off and catch another boat to Tonga. We left California towards evening. It was thrilling to finally be on the high seas. At times the ocean was a little rough, but generally we had a smooth voyage. I enjoyed visiting with the other Elders. One of the cooks tried to convert me to his type of meditational religion, but I couldn't understand him very well and he wasn't interested in my church, so after that we just ate.

We had been out of sight of land for twelve days when one morning the mountains around Pago Pago, American Samoa, came into view. I was excited to be in the islands of the South Pacific!

It was early morning when we pulled into Pago Pago harbor. I was anxious to find out how I was to get to Tonga and fully expected someone to be at the wharf to meet me. I looked and looked and with disappointment soon realized no one was coming.

The crew started unloading the cargo. They took my trunk off, put it on the wharf, and told me this was as far as my ticket would take me. I tried to explain that I was going to Tonga, but they said they were only to take me to American Samoa, "and besides, we aren't going to Tonga."

I got off the boat and asked people on the wharf about boats to Tonga and about any Mormon missionaries around. One person said there had been a boat to Tonga, but it left six weeks ago. When I mentioned Mormons, several pointed to the far end of the bay. I kept waiting for someone to come, but no one ever did. Noon arrived and the captain said the boat was leaving. I had grown pretty close to the six Elders on the boat, and they protested that I shouldn't be left alone, but the captain said that wasn't his concern. Since I had an American passport, there was no problem staying in American Samoa, but I was worried about where to go and what to do.

The crew pulled up the gangplank and ordered the ropes slipped from their moorings, and the boat started down the harbor on its way to New Zealand and Australia. I felt very lonely. There were a few tears as I waved good-bye to the other Elders. The boat got farther and farther away and then disappeared from view. I was left alone with my trunk on the wharf.

A young Samoan boy who worked on the dock and spoke English said, "There are some Mormons who live at the end of the bay. If you want to go find them, I'll guard your trunk." I felt I had no choice, so I started walking according to his directions. It was hot, and the end of the bay was a long way away. It probably took only thirty minutes to get there, but in the heat it seemed like hours.

The boy had described a house next to a church. I finally found such a house and felt I was in the right place. I started to knock on the door, when I heard some yelling and arguing. I thought I must be in the wrong place. I heard someone throw something, then the door crashed open and a man charged out. He apparently didn't see me because he went right by and marched on down the road.

I hesitated but decided to knock anyway because the house fit the description I had been given. When I knocked, a lady yelled, "I told you not to come back!"

I replied, "I'm just trying to find some Mormon missionaries." There was silence.

A woman came to the door and said, "Who are you and what do you want?" I explained that I was a Mormon missionary on my way to Tonga, but our boat was about two months late arriving and I guessed I had missed my connection.

She looked at me unbelievingly. "What's your name and where are you from?" (We had no name tags in those days.) I told her I was Elder Groberg from Idaho Falls, and I needed to find a way to Tonga and a place to stay until I did. She said she and her husband were Mormons, but they didn't have any room and I couldn't stay with them. Besides, no one had told her about my coming.

By this time it was fairly late in the afternoon. I hadn't had anything to eat since breakfast. I asked if she had something to eat. She shot back, "No, we don't have any extra food, and there is no place to stay here. How long do you plan to be around?"

"I don't know," I said. "I'm supposed to catch a boat to Tonga."

She replied, "I don't know of any boats going to Tonga from here. If you're really a missionary and you need a place to stay and something to eat, go on down the other side of the bay. They're building a chapel there and you can probably work with them. Maybe they'll give you a place to sleep and some food to eat." She pointed down the harbor and slammed the door.

I was really discouraged now. I was thirsty, hot, hungry, and tired. My friends had all left, and I was worried about my trunk. I couldn't figure anything else to do but walk on around the bay and see if I could find a chapel under construction.

It was late afternoon when I finally found a group of young Samoan men hauling sand and making cement blocks. I asked if they were Mormons. Some of them spoke English and said, "Yes, we are. And who are you?" I told them my story and explained about my trunk and asked if I could have something to eat and drink.

They were nice. Someone gave me a boiled banana and another gave me a green coconut to drink. They tasted great!

Before long another man came by in a pickup truck. He seemed to be the boss. The others explained my predicament to him in Samoan. The boss spoke good English and said, "We had no word about your coming, but I believe you. Hop in and we'll get your trunk and bring it here. If you are willing to work with us, we will give you food and a mat to sleep on on the beach with the rest of us." It sounded good to me.

We went back to the wharf. The young boy was still there watching my trunk. It was long after work hours, but he had stayed as he said he would. I have always felt good towards Samoans since then. He was happy that I had found some other Mormons and said he was a member also.

It was dark by the time we got back to the construction site. They had a fire on the beach and gave me some more of their food. They gave me a mat and a sheet and showed me where the outhouse was and where I could shower and change.

For the next several days I hauled sand in buckets, mixed it with cement, and shook forms to make cement blocks. It was hard work, but I got food and a place to sleep and felt I was among friends. I remember thinking, "I didn't know missionary work was going to be like this."

After a few days someone came from the Church ranch at Malaeimi, on the other end of the island. He said he had heard I was a proselyting missionary on my way to Tonga. He told me the Samoan mission president would be coming in a few days, and he thought I might be under a better influence if I were living with him rather than with the building missionaries. I told him it didn't matter to me, but he seemed to be in charge, so he took me to the Church ranch and I helped him herd cows, throw coconuts on carts, and do other farm work for a couple of days.

Soon the Samoan mission president arrived. I had a chance to talk with him and explain my circumstances. He said, "There aren't any boats from here to Tonga. Come with me to Apia, Western Samoa, where the mission home is, and I'll see what we can do."

We traveled by boat to Apia, which only took one day. We went to the mission home—a large, wooden, two-story, German colonial building with lots of rooms. I thought it was beautiful. The mission president assigned me to a room and said he would check if there was a way to get me to Tonga.

The next day he said, "There aren't any boats going to Tonga from here. Why don't you just stay here?"

I said, "Well, my call is to Tonga. I probably ought to go there."

He replied, "Well, okay, if that's the way you feel, let me do some more checking. In the meantime, just be as helpful as you can around here." I was there for several days and helped in the kitchen, washed dishes, and did yard work.

After a while, the mission president realized I didn't have much to do, so he assigned me to keep his big, black car washed and clean. None of the roads were paved, so each time the car went anywhere it came back dusty. Keeping it clean turned out to be almost a full-time job. I remember one day washing that car seventeen times! Again I thought, "This sure is different missionary work than I supposed I was going to be doing."

A few days later the mission president said, "If you go to Fiji, there are occasional boats from there to Tonga. We just sent two missionaries to Fiji last month to open the work there. They can help you. I'll telegraph them and they'll be there to meet you." He put me on a boat to Fiji the next day and said I should be there in two or three days.

I was excited to be on a boat that supposedly was getting me closer to Tonga. I had a small cabin way down by the waterline. It was very hot, so I spent a lot of time on deck where there was a breeze. I

*The freighter S.S.* Ventura, *on which*
*we traveled to Samoa.*

met a young island girl who spoke good English and who was very friendly. At first I was happy to have someone to talk to. I told her what I was doing and where I was going. It soon became apparent that she had things other than religion on her mind. When she started asking me to come to her cabin, I realized this was going in the wrong direction, so I excused myself and stayed in my cabin the rest of the voyage.

The day before we got to Suva, Fiji, was a Sunday. I had been alone in my hot cabin for a long time. I didn't feel like going back on deck. How I missed church that Sunday! Suddenly the thought occurred to me: *You're a missionary. You have the priesthood. You can have church.* I don't know if it was right, but I got some bread and water, a plate and a cup, and my scriptures, and held my own church service. I taught myself a Sunday School lesson, sang a song, and gave the opening prayer for sacrament meeting. I then sang a sacrament song and blessed the sacrament and partook of it. Then I gave a talk, sang a closing hymn, and gave the closing prayer.

I felt great! The cabin didn't seem nearly so hot. I was less discouraged, as I felt God had sent His Spirit to that little sacrament meeting on the high seas just out of Suva, Fiji. Still, I looked forward to seeing those two missionaries the next morning.

# 4

## The Gangplank

When the boat arrived in Suva, I looked and looked but saw no Elders. An hour went by, then two, then three, but still no Elders. The captain kept telling me to get off the boat, as they were leaving soon. I told him I would be met by two young men, but they didn't come.

Finally, noon arrived and the captain was ready to leave. "Get off," he said, "you only have a ticket to Suva. I'm leaving, and you're staying here."

With great fear, I started down the gangplank, only to be met by immigration officials. "Let's see your visa, your onward ticket, and the money to keep you while you're here," they demanded.

I had no visa. I had no onward ticket. I didn't have sufficient money. I assured them that two young men would come right away with whatever was needed. How I prayed! But they didn't come.

"Back on the ship, then," they insisted.

"Not on my ship!" bellowed the captain.

I can remember standing in the middle of the gangplank and looking up at the folded arms and glaring eyes of the stern captain, and then looking down at the equally determined faces and set jaws of the immigration men.

I looked at the ocean under the gangplank. I wondered how long I could tread water. I was pretty scared.

In the end, the captain proved to be the toughest. Amidst cursing and yelling and banging of bags, the gangplank went up, the ship departed, and I found myself in the not-too-friendly hands of the immigration officials.

There was a long discussion among them, most of it in a foreign tongue. Finally, one of the younger men, who seemed more friendly, came over and explained that for now I would have to move with my things into the customs shed, where things went that weren't allowed into the country until tax was paid on them. He assured me that he felt the two young men I referred to would be along soon and everything would be fine.

The afternoon wore on. I tried several times to figure out a way to contact the missionaries, but to no avail. I know missionaries are supposed to be brave, but right then I was scared, tired, and hungry. The sun was getting low. It seemed the lower it got in the sky, the lower my spirits became. I knew I wasn't really in danger or in prison, but to one used to lots of freedom it seemed like it.

The pungent odor of curry, *copra* (dried coconut meat), drying fish, and the myriad other sights, sounds, and smells of an oily tropical wharf seemed so foreign to the cool, fresh smells of my Idaho home. I knew I was homesick. I wanted to cry, but knew that wouldn't do any good.

Finally, the whirring of winches, the groaning of blocks and cables, the banging of cargo, and the sputtering of machines ceased. The dock workers began to leave, followed by the immigration people, until just a few watchmen and supervisors were left. It was silent now. I really felt alone.

I tried to lie down on the dirty, uneven cement floor. I prayed to know what to do. There seemed to be no answer. I watched the last rays of sunlight as they broke through the clouds and blazed across the ocean and through the holes of the metal customs shed.

"How long will the light last?" I thought. Then I wondered, "What will happen when those last rays disappear and fold into the night? Maybe if I close my eyes, I'll just disappear or at least circumstances will change." I closed my eyes. However, nothing happened, so I opened my eyes and said, "I must have hope. Things must turn out all right."

I closed my eyes again, this time in prayer. Suddenly I felt almost transported. I didn't see anything or hear anything in a physical sense. But in a more real sense, I saw my family in far-off Idaho kneeling together in prayer. I heard one, acting as mouth, say as clearly as anything can be heard, "And bless John on his mission."

As that faithful family called down the powers of heaven to bless their missionary son in a way they could not physically do, the powers of heaven came down, lifted me up, and in a spiritual way allowed me for a brief moment to once again join my family circle in prayer. I was one with them. I was literally swallowed up in the love and concern of a loving family and sensed for a moment what being taken into the bosom of Abraham might be like (see Luke 16:22). I was given to understand also that there are other circles of love and concern, unbounded by time or space, to which we all belong and from which we can draw strength. God does not leave us entirely alone—ever!

Tears of joy flowed freely as I had restored to me the warmth of family, the light of love, and the strength of hope. When I again felt the hard, uneven cement beneath me, there was no fear, no sorrow, no trepidation, only deep gratitude and assurance.

I waited. Within half an hour I saw the young immigration man who had befriended me coming towards the shed with two Elders behind him. How happy I was to see them! It seems that on his way home he "just happened" to run into two young Americans with white shirts and ties and told them about another one just like them down at the wharf. They had received no telegram, but they believed him and followed him to the customs shed. Soon all was straightened out, and I went with the Elders to their flat in Lami, Fiji. They got another bed for me and were happy to have me there.

They explained that our assignment in Fiji was to go around the island and find out how many members there were. Each day we went about asking, "Are you a Mormon or do you know any Mormons?" In this way we located several members. We also found quite a few part-member families whom we were able to teach, as well as others who were interested in learning about the Church. This was my first opportunity to teach the lessons since California, and I enjoyed it.

I remember those two Elders taking me to an Indian restaurant (about half of the population in Fiji is of East Indian ancestry). They said I had to put more curry on to make the bland food taste good. I should have been aware of that old missionary trick, but I wasn't. When I took that first bite of food with its huge amount of curry, I thought my mouth was literally on fire. I couldn't drink enough water to quench the flames. They laughed and laughed, but we were still good friends.

We worked together for a couple of weeks. Each day we checked to see if there were any boats going to Tonga. Finally, we were told of a freighter going there in a few days. It had no passenger accommodations, but they said if I would sign on as part of the crew and work my way over, I could go. I jumped at the chance.

The boat was old and I could see why they had crew vacancies. It had a load of lumber, and I was assigned to a fellow crew member named Swede. Swede spoke broken English, but we understood each other sufficiently.

Swede told me he was born at sea and had lived all his life at sea. "It's nice," he said. He was considerably older than I was. Our job was to check the lashings on the timber. My responsibility was only minimal, because Swede actually did the work. Our shift was about six hours on and six hours off. There were several others doing the same work on different shifts. Most of the lumber was 4x4s and 8x8s, twelve to sixteen feet long. It was important to keep them firmly tied, for if they ever got loose on a rough sea they would become like giant javelins and pierce through the ship, especially the superstructure, and could sink it.

Swede and I shared the same room and usually went on our rounds together. We became pretty good friends. We couldn't communicate well enough for me to give him the missionary discussions, but pretty soon he realized I had a Bible and a Book of Mormon and a bent toward religion. I tried to explain the Book of Mormon to him, but he wasn't interested.

We had a lot of time to talk and visit. Finally he said, "Now, tell me again, you're a missionary? You're going to be a missionary?"

I said, "Yes," and tried to explain to him what that meant. I could tell he was getting angry. Finally, he said, "Come with me." He got a small picture book out of his drawer and said, "You don't want to go to Tonga. You don't want to be a missionary. You come with me. You're a good worker. I'll get you a full-time job on this boat." He then opened the book and showed me pictures of all "his girls." Most of them weren't the type of pictures missionaries should look at.

"This one's in Ecuador. This one's in Peru. This one's in Tahiti. This one's in Tonga. I can line you up with her and her and her. You'd enjoy that life a lot more than missionary life!" I tried to explain to him that it had taken me such a long time and so much effort to get this close to Tonga that I wasn't about to change now. I told him that his kind of life wouldn't bring true joy or happiness, but that the kind of life I had could bring eternal happiness.

When he realized he couldn't convince me, he became almost violent. He started railing on me: "You missionaries! You and your Bibles wreck all the fun for guys like me. You'll get to Tonga and teach all those girls about these silly things and about not going out with guys like me. You'll teach them they're supposed to get married and supposed to blankety-blank-blank!" He used some pretty descriptive language. I didn't understand all of it. He finally calmed down.

We were nearly to Tonga, but the last hours of the voyage were quite miserable. I was not fearful that Swede would hurt me in any way, but he was pretty upset. The next morning we arrived in Tonga.

Before I got off the boat, Swede tried again to talk me into staying on. He said he had talked to the captain, who told him it would be fine for me to stay on as they always needed more crew members.

I said, "No, I'm getting off here." This time, instead of getting angry, he said, "Well, I don't agree with a thing you're doing. You are making the world a worse place rather than a better place from my point of view. But I admire you for sticking with it and wish you good luck." We shook hands. I told him my great-grandparents had joined the Church in Sweden and came as Mormon converts to the United States. He laughed and said, "I should have known it—stubborn Swedes." We parted on a friendly note.

As I went down the gangplank, I checked the date. It was November 17. It had taken me exactly three months to get to Tonga from the time I left home. I was glad to be there. I looked around, but again there was no one to meet me. The Elders in Fiji had said they would send a telegram. I didn't know what had happened, but at least I had a landing permit for Tonga. I got off the boat and went through customs and immigration.

I started asking about the Mormon mission home. It was a lot easier here than in Fiji because people knew where it was. I stopped at a store owned by a member who spoke English. He said to wait there while he got the mission president, who didn't live very far away.

When the mission president arrived, I was immediately attracted to him. He said, "Elder Groberg, I expected you two months ago. Where on earth have you been?" I felt like saying, "If you have a few hours, I'll tell you where on earth I've been." But I just said I was glad to be there and looked forward to a good mission.

He took me and my trunk to the mission home. After we had a nice visit, he said, "I have prayed about it, and I have just the place for you. It's a little island named Niuatoputapu. It has about 700 people and is the most distant Tongan island from here. As far as I know, there are no white people there, and no one speaks English." I remember wondering, "Why is that just the place for me?" But I didn't say anything. I trusted my mission president.

He continued, "The boat for there is leaving soon. It will take seven or eight days to get there, as they stop at Niuafoʻou island on the way. I'm going to assign you to a companion named Feki Poʻuha. He's a good man. He's on a building mission now, but I don't want you to be alone in your first area." Then he said solemnly, "I am giving you two assignments. First, learn the language as soon as possible. Second, build the kingdom. Do you have any questions?"

"No."

"Fine, then I'll take you to Liahona to meet Feki."

As soon as I met Feki, I knew I would like him. He was so positive! The boat was to leave for Niuatoputapu in about a week, so in the meantime Feki and I stayed at the Church school, named Liahona. The mission president did not want me to teach at the school but rather to proselyte with Feki in the surrounding area, so even though the labor missionaries were still working at Liahona, Feki and I traveled each day to the outlying villages and proselyted. I suppose that given my experiences thus far, I should not have been surprised when the departure of the boat kept getting delayed again and again. I had to learn more patience.

# 5

## *Feki*

I don't see how anyone could have a better companion than I had in Feki Po'uha. He was patient, kind, hardworking, and obedient. Feki was a priest in the Aaronic Priesthood. He was worthy to be an elder, but at that time in Tonga men were ordained elders only when they got married. He became my first, last, and only regular missionary companion.

I learned to love Feki's infectious smile, his sparkling eyes, and his "can do" attitude. I marveled at his ability to speak Tongan, even though it was his native tongue. I marveled even more at his obedience.

The mission president told Feki he wanted me to learn to speak Tongan, so he asked Feki to speak only Tongan to me. Feki spoke some English, but during the thirteen months we were together he spoke only Tongan to me.

It is hot and rains a lot in December in Tonga. Sometimes as we walked from one village to another, we would hear a thundering sound like a herd of galloping horses behind us. The rain would come so quickly and in such heavy waves that there was no way to escape, so we often got drenched.

At first I was irritated at getting wet so often and wondered why we didn't use umbrellas. But when I saw Feki's dancing dark eyes and felt his unrestrained, gleeful attitude, I couldn't help but feel the same. A hot sun usually followed each deluge, so we were generally pretty dry by the time we got to the next village. Feki laughed, "Why not enjoy it? Umbrellas are a nuisance. Tongans love to play in the rain! It's like a free shower."

Mud and bugs were everywhere. With the heavy rain and hot sun, I soon learned why old clothes and old shoes (or no shoes) were better than something you wanted to keep clean or dry.

Although I understood very little of what was said, I understood the joy of being with Feki and of doing missionary work. Tongans love music, and it had been suggested I bring my trumpet on my mission. Feki often asked me to play it at cottage meetings. Playing my trumpet always brought lots of extra people out, most of whom left when I quit playing and the meeting started, but some stayed and listened.

Since there were no phone lines to Liahona, we rode bicycles to Nuku'alofa nearly every day to check on the boat. It was about fifteen miles round-trip, but we soon got used to it.

While we were waiting for the boat to Niuatoputapu, the mission president received a cable message stating that President and Sister David O. McKay and a few others would arrive on the SS *Tofua* in one week to visit the Tongan Mission. What an event! Everyone jumped into action and worked hard to have things just right for the prophet's visit. It was great to see how united and happy everyone was.

Feki and I were assigned to help clean the grounds at the Church school, as well as some of the paths at the Church ranch, which had been the site of the former Church school, Makeke, when President McKay visited Tonga in 1921.

A few days later President and Sister McKay arrived. What a splendid man he was, and what a lovely lady she was! His white hair, regal bearing, and piercing eyes made him the model of a prophet to me. How could anyone doubt?

The walks were covered with *tapa* cloth and lined with school children and missionaries. When President and Sister McKay walked down those aisles of smiling children waving palm leaves, tears came easily to their eyes.

President McKay sat through a traditional *kava* ceremony and drank some *kava*. (They mix a type of pepper root with water and serve it according to rank.) In fact, he said, "Give me a bigger serving. Some people say *kava* is against the Word of Wisdom, but it isn't, and I'll be the first to show that." He was so gracious and appreciative of the food and entertainment and all that was done for him.

There were very few missionaries, so we were always seated close to him. When I was formally introduced to President McKay, he said without a moment's hesitation, "I knew your father—no, your grandfather—in Ogden. We worked together in the Weber Stake Sunday School. He was a great man. Do him proud." I was impressed.

Later he asked me to hold his hat while he inspected the hooves of some cows at the ranch. As I held his hat, I mentioned I had done this before at the Idaho Falls Temple cornerstone ceremony. He looked at me knowingly and said, "You were lots smaller then." His eyes were something else!

He told the mission president to start ordaining some of the men to the Melchizedek Priesthood and make application to build some brick chapels. He held lots of meetings with the Saints and shook hands with nearly everyone.

Once he met separately with the *palangi* (white) missionaries, who consisted of three proselyters and about ten schoolteachers. I remember we were all sitting on the floor; as he spoke, chills of wonder went through me. He looked at each missionary individually, and when his eyes met mine and he talked about being a good missionary, it was as if I had received a new charge from God Himself! How could I do anything less than be a good missionary?

After a few days, President and Sister McKay departed for other islands, but left a great legacy of faith and love and resolve among us! About a week after they departed, we received word that the boat would sail for Niuatoputapu the next day. I felt the boat had been delayed so we could meet and hear President McKay.

The boat we were to sail on was a relatively small copra boat with a cargo of pigs and other animals, as well as a deck full of passengers. I was repulsed by the smell, but still anxious to get to our assigned area. We boarded and soon were on the high seas.

I had been a little seasick on the large boats coming down to Tonga, but not too bad. Those boats were relatively large and had good places to sleep—and a tolerable odor. By contrast, this boat was small, the sleeping quarters were a joke, and the smell was something else—a mix of pigs, chickens, copra, diesel, and people throwing up.

Within a day I learned again the classic definition of seasickness: At first you're afraid you'll die; then you get so sick you're afraid you won't. When I wouldn't or couldn't eat on my own, Feki would come with a crew member: one would hold my nose and the other would pour soup down my throat. "We don't want a dead man on our hands," the captain said. I am sure they knew best, even though I didn't appreciate it at the time.

For eight days and nights we rolled and tossed across the ocean, making only one brief stop at Niuafo'ou (Tin Can Island) before arriving at Niuatoputapu. I had been deathly ill most of the way. I resolved if I ever got on dry land again, I would never leave.

Finally the boat anchored off Niuatoputapu, and we came to shore on smaller boats. I had envisioned a large group of grateful Saints warmly greeting us and letting us know how much they appreciated what we had been through to get there—maybe even singing and putting leis on us and having something for us to eat and drink.

I looked around. No one. I asked Feki, "Where are they?"

"Who?" he replied.

"The Saints we have come to be with!"

"They're not here. I've asked around, and they didn't know we were coming. The telegraph is broken, so the message didn't arrive." Since the telegraph ran on a car battery, when the battery ran out of power there were no telegrams until a fresh battery came on the next boat.

We dragged our things up the sandy beach, away from the lapping waves. "You stay here and watch our things," Feki instructed me, "and I'll go and find the branch president. We'll come back with a *saliote* (horse-drawn cart) and take you and our things to wherever we are to live. Don't let anyone take our things and don't wander off. Stay right here!"

I had no choice, so I sat down on the sand—tired, hungry, thirsty, and very disillusioned. My dream of the greeting party and their gratitude for my being there was shattered.

The only people around now were some children, a few of whom came up and touched me and laughingly said, *"Palangi, palangi!"* Some of the smaller children got close and then started crying and ran away as their mothers threatened, "Come away or the *palangi* will get you!"

I didn't understand a lot, but I understood enough to know that, far from my expectations, I wasn't very welcome here. I could sense a mixture of pity, fear, curiosity, and aloofness from most of the people around me. The few words I understood from the little comments I heard didn't make me feel any better.

Some people came and asked a few questions or offered to help, but my fears had started to rise and I saw everyone and everything as an attempt to steal our things or cause us trouble. I remembered Feki's words, "Stay right there and don't let anyone take anything," so I warded everyone off.

Time passed. The crowd on the shore thinned out. The sun was hot. I wondered if Feki had left for good. I felt alone again. I wanted to cry but knew I shouldn't.

I had noticed a few mosquitoes while I had been moving around to protect our things, but they hadn't seemed too bad. Now I was sitting more quietly and the mosquitoes were coming in hordes—hundreds, thousands, millions! It seemed as though they were trying to carry me off. I imagined their leader telling his troops, "We've had lots of Tongan blood, but seldom do we get the chance to have white man's blood! Feast up, everyone! Attack, attack!"

The more I struck at them, the more they seemed to come. It was getting hotter and more miserable. Feki was not back. It had been over an hour since he left. The people were mostly gone. I could tell the boat was about ready to leave.

Suddenly true panic hit me. *What if Feki doesn't come back? The people don't seem to like us. What if there aren't any Saints here? What if they've all left the Church? What if we're in the wrong place? What if the boat leaves and Feki doesn't return and no one will help me and the mosquitoes keep coming and I just sit here on the beach and slowly die?*

Satan has a way of combining things to bring out our worst fears. In that panicky state, I jumped up and thought, "If I run fast, I can make it to the boat before it leaves. At least I know a couple of crew members, and I'm sure it's going back to Nuku'alofa. I'll just tell the mission president what happened, and he'll be happy to have me back. I won't stay here and die from hunger and thirst and mosquitoes and heat."

I was about ready to bolt and run, when another feeling hit me: *Eight more days of seasickness?* I thought of my resolve to never leave solid land again. I felt a swirling confusion of fears, heat, mosquitoes, uncertainties—all of which pummelled my panicky feelings. I didn't know what to do. I wanted to run, but my churning stomach said, "Eight more days of seasickness? No way!"

I slumped back to the sand. I should have prayed, but instead I cried. Finally between sobs I asked, "Father, what should I do?" I didn't seem to receive any answer but just sat there rather stupefied and watched the boat leave.

Now I was totally alone. *What have I done? Why am I here? What have I gotten myself into? Where is Feki?* I hit a few more mosquitoes, then lay down and resigned myself to whatever fate lay ahead. *You mosquitoes! Go ahead and enjoy your white man's blood. You mothers! Go ahead and scare your children, telling them if they are not good the* palangi *will get them. You others! Go ahead and poke me and make fun and steal our things. I don't care! I don't care about anything anymore!*

Then I thought of home—beautiful Idaho. *It isn't so hot there.*

*President and Sister McKay leaving by boat*
*after visiting the Tongan Mission in January 1955.*

*There aren't as many mosquitoes. My family wants me around. They speak English. Mom has a fresh loaf of whole wheat bread just out of the oven. There is butter and honey. The loaf is broken apart. See the steam rise. Smell the freshness. Watch the butter melt. Taste that heavenly bread with honey—uh, huh!* I closed my eyes as tears of homesickness welled up again. *Why am I here? Why am I not there?*

I could see my parents, my brothers and sisters, my girlfriend and other friends. I remembered my farewell and vaguely recalled someone saying, "Even if you get homesick, stick it out. Do what is right and God will protect you. We'll be praying for you." *That was fine when spoken at a farewell among friends, and maybe it was true sometimes, but how do you know what is right under these circumstances? Should I even be here?* I closed my eyes again as though to blot out my fears.

Someone poked me. I jumped up. They pointed down the trail. There was a cart coming. It was a long way off. *Was that Feki with another man? I think so. Oh, Feki! Feki, you are alive! You have come for me! Yes, that's him! That's his smile!* I looked at the boat, now far out in the channel. I was glad I had stayed.

# 6

## *Starting Out*

The *saliote* got closer. Feki ran up and explained that even though the telegraph was broken and the Saints hadn't known we were coming, they were happy to have us. It had taken him some time to find the branch president, more time to get the horse, find the harness, hook up the cart, and quite a while to come from Vaipoa, especially since the horse went at its own pace, which varied between slow and very slow.

We loaded our things onto the cart. Feki introduced me to the branch president, who smothered me with hugs and Tongan kisses (rubbing noses and cheeks). He hadn't shaved for a couple of days, so my face was thoroughly sandpapered!

We eventually got to Vaipoa, where most of the members lived. They moved us into one end of the branch president's house. Even though I was tired and just wanted to sleep, it was obvious there would be none of that until they fixed a big meal. We sat cross-legged on the ground outside in a large semicircle with several smoking coconut husks by us—supposedly to keep the mosquitoes away.

We ate and talked. They were appalled that I didn't know Tongan and couldn't answer their questions: "Where do you come from? How many brothers and sisters do you have? What ages are they? What is your father's name? What titles does he hold? How big is your island? Who has the most pigs there? How long have you been a member? What kind of fish do you like? Why don't you speak Tongan?" Feki explained all he knew and they seemed somewhat satisfied.

Finally, after what seemed forever, especially to my crossed legs, someone suggested I might be tired and like to sleep. I agreed. I tried to get up but couldn't because my legs were asleep—that brought some laughs. They showed me where the outhouse was, where the tub for a shower was, where the well to draw water was, and where my mat, blanket, and pillow were. They had lots of ceiba trees there, which produce kapok, a light, cottony substance which the Tongans used to stuff pillows. I suppose some of their pillows didn't have seeds and husks in them, but I never felt one.

I told Feki I was too tired to shower, so I would just go to the outhouse and then to bed. Several men accompanied me to the outhouse and waited to accompany me back. "You sure you don't want to bathe? We'll get water for you."

"No, I'll just go to bed," I said.

"Okay. But you'll rest better if you bathe." I had slept for several days in my clothes on the boat, so I suspect there was a reason for their insistence. Tongans are generally very clean and conscious of odors. But I just lay down, took off my sandals, said my prayers, and immediately fell asleep.

The next morning I did want to bathe. I thought there must be someplace besides the galvanized tub in the middle of the yard, but there wasn't. Feki said he'd get water. As far as I knew, I was the only *palangi* on the island, and the local people seemed fascinated with the opportunity to watch me bathe.

I hadn't taken a bath with people watching since I was a child. But now I faced a new dilemma. I was the only one on the island who had been through the temple. I didn't want to be disrespectful, but was unsure what to do. The first day I decided to take my garments off in the tub. They would have to be washed anyway. But I couldn't figure out how to put new ones on in the tub without getting them wet. I finally decided to change in the house and go back and forth with a *tupenu* (large cloth) as a covering.

After a few days, I talked Feki into building a protective screen of coconut fronds around the tub. It kept the adults from my view, but I soon became aware of smaller eyes peering through the openings to see what a *palangi* looked like while bathing. Eventually I got used to bathing with an audience.

I suppose you can get used to anything, and before long bathing wasn't an issue. I don't know whether their curiosity was satisfied or whether I didn't care anymore. Probably some of both.

I found that the mosquitoes were as bad in Vaipoa as on the beach by the wharf. I also found that while it was nice to live in one end of the branch president's home, it left us (and them) no privacy. It also meant that if he had something he wanted us to do, it took precedence over our plans. It was not the best situation.

Feki and I walked around those first few days to see the other two villages and the rest of the island. You can walk around the entire island—a distance of about fourteen miles—in a few hours. I found there was no running water, no electricity, no cars, no motors, nothing mechanical—except the telegraph, which worked sometimes. There were no stores, so you couldn't buy anything, no matter how much money you had. People basically didn't use money there at that time.

I sensed the villagers were both curious and reserved as far as we were concerned. They were interested to know who we were and why we were there but generally scared and unwilling to listen when they found we wanted to talk about "Mormonism" and Joseph Smith. Most people were kind when they sensed we needed food or water. I soon felt I knew a few people and had some friends. Feki, of course, was my main support.

It was very hot. Everyone but the small children wore a *tupenu* wrapped around their waist. It was not uncommon for men and women of all ages to go without clothing above the waist. If the women knew I was around, they often covered up in some way, but much of the time they didn't. As it got cooler, people covered up more, much to my relief.

It is hard to remember just how the transition took place, but it didn't take too long before I felt somewhat at home and began to see past the newness and strangeness into the reality of different personalities with their various problems and concerns. I soon realized that while the setting was different from my Idaho home, the everyday problems of living and dealing with personal interactions were about the same as anywhere else.

I realized that some people were selfish; others were generous. Some were kind; others less so. Some were trying to live Christian lives according to what they understood, and others didn't seem too concerned about it. Some were open and gregarious; others closed and distant. Some were friendly; others were suspicious. The whole gamut of life and personality was evident, even among only seven hundred people.

I quickly learned to be friendly to everyone and stay on their good side, partly because that is what a missionary is supposed to do and partly because I knew that was the only way I would get food. When you can't buy food with money but can only get it through the goodness of others, it helps your attitude towards them a lot. Everyone was related to everyone else, so if you said anything bad about anyone, you were in trouble. The branch president and the members carried the main burden of our care, but nearly everyone on the island was solicitous of our needs and helped whenever they could. Feki was related some way to the chief magistrate and that helped.

Basically we ate four types of foods: (1) fruits such as pineapples, oranges, mangoes, and bananas; (2) tubers (starchy roots) such as *talo* (taro root), *ufi* (like a huge potato, eighteen inches or more long, four or five inches in diameter, and fluffy when cooked), and *kumala* (similar to yams or sweet potatoes); (3) leafy greens such as *lu* (similar to spinach) and seaweed; and (4) seafood from the lagoon, such as fish, crabs, lobsters, and the like. One of my favorites was a sardine-like fish baked whole for two or three days so you could eat it all like a breadstick—head, innards, tail, and all. It was a real treat.

Most of the time we ate *hamu* (fruits and vegetables only) without a *kiki* (meat from an animal source, such as fish or lobster). But a couple of times a week we would have some type of fish and once or twice a month we might even have chicken or a little pork, especially if there was a funeral or marriage where a pig was roasted. We had no milk, beef, or dairy products of any kind. There were, of course, no refrigerators, ice, or coolants.

I had excellent health and felt about as good as I ever have. I noticed that the people were generally very healthy with straight, white teeth, beautiful hair, clear complexions, strong bodies, and almost inexhaustible energy. We mostly drank coconut juice. There were a few barrels to catch rainwater, which we also drank. It was sweet, but often had to be dumped out when rats or other animals crawled in and drowned. If it didn't rain for a long time, we drank well water, which was quite brackish, but when you're thirsty, you don't mind.

Our church meetings were wonderful. The branch president did his best to conduct them in an appropriate way, and the Spirit of God prevailed despite some obvious problems. I remember asking the branch president what time sacrament meeting started. He looked to the west, pointed partway down the sky, and said, "When the sun is about there."

I learned that was the best way. Everyone understood and could see the sun. It was a clock everyone could afford. My watch soon rusted out. I threw it away and didn't get another until I returned to the United States. People were nearly always "on time"; that is, they arrived at church when the sun was "about there." If everyone was present, we might start early; if everyone wasn't there, we waited. Attendance averaged from twenty to twenty-five depending on sickness and investigators. The meetings varied a lot and lasted until they were done. On small attendance Sundays, that was until everyone had participated; on large attendance Sundays, that was until the *umu* (meal) was *moho* (baked well).

It was a marvelous thing to see how united everyone was. No one had watches, but everyone knew when the church service should be over. It was a united sense that everyone felt. I suppose sacrament meetings were somewhere between one and two hours, but they never ended too soon, nor went too long. You learn to feel things together in this more communal setting than when there are watches and individual time schedules. The one rule they never broke was this: when the smell from the *umu* came through as being done, the closing song and prayer followed rapidly.

Meal preparation was an art, especially for the Sunday meal. On Saturday they dug a hole, put wood in, and added rocks on top of the wood. They burned the wood, leaving hot rocks. They then lined the rocks with banana leaves, put in tubers, fish, sweet potatoes, or chicken, wrapped in more banana leaves. They then put more banana leaves on top of that and covered the whole thing with dirt. It steamed all night and into Sunday.

Each family or extended family had their own *umu,* but lots of sharing took place. If someone caught a large fish on Saturday, they shared it with most of the close-by families.

One of the status symbols of the day was to have a meal good enough to invite the *Faifekau* (preacher, minister, or missionary) to eat with you. The established preachers ate very well. We weren't in that category at the beginning of my mission. This practice was also a source of hard feelings for those families who invited the preachers to eat with them and were passed over for another family.

The villagers often speculated with great interest, "Where is the preacher going to eat today?" I wondered how the preachers chose. At first I thought it was who extended the initial invitation; then I thought an important factor was who had the best meal; I finally realized that probably the main factor was which family donated the most money at revivals.

I had several experiences that taught me that there were deeper feelings of love and hurt, kindness and revenge among the people than I had suspected. Most of the reasons for hurt feelings seemed pretty silly to me.

I learned you can choose to argue over anything or be offended in any manner. I saw hurt feelings that festered for years when the *Faifekau* chose one family's meal over another or other similar situations. They seemed like insignificant things to get hurt feelings over, but I soon realized some of the things we choose to get hurt feelings over in our culture are just as crazy. I suppose it's silly to be offended or get hurt feelings over anything. I was glad I didn't have to worry about the politics of village life. I just wanted to preach the gospel, but I also hoped I could get enough to eat.

I tried to understand what was going on around me, but everyone spoke so fast that I couldn't keep up. We tried to go out and visit every day, but sometimes it rained so hard that we could hardly move, and other times the branch president insisted on us helping him with his chores. We felt duty-bound to help him because he had done so much for us. He was a good man and I liked him and his wife and daughter.

I tried to obey the mission president and Feki but felt very inadequate and wasn't sure how much good I was doing. I studied the language as much as I could and tried to speak it often, but felt I was not doing too well. Sometimes I felt I was making progress, and other times I felt I was going backwards. Thank goodness Feki was always happy and supportive. I learned that when people are discouraged, they don't need criticism or lectures—they need positive examples of happiness.

# 7

## *Despondency and Deep Feelings*

For several weeks things seemed to move along quite well. There was something new to learn or someplace different to go each day. Before long, however, I began to realize that everyplace we went, we had been before and everything we did we had done before. Seven square miles is a fairly small area, and doing the same things and visiting the same places over and over again became quite monotonous. After a while that old devil homesickness, and the accompanying discouragement, began to set in again.

It rained a lot and was hot and humid—everything began to smell musty to me. The language still seemed to run together with no real meaning. The days seemed interminably long, the food less palatable; everything appeared flat, dull, and unmeaningful. I tried to study hard, and I tried to act enthusiastic and seem excited about going out and visiting, but the fact was I was starting to feel I couldn't stand the weather, the mosquitoes, the smells, the food, or the strange words any longer.

As I started to sink into the hole of self-pity, I found my main solace in prayer and scripture study. Letters were few and far between as the boat came only about once a month. There were no visits from the mission president, and my companion refused to speak to me in English. I was frustrated and discouraged. Why couldn't I understand? Why didn't I feel better about things? What good was I really doing? This was such a small place, so few people, so far away, so different. What was I doing here? The old question of Should I even be here? kept recurring. In the back of my mind I could hear the mission president saying, "I have prayed about it and I have just the place for you." I respected him, and to some degree that statement kept me going.

Some days seemed better than others, but generally there was a downward drift, down to discouragement, discontent, and despondency. I had a feeling that no one really cared about me, nor even knew where I was or what I was going through. I tried to fight these feelings but found myself giving in to them more than overcoming them.

I remember well one morning waking to the sound of rain. A leak in the roof had developed near my feet, and they were wet. Everything felt and smelled dank and dark. No one was moving, and I sat up and thought, "I can't stay here any longer under these circumstances. Something has to change. I must get out of here. I can't stand it any longer!" It was still dark. I got up and lit the kerosene lantern. I swatted at the swarming mosquitoes and tried to read some scriptures.

I opened the Book of Mormon and read a little. Eventually my eyes fell on some verses from Ether that seemed to irresistibly pull at my attention. I read over and over again Ether 12:27: "If men come unto me I will show unto them their weakness. I give unto men weakness that they may be humble; and my grace is sufficient for all men that humble themselves before me; for if they humble themselves before me, and have faith in me, then will I make weak things become strong unto them."

If anyone was weak, I was. If anyone needed strength, I did. For some reason this verse seemed to kindle a determination in me to either "do or die" and find out whether I should even be here. I guess part of humility is knowing that you don't know everything, and there were lots of things I didn't know. I felt I had to receive an assurance that I was doing what God wanted me to do and I was where He wanted me to be, no matter what it cost. I don't know why or how that feeling came, but it came and it came very strongly.

I determined I would fast and pray and read the scriptures all that day. It was raining and I didn't know that I could do any good visiting the people anyway. I told Feki of my decision. He just smiled and said, "Okay," and went about his work.

I neither can nor should go into detail as to what happened over the next few days. The thing that is important is that I learned, as all people can learn, that God hears and answers prayers. It may not always be in the way we hope, but it is always in the way that is best for the person praying.

If we anticipate voices or visions or things spectacular, we will likely not receive them. But if we humble ourselves before God and sincerely ask for His help, He will help us. First, He will help us see ourselves as we really are, which is at the same time one of the hardest and one of the most blessed things we can understand. I reflected on Nephi's words in 2 Nephi 4:17–19: "My heart sorroweth because of my flesh; my soul grieveth because of mine iniquities. I am encompassed about, because of the temptations and the sins which do so easily beset me. And when I desire to rejoice, my heart groaneth because of my sins; nevertheless, I know in whom I have trusted."

As the days wore on, I read the rest of Nephi's psalm and David's and many others. There is a valley of darkness through which all of us are led, but if we trust in the Lord, we will get to a point where we will "fear no evil," for we will know that His "rod" and His "staff" do comfort us (Psalm 23:4).

Suffice it to say, when a small price had been paid, when sufficient effort had been put forth, the Lord in His goodness comforted my soul. What greater blessing could there be? What greater blessing is there?

I knew that God knew who I was. I knew that Jesus knew me (weaknesses and all) and still loved me, as He does all men, women, and children. I knew that He died for me and for all mankind. I knew that He freely suffered and gave His life for me and for everyone. I knew that His love was unlimited—broad, wide, and deep as all eternity, without any bounds. I knew He was my friend.

There was much struggling of spirit and many tears, often tears of joy, and then more struggling to express that joy. Words cannot adequately express feelings, but as I finished my determined course, I could hardly contain myself when I read 2 Nephi 4:34–35: "O Lord, I have trusted in thee, and I will trust in thee forever. I will not put my trust in the arm of flesh; for I know that cursed is he that putteth his trust in the arm of flesh. Yea, cursed is he that putteth his trust in man or maketh flesh his arm. Yea, I know that God will give liberally to him that asketh. Yea, my God will give me, if I ask not amiss; therefore I will lift up my voice unto thee; yea, I will cry unto thee, my God, the rock of my righteousness. Behold, my voice shall forever ascend up unto thee, my rock and mine everlasting God."

Sometimes when things aren't going right, we think we need to get away from a place or a person. Sometimes that helps, but most of the time what we need is to get away from our old self and our selfish feelings. We can leave a place behind, or we can stay in that place and leave our selfishness (often expressed in feeling sorry for ourselves) behind. If we leave a place and take our selfishness with us, the cycle of problems starts all over again no matter where we go. But if we leave our selfishness behind, no matter where we are, things start to improve.

During this time neither my companion nor the local people bothered me. They just left me alone and only occasionally asked if there was anything they could do to help. When I shook my head, they left and said no more. My experience is that Tongans generally are much more attuned to people's feelings than *palangis,* and they instinctively seem to know when to leave people alone and when to press to do things with them.

From that moment on I tried to never look back. I realized that any small place or any small number of people was more complex than I could comprehend and contained more potential than I could possibly realize. The infinite cost of the Savior's suffering and dying for all of us makes even one soul anywhere of infinite worth and deserving of all the energy, effort, sacrifice, and love our whole lives are capable of giving. There is no such thing in this universe as a place too small or a people too few to not warrant our full effort and more. I now knew that for sure!

True love, God's love, is the answer to all concerns. It fills the universe and should fill our lives and our thoughts and our actions. To know that He suffered and died for others as well as for us is the greatest single force in the universe to give us the desire and the power to help others. We all fall short in many ways. We all love much less than we should. But the Savior did not fall short, nor love one whit less than He should. Literally, the universe is filled with His love, and we should be filled with love because of Him. Oh, how we should try with all our hearts to become part of this infinite love! I was determined to do so.

When I returned from my odyssey back to the branch and my companion, I was quieter and more subdued in my conduct. I seemed to weep more—and to listen more. I seemed to feel more of what was going on around me and be more empathetic with the problems others were experiencing. I tended to look deeper into people's eyes and tried harder to testify to them that God lives and loves them. I tried with all of my heart to let them know that Jesus lives and loves us, and because of Him all will be well—eventually. I tried to have faith and to

*A typical "saliote" or horse-drawn cart—*
*big wheels were needed for the mud and ruts.*

show love and patience in all things. I felt I understood, at least a little better, the importance of faith, hope, and charity. I tried to impart the fruits of as many of these qualities as I could.

I wish I could constantly be surrounded by that aura of warmth, love, and certainty that I felt then. I was now ready, in a new way, to go to work with Feki and teach, testify, love, and help for a different reason than before. I hoped I was ready not to complain anymore, or at least not as much.

# 8

## "The Angels
## Have Recorded"

After I caught my second spiritual wind, we worked harder
than ever. As we spent more time out visiting and sensed the conflicts
this caused with the branch president, we realized we should have our
own house. We knew the only way we could have it was to build it
ourselves, so we determined to do so. When we announced our intentions, it caused deep and mixed emotions. The branch president did
not want us to leave his home, but when we agreed to build our house
near his, he was more cooperative. There were about thirty members
of the branch, most of whom were active, at least in the sense of acknowledging they were members and coming to meetings. Some of
these members volunteered to help while others did not.

To begin construction, we needed several strong poles of considerable length for the outside supports. Experienced people told us that
ironwood poles were best. Ironwood is aptly named. It grows in the
swamps and lasts a long time both above and below ground. Since
there were no saws, the only way to get the ironwood out was to wade
into the swamps and cut it with machetes. The wood was so hard that
the first few blows of even the sharpest machete hardly made a dent.

Several of the priesthood brethren finally agreed to a pole-cutting
project. Early one morning, eight of us met to go two-by-two into the
swamp. Each team was to bring back four ironwood poles of five to
six inches in diameter and ten to twelve feet in length. It was a formidable task, but we were all agreed. We had something to drink, ate
some left-over *talo*, and left for the swamp.

The branch president had made team assignments. I was assigned to a strong young man. We all noticed that Feki was assigned to the laziest one of the group. We smiled, as we knew Feki was by far the hardest worker.

It gets very hot and the mosquitoes are terrible in the swamp, so we were all anxious to cut the poles and get out as soon as possible. While we were gone, the Relief Society sisters agreed to weave *polas* (woven coconut leaves) to use for the roof and walls of our thatched home. They also said they would have a nice meal ready for us about midafternoon, when they estimated we would return with the poles.

Each team separated to a different part of the swamp and started hacking away. I would swing a hundred times or so while my partner rested—if you can rest while knee deep in a hot, smelly swamp with mosquitoes constantly swarming around you! After my hundred swings, my partner would swing while I tried to fend off the mosquitoes. Even though my arm was awfully tired at times, it seemed preferable to be swinging than standing. I suppose we were bitten with about the same frequency, whether standing or swinging the machete, but you didn't notice the mosquitoes, the heat, or the smells so much when you were working hard.

Eventually, we finished cutting our trees. We removed the limbs and had four poles of sufficient length and diameter to meet our goal. It was probably about three in the afternoon when we came dragging our poles back. One team had arrived shortly before us and another came soon after. We waited and waited, but Feki and his partner did not come. The Relief Society had the meal ready, but we decided to wait until Feki and his partner returned. The ladies were still weaving *polas,* so we helped them as we waited.

Weaving *polas* is an interesting process. You weave the individual coconut leaves together and then periodically break the hard back of one of the leaves and stick the broken stem into the next leaf so it holds together. Some do the weaving tight and strong, and others make the weave too loose. Over the several weeks of building our house, I wove a lot of *polas* and became fairly proficient at it.

We waited, wove, and talked for a long time. An hour went by— no Feki. We were hungry and the food was ready, but we waited. Two hours. *Where was Feki?* We all knew what had happened and why it was taking so long. We said as much as we got hungrier and hungrier.

Finally after nearly three hours, Feki and his companion came dragging four nice poles. Almost in unison we called out, "Finally! What took you so long?" We all knew Feki had done nearly all the work, and we were pushing him to tell us how lazy his partner was, but he just smiled as they placed their poles alongside the others.

We kept pushing him as the Relief Society sisters spread the meal, but he said nothing. Finally I said, "Ah, c'mon, Feki, tell us why it took you so long. Didn't your partner work at all?"

Feki looked me straight in the eye. He looked at the others, too, then softly said, "What difference does it make to you why it took us so long? We have our poles. The angels have recorded the work done this day, and that is all that counts." He smiled broadly and sat down. We all looked at one another, somewhat embarrassed, realizing in our hearts that he had spoken the truth and said something quite profound. I had never thought of Feki as being profound before, but I did now. The atmosphere abruptly changed from one of needling to one of contemplation.

The meal was ready, so after prayer we all ate and began to laugh. We talked about the varied events of the day. We had happy feelings, as the food was good, our hunger was satisfied, and the poles were in.

But during occasional moments of silence that evening, I pondered the power of Feki's statement: "What does it matter to you? The angels have recorded the work done this day."

I thought of the many things we do in school, with friends, in business, even in Church, which are largely for show, to get credit, or to be the top of the class. The Savior's teachings flooded my mind: "Where your treasure is, there will your heart be also" (Matthew 6:21); "No man can serve two masters" (Matthew 6:24); and more. I thought of the Pharisees, of the pomp and the trumpets. I thought of the widow's mite, and then I found my mind resting for a long time on the publican. I could all but literally see him and hear his cry as he smote his breast and cried, "God be merciful to me a sinner" (Luke 18:13).

As dusk deepened to darkness, I looked across the small fire into Feki's dancing eyes, and my heart melted with admiration. He had absolutely refused to downgrade another. I knew I could trust him. Yes, the angels had recorded the work, the words, and the feelings of that day, and they were good.

# 9

# *Building Our House*

We continued to visit people each day, but most of our time for the next several weeks was spent building our house. Deciding on the size and shape of our *fale* (house) and placing the ironwood poles accordingly was the first step. We had to dig deep holes and pack the poles firmly with rocks and dirt so they were solid and could withstand weight, wind, time, and other forces. It took a long time, but eventually we got the main outside poles up and began working on the rest of the house.

Feki was a master planner and builder. People on Niuatoputapu marveled at his talents and ideas, as did I. I had worked some in construction in Idaho, but my experience with saws, hammers, nails, and dimensional lumber was largely useless here, sometimes to my embarrassment, so I followed Feki's lead. Inside the main poles we dug additional holes and placed a series of much shorter poles in them, upon which we built a floor about two feet above the ground. The floor was made from split coconut logs and was covered with several layers of coconut fronds and mats.

We next built the roof. We measured the exact size and then built the roof superstructure on the ground using many medium-sized poles. It was a standard inverted **V** configuration. When all the poles were tied firmly together and the superstructure was tested for strength and firmness, we tied hundreds of *polas* to it, one on top of another, only a few inches apart, much like shingles. At the apex, we placed some specially prepared *polas* that evenly divided the rain, so it would run down both sides. It rained a lot, so the roof was thoroughly tested on the ground and any gaps filled before we lifted the whole roof structure up on the main poles and secured it in place with more sennit.

We next built walls by attaching small poles with coconut sennit horizontally to the perpendicular main poles. (The sennit was a braided cord made from coconut husks.) We then brought the dried *polas* the sisters had woven and tied them to this framework in sections. We left a space for a door and tied the *polas* on the poles to about four feet above the floor, leaving the area between there and the beginning of the roof open for ventilation.

There were no nails used in the house, just local materials. I guess some had tried nails before, but they split the brittle wood, rusted, and seemed inferior to sennit binding. During construction, I noticed how useful the coconut trees were to the Tongans. Not only did they provide shade and beauty, but the trunks furnished poles for houses; the leaves furnished *polas* for roofs and walls; the coconuts furnished drink, food, and oil; the husks furnished material to make rope or string (sennit) bindings, and what was left furnished firewood for cooking.

Some of the sennit lashing designs Feki and others made on the rafter poles were absolutely beautiful and to me were works of art. Not only were the cross beams held securely by the sennit, but the pattern and design developed in the careful overlaying of various colored (dyed) cords was magnificent to behold, much like a beautiful painting. Feki, as well as others, took great pride in this work.

After we raised the roof and secured it with sufficient lashings, we had a structure that looked and felt like a house. We next placed a series of loose *polas* from the roof that could be let down to cover the open space in case of heavy rain or wind. We still needed a door and some steps to get up the two feet to the main floor, but we started to sleep in our house anyway.

We soon found that the pigs and chickens loved to stay under the raised floor. They made a lot of noise, to say nothing of the smell and mess they left. We decided that wouldn't do, so Feki and I got a large number of small poles, cut them into four-foot lengths, and sharpened one end. We then made some large, wooden mallets, and for days we pounded poles into the ground around our house. We wore out several mallets but eventually had a fairly large area around our home enclosed with hundreds of poles close enough together that pigs, dogs, and chickens could not get in.

*Coconut fronds were woven and then
dried in the sun to be used to make
the roof and walls of the house.*

*The roof was built on the ground,
then lifted into place. Dried polas
were attached much like shingles.*

Feki figured out an ingenious way to make a gate and a door, and soon we had a real house. The whole project took several weeks. We had quite a bit of help from members and nonmembers alike, but Feki still did most of the work. I helped the best I could, which probably wasn't very much.

It makes you feel good when you have finally accomplished something quite challenging. I wish more missionaries could have the experience of building their own homes. You appreciate a home much more when you have labored for a long time to build it. Of course times and circumstances have changed now, but I still think missionaries generally should take more pride in their living quarters.

When the house was finished, we officially moved our things from the branch president's house to our new home. It was quite a day—

*Feki pounding small poles for perimeter fence to keep animals out.*

*Feki tying dried* polas *to form the walls of our almost finished house.*

moving is traumatic no matter where it occurs. Our house was close to the branch president's home but far enough to be separate and provide needed privacy for everyone.

We held a dedication service for our house to which we invited the branch members and several other friends. Many people had helped and most of them came to the dedication. We were obligated to furnish a feast for those we invited, so we had extra work to prepare the food and drink. The priesthood brethren and Relief Society sisters helped as much and as happily with the feast as they had on the building of the house. As a result, the dedication was a big success. We asked the branch president to offer the dedicatory prayer. He did a good job, and from then on he felt better about everything. We were now officially on our own. It felt good to be in our own home.

# 10

## The Boy and the Mango Tree

Shortly after moving into our house, I received a great lesson in Tongan faith. It happened like this: the day was hot, the mangoes were ripe, and life moved slowly forward. Feki and I had just returned from visiting when suddenly we heard some yelling and knew something unusual had happened.

The noise of a small crowd was getting closer to our house. We went outside to see what was going on just as a member, his family, and a few others arrived at our *fale*.

The father carried the seemingly lifeless body of his little ten-year-old boy wrapped in a large *tupenu* (piece of cloth). As the father lowered him from his shoulder and put him into my arms, he said, "He has fallen from high in a mango tree and hit his head and back on the hard roots. Here, make him well and bring him back to me."

I looked at the limp body and said, "He's dead. What can I do?" The father just looked at me and said, "Whether he's dead or not, I do not know. What I do know is I want him well again, and you have the power to do it."

I said, "Life is from God. If God has allowed his life to leave, we should be reconciled." He responded, "I've talked to God. I want my boy back now more than God wants him now. Make him well. It's fine."

I didn't know the words in Tongan to administer to his son, and I was looking for some way to get out of this uncomfortable situation. I had not personally experienced this type of faithful determination before and I just wanted to leave, but the look of expectation on the faces of his father, mother, brothers, sisters, and friends was so intense that I felt tremendous pressure to do something.

"We should get the branch president," I said, stalling for time. No sooner had I said this than the branch president walked up. He had been working in his garden when he heard the disturbance and came to see what was happening.

Feki quickly explained the situation. In a sort of panic-stricken state, I said, "You're the branch president. This is your responsibility."

I tried to give the child to him, but he said, "No, just hold him. I'm going to shower, clean up, and put on my Sunday clothes. Then we'll administer to him, and we'll see what God's will is."

I couldn't believe him. I complained, "He's dead, or dying, and you want to clean up first?" He looked at me with compassion (and maybe a little disdain for my lack of faith) and replied, "It is a sacred work to administer to someone. I am not going to approach God all sweaty and in my dirty clothes."

I waited for what seemed hours (but was probably less than ten minutes). Everyone else was calm and quiet, but *my* heart was pounding fiercely. There was no movement from the child. Finally the branch president emerged in his clean white clothes with a bottle of olive oil. Feki, who was a priest, helped me with the Tongan words as I anointed the boy, and the branch president sealed the anointing and blessed him.

I didn't understand all of the words of the blessing, but I did understand when the branch president finished and said to me, "Take the boy. Pray. Exercise your faith, and it will be according to God's will, his parents' faith, and *your* faith."

In all this time, I had not felt a heartbeat or breathing or any movement from the boy. I despaired as all eyes turned to me. The logic of my thinking was to tell them, "Dig a grave. This boy is dead. Don't make me do this."

But the faith of the Tongans caused me to go into our house with Feki, carrying the boy's limp body. It was almost evening. We closed the door, let the blinds down, and sat there in a sort of stupor as I thought of the father's last words, "We'll wait right here for as long as it takes. Just bring my boy back to me alive and well." I laid the boy wrapped in his *tupenu* on the floor. I could see no movement at all.

I have been scared on many occasions—such as car crashes, near drownings, scholastic tests, and the like—but I'm not sure I have ever been more scared than at that moment. This was life. This was faith.

This was priesthood power on the line. And there was only me, my companion, a seemingly lifeless body—and God.

I prayed as I had never prayed before, "Help me out of this. What should I do?" Tears followed—tears of sorrow for the family and the boy and also tears of fear. What could I do? My faith simply was not strong enough. Feki sat in the corner waiting silently.

Little by little the fog of my mental despair began to dissipate. I began to feel: This is God's work. I am on His mission. The branch president holds the priesthood. So do I. These people have faith. God wouldn't leave us without some way out. These people can be made to understand. It won't be that bad. Something will work out somehow.

Then I reflected: God lives and loves us. Jesus lives and loves us. He healed the sick. He brought back the dead. As my mind caught hold of that thought, a light began to appear. Fear began to recede. Faith began to motivate my prayers.

The more earnestly I prayed, the brighter the light became. My thought was no longer, "How do I get out of this?" but rather, "What is God's will? What should I do? I'll do it, no matter what it is." I felt much better. I was still shaking, but light and courage were now replacing darkness and fear.

Time went by, then a very faint impression came, "Give him artificial respiration." I waited, but the impression stayed. The only artificial respiration I remembered was when I was a Boy Scout and we learned to push on the back of the rib cage and say, "Out goes the bad air, in comes the good." It seemed silly, but I felt I should try. I didn't even think about the possible damage if he had broken bones. I turned him on his stomach and put his head to the side with his arms at right angles. I could sense the limp, cold feel of death, but I also felt the warmth and power of faith that seemed to be pouring through the very walls of our house.

I couldn't remember exactly what to do, except to push on his back and say, "Out goes the bad air," then release and say, "in comes the good," so that is what I did. For several minutes my hopes rose, but as time ticked by and nothing happened, that former dark feeling of fear began to return. "No!" I said. "Get away! You can't be here, not with their faith!"

Suddenly, I felt a little twitch. Was it one of my muscles? Silence. More artificial respiration. Another twitch. *That's not me,* I thought. Then another twitch, and another, more definite now. It must have been an hour since he was first placed in my arms with no sign of life.

More artificial respiration. A stronger twitch, then all of a sudden a violent retching and a great gush of half-digested mango pieces and gastric juices spewed onto the floor. It came and came. There seemed to be more than it was possible for one little boy to hold.

The smell was terrible, yet sweet, for what did I notice as the retching subsided? Tiny shades of breathing? Slight rising and falling of the back? Could it be?

Faithful Feki moved from the corner and with a rag, a bucket, and water began cleaning up the mess.

The night wore on. At times I thought there was regular breathing. At other times I thought I was deceiving myself. Prayers ascended all night. The fight between the light of faith and the darkness of fear continued. Finally the first glimmerings of dawn began to appear. There was still no sustained movement. But as the daylight became a reality and the darkness faded away, so did the light of faith reign and the darkness of fear depart.

There was definitely a hint of breathing and a little warmth where his heart was. We had no thought of eating or drinking, just fasting and praying and the spiritual sustenance of faith to keep us going. Throughout the day we could hear the family outside, but never once did they complain or even inquire. They just waited, prayed, and believed.

Again, twilight came. But as the light receded and the soft cover of darkness enveloped our small *fale,* this time it did not bring with it fear but rather a sweet assurance that things would be all right.

The prayers continued, increasing in faith through the second night. We kept up a constant *mili mili* (rubbing or massaging of the back). Finally, as the light returned the second morning, there was a little movement of the boy's head, a tentative moan, and a tiny flutter of the eyelids. As the first sunbeams of the light came through the cracks of the coconut frond blinds and streamed across the floor up to the young boy's face, almost on cue his eyes popped open. He looked about for a moment, still without moving, and simply said, "*'Oku ou 'ife?*" ("Where am I?")

His eyes closed again for a while, then reopened. His head moved. He rolled over on his back, then on his side. He tried to get up but couldn't. He was too weak to walk, but he was alive! I picked him up and carried him to his parents outside. As Feki opened the door, the whole family stood waiting. I simply handed the little boy back to his father and said, "*He'e, ko ho foha. Kuo sai.*" ("Here is your son. He is all right.")

With tears of gratitude, they thanked me profusely. With as much sincerity as I have ever felt, I replied, "Thank God, not me. He healed him. In an eternal sense, only He can truly heal. That is who the Savior is—the great Healer of all mankind and of all our problems. If we will only have faith in Him and do as He says, He will heal us all of all our problems." They listened respectfully.

It is hard to comprehend the feelings of that moment, for they were deep and full of love, faith, tears of joy, and the Spirit of God. Feki and I returned to our house, and after prayer we slept and slept and slept. No one bothered us. How sweet sleep is when you have done your duty and followed God's will—no matter what was required!

I don't know why this incident occurred, or exactly how. All I know is that it happened. I have seen just as much faith on many other occasions without the same results. I have learned that true faith in God does not require specific physical benefits but rather a sincere desire for God's will to be done, knowing that He knows best. The great faith behind the sublime statement, "Nevertheless not my will, but thine, be done" must find place in our hearts and lives (see Luke 22:42). When we understand His will through faith, no further questions or problems exist, for even if His will is different from our original will, His will becomes our will.

In this and other similar situations in Tonga, I felt more like a bystander than an active participant. I felt like I was standing on the shore of a mighty river while watching the powerful flow of faith go by. That river of faith was like an unfathomable current that I could see and feel, but not fully understand from where it came or to where it was going, yet every part of me felt its force and beauty and power. It was marvelous!

In a few days the boy was running around and climbing mango trees again.

There was no huge stir among the people of Niuatoputapu, even though they all knew of the event. Outwardly, at least, not much changed. A few more doors were opened to us. Most were still closed, but I felt a subtle change.

I heard little whispers, both good and bad, everywhere we went. People didn't turn us away quite so curtly. A few more questions were asked. Some listened and a few were baptized. The opportunity to teach and bear testimony was a little greater, and the work of God and the building of His kingdom moved forward.

# 11

## A Quick Remedy

We continued to visit and continued to get turned away by most everyone. Occasionally a family would agree to listen, and when they did, we stayed and talked as long as we could. One evening we visited with a family in another village until quite late. They asked if we could stay with them that night. I was unsure, so I looked to Feki; he nodded his approval, so we stayed. They fed us a great meal and spread some mats for us in one end of the house. After prayers, we were soon fast asleep.

I was sleeping soundly when I sensed a movement. I rolled over and tried to go back to sleep, but I felt uneasy. There was a bright moon out and the end of the house we were in had some open ceiling, so it was fairly easy to see things. As I looked to where Feki should be, I realized he was gone. I then looked on the other side and saw that a new mat had been pulled in and a beautiful young woman was sleeping there. She had a sheet over most of her body. As she sensed me turning that way, she smiled and moved the sheet down some.

I was devastated. *Where was Feki? How long had he been gone?* I couldn't stay, but I feared getting up and walking out as I knew she was awake. If I obviously spurned her, she could start some bad rumors, and I wasn't sure what she or the other family members would do. *How had I ended up in this situation?* I quickly closed my eyes. Maybe she hadn't realized I was awake but was just responding to my turning.

I prayed with all my heart. *What should I do? Please help me get out of this. I didn't try to do this.* I felt myself getting warmer and warmer, then all of a sudden I had terrible stomach cramps. I knew I was going to throw up. I sprang from my mat coughing and trying to keep from vomiting. I raced outside to the nearest bushes, where I heaved and heaved until I thought my whole insides would come out. Soon a small crowd gathered, including Feki, the parents, this girl (now appropriately dressed), and several others. They could see how much pain I was in and really showed concern when they saw some blood in what I was throwing up.

I was finally able to settle down some, but I was still shaking and sweating and felt semidelirious. They helped me to a nice mat outside in the open. Feki and one or two others started fanning my burning brow and put some wet towels on my forehead. They stayed the rest of the night with me as I fitfully tossed and turned.

It was almost light before I dozed off and was able to sleep for a few hours. When I woke, it was daytime. Someone had made a canopy of sheets over me with four poles. Feki and two others were still there watching. They were all smiles as I opened my eyes.

What a beautiful sight to see Feki with his contagious smile, pearly teeth, and sense of self-assurance. I closed my eyes again and thanked God for His help. I slept some more, and when I woke again only Feki was there. My stomach wasn't churning anymore, the fever was mostly gone, and I felt fine. I asked Feki where he had gone during the night. He said the father had asked him to come and help on a project; while they were working on it, I had come out and began throwing up. I never told him what happened and doubt he had any idea.

I learned that God will always provide a way for us to escape from danger if we seek him sincerely, even though the means he uses may sometimes be quite unusual. I also realized more fully why missionary companions should always stay together.

I eventually got up and walked around a little, still somewhat unsteadily. The family came and apologized. They thought they had fed me something poisonous. "Strange, though," they mused, "we all ate the same food and no one else got sick." They asked how I was feeling, and I assured them I was fine. They were very relieved and expressed their happiness that I was feeling better now. The girl who had been there the night before was among those who seemed relieved that I was feeling better. Nothing more was ever said about the incident. We never slept at that house again.

# 12

## *Tangi Lau Lau*

By now, I could communicate some in Tongan, but not in much depth. We had been in our house only a few weeks when a delegation came from the village of Falehau and asked if we could come and help a very sick man. Knowing there was currently no doctor or hospital on the island, we agreed and immediately went to Falehau. When we arrived, I noticed many people sitting around looking at us skeptically but expectantly.

The sick man was around fifty years old. He had developed a large boil on his neck that had grown inward and was cutting off his throat passage. He could not eat or drink and was having difficulty breathing. He seemed to be starving to death and was nearly nothing but skin and bones. Unlike the family and friends who gathered when the member's boy was hurt, this group was not united by faith. I was scared—I had no idea what to do, and I realized they expected me to do something.

The main contact Tongans on this island had previously had with white people was during World War II when some Allied soldiers set up a tracking station on top of the mountain. After a few months the tracking station was moved farther west to the Solomon Islands. Even though the soldiers were there only a short time, they left a reputation for three things: (1) being womanizers, (2) teaching the local youth how to use pineapples to make "bush beer" or "home brew" (which proved deadly at times), and (3) giving out pills and medicines. I suppose these people felt that as a white man, I should have some pills or potions to help make this man well.

When I told them I had no pills, their countenances fell, and I became even more scared. I asked Feki to explain that even though we had no pills, we would be happy to pray for him. They scoffed at the notion of our praying and insisted I try something else.

There was a smoldering fire close to the house with lots of smoke to keep the mosquitoes away, and it was hard for me to breathe. I felt this smoke was not good for the sick man with his already difficult breathing and told Feki so, but he told me to not say anything about that. He encouraged me to try something else.

As much as I prayed and tried to think of something, I received no impression of anything to do. They asked me to examine the man more closely. It was a miserable ordeal. I was sure he was in the last stages of dying: he could hardly move or breathe, and there was a terrible smell about him. I wondered whether they could get into his throat with a knife and lance the boil, and whether that might help. But I couldn't explain how to do that, and I wasn't sure it was right anyway, so we dropped it.

We stayed several hours until early evening. I never could figure what to do. Finally, after they could see I either couldn't or wouldn't do anything, they let us go. As we left, I felt a darkness from the expressions of the family and friends and a sense of anger in their eyes.

We arrived back home about midevening. After the normal chores of hauling water, gathering firewood, sweeping the house and yard, and bathing, we read scriptures, said our prayers, and retired for the night.

I could not sleep. The thoughts of that suffering man, the awful smell, the smoke, and the angry eyes of his family and friends following me—all combined to create a nightmare. I prayed for relief and explained to God that I had tried my best but just hadn't known what else to do. It all seemed to no avail, and the oppressive feeling of darkness got worse. I would fitfully drift off for a moment and then suddenly awaken with a feeling of dread and fear.

Sometime during that long and frightful night, I sat up with a start. I was aware of an eerie sound. It seemed to ooze from the walls, the ground, the sky, everything around me. At first I sensed it more than heard it. This fearful, almost unearthly, sound got louder and louder. I was not dreaming . . . it was real!

Such howling and mourning and crying! It seemed to bounce off the trees and fill the island, then rush into our house and engulf me with the darkest of fears. I noticed Feki stirring. Frantically I asked,

"What is it?" He replied, "It's a *tangi lau lau* (mourning for the dead)." I shivered and wondered what it all meant.

The sound was getting louder and closer. In my fear, I imagined the dead man's family and friends coming after me. *But why and how? What are they going to do? What can I do?* I couldn't hide—there was no place to go. Besides, they were almost here.

I trembled with fear. I was certain that since I had failed them they were going to see that I paid. *But in what terrible way?* My imagination and fear ran wild. Almost hysterically I clung to Feki. "Help me, help me, they're coming! Listen to the howling and crying! What should we do?"

Quietly Feki put on his *tupenu*, opened the door, and stepped out into the heavy darkness that was now filled with wailing and shrieking such as I had never heard before. I thought of how brave Feki was, walking into the very jaws of a dark, tumultuous hell, or so it seemed to me.

I heard some subdued whispering, a few questions, and some responses. I could not understand much of the exchange. Then the howling started again as Feki returned to the room. Had he sold me out? What would happen? Feki wouldn't do that. Or would he? Maybe they had used some magic on him. What should I do?

Feki's face was somber. He sat down and looked at me for a long time. I was perspiring. My breath came short, my heart was pounding unmercifully. Then quietly and with dignity he said, "The man we visited this afternoon has just died. There has been some arguing. Some say they should have let us stay and pray; others say our coming speeded his death; still others say his death was inevitable and we had nothing to do with it. Finally, the head of the family told them we had tried our best to help, but it was God's will that the man die, and they should invite us to the wake and the funeral. They have sent a delegation and are asking us to come right now."

Feki continued, "Get dressed and follow me. Don't worry, they understand. No harm will come to you. Everything will be fine."

I wasn't totally convinced, but I trusted Feki. After the terrible imaginings I had just been through, I was ready to grasp at any straw of hope. The sky was starting to lighten as I got dressed and tremblingly followed Feki down the trail to Falehau. In the half darkness, shadows and sounds were magnified hundreds of times and seemed to literally jump out at us. With absolutely nothing mechanical on the island to interfere with the morning stillness, I could hear almost everything and imagined everything else. The weeping and wailing we were headed for seemed louder and fiercer than ever. I followed Feki. I had to trust him. I had to.

By the time we got to the funeral, a large crowd had gathered. It was quite light now. A new day had begun.

They asked us to sit close to the bier of the dead man, who was covered with mats and *tapa* cloth. Relatives and friends came by the score. They were disheveled, with wild hair and old clothes. They wore the dingiest of mats, tattered and dirty. Their clothes were black, ragged, and torn (the older and dirtier, the more respectful, I later learned). They wailed and threw dust in the air and on their heads. Some ripped their clothes and showed other signs of deep emotion and sorrow.

My fear was now beginning to move into shades of wonder. I was still not sure what was going on, but I was getting caught up in the emotion of the whole event. Some came and threw themselves on the dead man's body, while others would lie at his feet and howl in a way I didn't think humans were capable of. Emotionally I was torn—fascinated and scared at the same time.

A group of five ladies arrived. They were dressed in black, with old mats and frazzled hair, their faces and eyes deep with sadness and mourning. What weeping and wailing came from them! I assumed they were sisters or aunts or even daughters of the deceased. How they carried on, with their wailing, so heartfelt and forlorn! "Oi, oi, Oiaueee," they wailed at the top of their lungs, holding the "eeee" sound up high till you would think their lungs would burst. Then they came down the scale like a sliding trombone until they got very low and very soft. They then took a few deep breaths and with renewed vigor shattered the skies with a tremendous outburst of even higher and louder "Oi, oi, oiaueee's" before eventually coming down again for more breath and another attempt at record length, height, and volume.

I marveled at what I perceived to be the depth of sorrow and mourning for the deceased. How they must miss him! I felt a little more at ease now that I sensed that the emotion of the people seemed directed toward the dead man and not me.

I had never experienced such literal "weeping, and wailing, and gnashing of teeth" (Alma 40:13). The howling and the sackcloth-and-ashes atmosphere felt like something from the Old Testament, and I thought of Isaiah's comments "howl ye inhabitants of the isle . . ." (Isaiah 23:6), "Ye daughters of Israel, weep" (2 Samuel 1:24).

I had been reading the Tongan Old Testament and comparing it to the English; in the midst of this mourning, I thought I could just as easily have been back in King David's time or in Abraham's. I felt that you can't really understand the Tongan people until you understand the Old Testament. The reverse is also true: You really don't understand the Old Testament until you've lived among and understood the Polynesian people. They truly are of the house of Israel. In their preaching, their mourning, their stories, and their actions, they refer a lot to the Old Testament and just naturally seem to understand it.

I was now becoming more and more a part of the whole event and could feel my own emotions changing from fear to wonder to sorrow. I almost felt as though I could join with them in their great lamentation over the loss of a loved one. I couldn't get Isaiah out of my mind: "Howl, O gate; cry, O city" (Isaiah 14:31). And these people did!

They had offered me something to eat, but I said, "No, I have come to comfort and mourn with you, not to eat." They said the *toupai* (pudding) would soon be ready and they knew I would like that. I still wondered if this was all a ploy to get me there, lull me into a form of security, then do something to me because I had not saved this man as they might have felt I could have done. I hoped not.

As I began to emotionally melt into the surroundings, I was even more fascinated at the intensity of the "oi, oi oiaueee's" of the lady next to me. Each wail was a crescendo, louder and higher and more hysterical than the last. I had never heard anything like it.

On one of the highest and loudest of her "oiaueee's," I felt there was no way a human voice could be held for so long. Finally, her voice started to come down, gradually becoming lower and softer. When she got to the very bottom, she took a deep breath (much to my relief), then unexpectedly turned to me and with anticipation whispered, "*Kuo moho 'ae toupai?*" ("Is the pudding done?").

I was stunned. I could hardly believe my ears. What had she said? The trance I had built for myself started to dissolve. I looked at her and replied, "*Te'eki ai*" ("Not yet"), and she immediately went into another long wail, higher and louder than ever before.

I found out later she was not a relative but rather a professional mourner. She was not so caught up in sorrow over the loss of a loved one as she was trying to do a good, professional job as a mourner. I often kid the Tongans that she was wailing more because the pudding wasn't done than because someone had died!

It turned out that all five of these ladies were professional mourners, and they were all very good. They came to help set the mood, to get fed, and to have something to do.

Of course, the family members and others were wailing sincerely for the loss of their brother, father, and friend. But I wondered if part of their wailing was knowing they had to feed so many people! The best thing to bring to a funeral in Tonga is a sack of flour or sugar, or a dozen loaves of bread to help feed the many friends and relatives who come and stay for days, weeks, or even months.

I soon came to the realization that these people were basically like people anywhere in the world. There are those who are sincere and those who are not. They needed the gospel as much as anyone to help them understand death as a transition and also to understand that the purpose of this life is to prepare for that transition.

I realized that these people were coming as the Israelites of old with weeping and wailing and gnashing of teeth, in sackcloth and ashes, but they needed help. They needed to remember some things encoded deep in their past. I understood again that the eternal question always has been and always will be not what people act like, or what they look like, or where they come from, or where or when they lived, or what language they speak, but what they are. Are they honest? Are they helpful? Have they come for their own account or to help someone else? I remembered Jesus talking about making Israelites out of rocks and realized again the significance of individual decisions.

I sat there for several hours, which was hard because I still wasn't used to sitting cross-legged and my circulation kept getting cut off. I felt I was learning some important things about human nature, such as the fact that sincerity is not always apparent, we often fear what we don't understand, and people are not always what they seem to be.

I remembered that the Savior spoke strongly against hypocrisy and said we must pray with "real intent," which I interpreted to mean having an eye single to His glory and being fully willing to do His will, no matter what it might be. If we have real intent, we have no hidden agenda.

I continued to listen and even ate some *toupai* as I reflected on these thoughts. I felt a deep kinship between their society and Old Testament times where a healthy expression of sorrow may have had a bigger place in life than we allow in our present Western culture. They buried the man before noon. However, the main part of the funeral lay ahead as the family hosted dozens of kin and friends. We visited with as many of them as we could, but before the sun set we returned to our home in Vaipoa.

*Funeral mourners. The frazzled hair and torn mats represent respect and
deep mourning for the deceased. The wreaths are later placed on the grave.*

The day had been an emotional roller coaster for me. First, fearing
that which never happened and never was intended; second, naively
assuming that all expressions of sorrow are sincere, when some are
and some are not; third, realizing that people everywhere cover about
the same spectrum when it comes to honesty of purpose; and fourth,
learning that generally things work out if we are patient and sincere
and willing to risk a little and listen a lot and feel for others more than
for ourselves. It was an educational twenty-four hours at the very
least.

# 13

## *"Toe Taha Mai!"*

I knew I had to learn the language better to be a good missionary. I could speak it superficially but was determined to heed my mission president's charge to learn the language well. I had memorized lots of phrases and understood a fair amount, but I knew I had a long way to go. I spent a great amount of time studying the language. Feki helped some, but generally he went out and worked with the branch president or other members while I studied. The only books I had in Tongan were the Book of Mormon and the Bible. I sat for hours and read and compared the English Book of Mormon to the Tongan. It didn't take long to recognize that the oft-repeated phrase *"Pea na'e hoko o pehe"* meant "And it came to pass."

I listened for words and phrases and wrote them down and asked Feki and others what they meant. As I learned more words, I started to understand the Book of Mormon in Tongan better than in English. I remember on one occasion thinking I knew what a verse in Tongan meant but was sure I was wrong because it didn't say the same thing in English. When I read the verse again in English, it suddenly dawned on me, "I think the Tongan is correct, and that's what it means in English. I just haven't understood it properly all these years."

I am convinced that learning another language helps us understand our own language better. We see things we have never thought of before. Experts say that learning another language expands our mind about as much as any activity we can undertake. I agree.

I was so fascinated by the different inflections of meaning in both the Bible and the Book of Mormon in Tongan as opposed to English that I made voluminous notes to remind me that there were different ways of understanding words and phrases. The principles never change, but the emphasis, at least in my mind, did.

Being raised in the western United States and coming from a multi-generational Church family, I naturally related to the pioneers and Joseph Smith and modern-day revelation and prophets. But reading the Book of Mormon and Bible in Tongan and living among those people cause me to relate more and more to the Old Testament. The Tongan Bible was translated directly from Greek to Tongan, not from the English King James Version. Because a number of clarifying manuscripts have been found since the King James translators did their work, the Bible in Tongan has many verses that have been translated more accurately than the King James Version. For instance, in Tongan the very first verse in Genesis reads, "In the beginning the Gods [using a word that means three or more] formed the heaven and the earth," which is significantly different from the English, "In the beginning God created the heaven and the earth." There are many such examples.

The main change in emphasis that came to me was seeing modern-day prophets and pioneers in their historical context and relating the scriptures and my experiences more and more to the Old Testament and the covenants made with Abraham, Isaac, and Jacob. The Tongans are of Israel, and almost everything about their culture, faith, thoughts, and actions ties in closer to the Old Testament and the Book of Mormon, which has a heavy Old Testament leaning, than to what I had traditionally been used to. It was a mind-broadening experience that strengthened my faith to see how logically everything fit together.

Often while I was studying, the branch president would ask me to come and help him with various projects. I tried to help but couldn't always understand what he wanted me to do. He got angry when he told me to do something and I just stood there not knowing what he meant. He would yell, wave his hands, and point, and eventually I figured out what he wanted me to do.

I remember once he had me hold a pole while he stood back and did some visual sighting. Then he yelled, "*Toe taha mai!*" ("A little closer to me!") I didn't know whether to drop the pole or move it to the left or right or what. I decided to move it back. That really got him angry, and he yelled, after calling me a few choice names, "*Na'aku pehe toe taha mai ikai koe toe taha atu!*" ("I said move it toward me, not away from me!") I tried moving it to the side and even turned it upside down, only to see his anger rising each time. I finally moved it forward and saw a big smile come across his face as he exclaimed, "*Ko ia!*" ("That's it!")

Even though it was a tough way to learn, I never forgot that "*toe taha mai*" meant a little closer to the person speaking, and "*toe taha atu*" meant a little farther from the person speaking. There were lots of frustrations, but what I learned, I learned well. I was amazed at how much patience the people had with me most of the time.

By now I could bear my testimony in a heartfelt way and understand much of what was going on. I could contribute some to our discussions, but as far as feeling that I could carry on an extended, meaningful conversation or explain anything in understandable detail was concerned, I had no confidence at all. I knew lots of phrases and some parts of various lessons, but Feki kept pushing me to say new things and participate more in the discussions. I tried but often felt I was more of a hindrance than a help.

One day while in the home of a family who had agreed to listen to us, Feki started to give his usual introduction. I was busy running the words of testimony and phrases of support through my mind when I heard Feki say, "You are such good people and we like you so much, I am going to turn the lesson over to Elder Groberg to explain the correct principles in clarity and truth." I was jolted from my mental complacency. I protested with my eyes and looks of bewilderment and even a little anger, but Feki just sat there smiling. The whole family looked at me expectantly. What could I do?

I hesitatingly started to speak. I gave a couple of memorized phrases and bore testimony of their truthfulness. I then stopped and looked at Feki. Beads of sweat were forming on my brow. My throat was dry. *Please help me,* my expression pleaded. Feki continued to smile, with an expression of confidence in me. The mother said, "I believe what you just said is true. Do you have more for us?" They looked at me with so much hope and trust and longing. I knew I had to say something, but what? How I prayed!

I closed my eyes and seemed to see a beautiful grove of trees on a clear, spring day. There was an aura of light and goodness about the scene. I started to speak and found myself describing Joseph Smith's desire to find which church God wanted him to join. Without realizing it, I began explaining about Joseph's feelings—his desires to please God and his confusion at not knowing for sure how to do this. I asked the husband, "Do you know how he felt?" He replied, "I sure do."

I went on and on, explaining and asking questions and hearing responses. It never consciously occurred to me that I was saying words and using phrases I had never used before or that I was threading sentences together in a way that brought meaning into the hearts of these good people.

I found myself saying, "Now I'm sure when you learn what Joseph Smith learned about God's true Church, you will want to do what he did and be baptized and follow God's will, won't you?" Only then did it hit me that a miracle had occurred. The husband and wife looked at each other, then at Feki, then back to me. They had tears in their eyes. They said, "Of course we will. You'll need to explain more, but we do want to do God's will just like Joseph Smith did."

I didn't know what to say. I knew I had been able to explain things so others understood. I knew I had even used the proper tenses. I felt like shouting "Hallelujah" or "God be praised" but thought it might not be appropriate, so I simply said, "God's Spirit has been here. I'll now turn the time back to Feki."

Feki smiled and quickly made arrangements for the next meeting. He thanked them for their attention and asked if we could all kneel in prayer. He asked the father to give the prayer. He didn't want to and asked Feki if he would instead. What a beautiful prayer Feki offered! He thanked the Lord for His help, for sending His Spirit, for loosening my tongue, for confirming His word, and for blessing this family with faith. There was not a dry eye, even among the children, as we concluded that meeting.

Feki said no more, but from then on I was expected to give every other lesson, handle every other door approach, offer every other prayer, and be a full partner in all that was said and done. I couldn't say or understand everything, but from that day on I could say all I needed to say and understand all I needed to understand.

This is the way God works in our lives. We don't understand everything, or even very much, but we can understand all we need to understand. As we gain that essential core of knowledge, we find it contains within it the seeds of all other knowledge. The testimony of Jesus is not only the beginning of all knowledge but also the essential life-giving material from which all other knowledge springs. Without that testimony, we can learn nothing of real importance.

I learned that many Tongans, who some may classify as uneducated or even illiterate, have a better core of true knowledge through a firmer faith in and testimony of Jesus than many so-called educated men. I don't know how the rest of the knowledge we need will come, but I do know that those who are firmly tied to the source of all knowledge, namely faith in the Lord Jesus Christ, can eventually obtain it, whereas those who aren't so tied cannot obtain it until they humble themselves and acknowledge Him, not only as their Lord and Savior, but as the fountain of all knowledge.

I learned that day that the gift of tongues is very real and very much alive in the Church today. I learned that the gift of tongues is much more than just saying or understanding words; it involves deeper understanding that comes from a divine source far beyond mere words. I learned that this gift also involves lots of hard work, hours of study, and a degree of discomfort, even pain, that tests our resolve almost to the breaking point.

I felt good, especially as I remembered the pleased looks on the faces of that mother and father and the heavenly smiles that shone from those beautiful children. I sensed a little better why Jesus loved the children so much. That scene and those feelings stayed with me poignantly through supper and prayers and was a deep comfort as I drifted off to sleep that night.

# 14

## My Aching Feet

It was so warm on Niuatoputapu that you could easily sleep without covers, but Feki told me to always have a sheet on at night and especially to always keep my feet covered. I wasn't sure why, but I believed him.

I soon found that a sheet did not keep the mosquitoes from biting. A thin piece of cloth was no major barrier for them! It was hard to sleep with their constant buzzing in my ears. We eventually got some mosquito netting from Tongatapu, but before that we just endured the best we could.

One night I must have pulled the sheet up around my head in frustration and left my feet uncovered. When I got up the next morning, something felt different. I stepped down and the bottoms of my feet split apart and started bleeding. I called Feki and he became very concerned. He asked me whether my feet had been uncovered during the night. When I said, "I guess so," he told me that rats had eaten the soles of my feet off!

I didn't believe him and thought he was joking, as I had felt nothing during the night. The whole thing seemed preposterous. What really happened, I guess I'll never know. What I did know was that I could not walk and my feet hurt terribly. The branch president was also very concerned, and he and his wife said I would have to have my feet seared, either by a hot iron or by the sun. I thought they were kidding, but they seemed very serious. I wanted nothing to do with a hot iron, so I chose the sun. I still thought the whole thing was crazy, but I knew I couldn't walk, and I knew something had to be done so I could walk again, and at least they *seemed* to know what they were doing.

The branch president gave me a blessing; then he and Feki tied me to a chair, which they then laid down so they could turn my raw soles towards the burning sun. They kept the rest of me covered except my feet. Someone was always there to keep the flies away and give me something to drink or care for any needs. They were very accommodating. At first the warmth felt good, but before long I realized that burning was taking place! How I suffered for the next few days! They rotated me about every half hour during the hottest four hours of each day so the bottoms of my feet were always facing the sun. It was terrible! I could see why they tied me the way they did. I almost wished I had taken the hot iron treatment and gotten it over with!

Finally, after several days, they said it was sufficient and I could just stay in and hurt rather than be carried outside and hurt. During these painful days I studied the language and read scriptures a lot. I also received visits from people, especially children, as I could understand them the best. I also played my trumpet and wrote letters—anything to take my mind off my aching feet!

The pain in my feet was excruciating, but eventually the soles scabbed over and I started to feel a little better. Feki and the branch president's wife constantly washed and rubbed my feet with special oils and aloe. After what seemed forever, they told me I could try to walk again.

I can still remember the deep sense of joy and gratitude that swept over me as I took those first few steps after so many days of not being able to walk. What a marvelous thing it is to be able to walk! I'm not sure we can truly appreciate something until we have lost it, or at least been without it for a while. I wonder if we can actually be grateful for something we have never been without? I know I appreciated the ability to walk, which I had always taken for granted before.

I still had to be very careful and walked only limited amounts for several days. During that time, I continued to study the scriptures. I thought a lot about gratitude. I remember reading in the New Testament where Jesus said, "My God, my God, why hast thou forsaken me?" (Matthew 27:46). I have heard lots of explanations, but I wondered if maybe even Jesus needed to feel what it was like to be without His Father, if only for a short time, in order to fully appreciate what it is to be with Him and be encompassed by His love. I had the feeling that we will appreciate our bodies after the resurrection more than we do now. I doubted, at least at that time of my life, that I would have appreciated the ability to walk until it was temporarily taken from me.

Time moved on, and little by little things got better. Within a few weeks, I was walking normally again. I often wondered if the story of the rats was true. Whether it was or not, I *never* left my feet uncovered again at night! The memory of the pain I suffered and the gratitude I felt when I first walked again is still very real.

About thirty years later, I developed a sore on one foot that would not go away. I finally saw a doctor who took a biopsy and found that it was cancerous. He removed the growth, which was smaller than a dime and the results showed that all the malignant material was removed. He told me he had never seen cancer in that location on the foot and wondered where it could have come from. I told him about the sunburn treatment. He said it was likely the cause of the cancer, since it can take twenty to thirty years for cancer caused by severe sunburn to show up.

Although I would never want to repeat it, that novel treatment did restore my ability to walk, for which I was and am very grateful. I still sleep with my feet covered—and probably always will.

# 15

## "Wise as Serpents, Harmless as Doves"

Tracting was often frustrating. Very few people were willing, let alone anxious, to listen to us. We would often go days without getting into a single home for a gospel conversation. The people, however, were generally kind to us, especially when they sensed we were hungry or thirsty.

Many would say, "We want to feed you, but we don't want to listen to your doctrine. We are members of such-and-such a church. Our parents and grandparents have been members, and we are expected to stay members. This is a small island and everyone knows everything about everyone. Social pressure is great, so even if we did want to believe your doctrine, we probably couldn't change anyway."

I felt a deep love and respect for these good people. They were generally honest and forthright and did not want to hurt anyone, but rather wanted to help others. They had close family ties, and in many ways I felt at home.

As I began to speak the language more fluently, I became even more frustrated at not being able to share the beautiful message of the gospel with more people. I felt we needed to do things differently, but *how* I couldn't figure out, so in the meantime, we continued to go out every day and ask for opportunities to teach, without much apparent success.

I remember one specific day when we were invited into the home of a good family to eat. They gave us the standard line about wanting to feed us but not wanting to hear the discussions. They were such a nice family. They had fed us a few times before, and I knew they sacrificed a lot to do so. This particular day I felt an extra strong desire to share gospel principles with them but was frustrated by their request that their neighbors and friends not see us teaching them. I recognized their problem and wondered how to overcome it.

Suddenly, as though a light turned on, a thought came to me. I said, "I realize the problem you have. You have been very kind, and we would like to leave a blessing on your home. Would it be all right if we did so when we say the blessing on the food?" They said that would be fine.

When the food was spread before us, we all bowed our heads and I offered a blessing. I thanked God for the food, for this family, and asked Him to bless them with every needful thing. I thanked God for the Prophet Joseph Smith, for the First Vision, for the Book of Mormon, and for the priesthood, which was again upon the earth. I thanked Him that we now had authority to baptize all those who had faith on Jesus, who truly repented of their sins so they could be cleansed and receive the gift of the Holy Ghost to guide them through the rest of their life as members of the true Church of Jesus Christ in these latter-days. I thanked Him for the atoning sacrifice of Jesus Christ and the opportunity His true followers have of renewing their baptismal covenant each week as they partake of the sacrament, and on and on.

I suppose that blessing took thirty minutes or so, but no one cared much except that the food got cold. We knew the neighbors were watching, but they weren't overly concerned because it was customary for the local ministers to pray for a long time. When I finished, I felt good. I could tell the family was touched by what they had heard and felt.

We were able to use this method of teaching some principles for a few weeks, during which several families became interested. After a while, however, word spread, and we weren't invited to eat as often in nonmember homes; when we were, the family would tell us they would offer the blessing instead of us.

Another common experience when tracting was to come upon a man working in his garden and hear him say he was too busy to talk to us as he had to hoe or plant so many rows before the garden inspector arrived. This was extra frustrating to me because he could be telling the truth and we didn't want him to get into trouble, but I felt as soon as we left he would likely go back to sleep or to a *kava* party and forget all about the garden.

Let me explain about garden inspections, which were a pretty big part of village life. Since there were no stores on the island and you couldn't buy food, and since everyone had to eat, it was a government decree that each family had to have a garden of sufficient size for their family, plus a little to spare. These gardens were inspected regularly by a government official. If a garden was not up to standard, the father was first warned, then fined, and if he didn't plant more, he was sentenced to jail. The rationale was that if they didn't have a big enough garden to feed their family, they must be stealing from someone else's garden to eat.

The jail was an interesting affair. It consisted of a small compound surrounded by a couple of low barbed wires, which could easily be stepped over. Everyone knew everyone else and there was no place to hide on the island, so no one tried to escape. In fact, the head policeman warned the prisoners that if they weren't back from their work detail before sundown, he would close the gate so they would be locked out of prison and would not get fed that night. No one was late getting back!

I was aware of very few people who ever went to jail. Some people were lazy and liked to go to prison to get the meals and have a place to sleep. I suppose every society has its cross section of workers and nonworkers, law abiders and lawbreakers, leaders and followers, trustworthy people and those not so trustworthy.

I remember one day, when we were tracting, a man told us he had to work in his garden and finish three more rows, so he couldn't listen to us. I was somewhat aggravated, but a thought struck me and I responded, "Those three rows will take you a long time. Do you have two extra hoes? We'll help and you can finish much faster."

He looked quizzically at us and shrugged, "Okay, if you want." So he gave us each a hoe; I could tell Feki was surprised but pleased. We began to work with him. When we got to a place in the garden that was beyond earshot of neighbors and friends, the man asked, "Why are you doing this?" I said, "Because we love you and have a precious message to share with you." He said, "Okay, I'll listen so long as we keep working. I don't want my neighbors to get suspicious."

We often worked several hours with men in their gardens, but felt at peace as it was good talking time. Almost always when we worked with people in their gardens, we were able to give the main parts of our message. If we couldn't give our message, we worked to the end of what we had agreed to anyway.

*Feki on a horse by a chapel we built with the Saints on Niuatoputapu.*

At other times we found people thatching roofs or walls who said they were too busy to talk to us. Often we volunteered to help. Most of the time as we worked with them, we got the opportunity to give some of our message, but even when we didn't we stayed and helped till the project was done. I learned that if you quit helping when they won't listen, you not only lose future opportunities but you lose the Spirit. You must sincerely desire to help and allow the Spirit to guide, which it always does. I thought of Ammon as he served the king until circumstances were such that the king was ready to listen to him.

Even though the people were loving and kind, most of them were resistant to our message. It took a lot of ingenuity, hard work, and guidance from the Spirit to reach them, but over time it started to happen. Somehow the Lord opens the way for good, honest people to hear the message of His gospel.

With lots of effort, we eventually got a few families to listen to us. At this point most of our serious contacts were part-member families or families who had some prior association with the Church. Usually we baptized the nonmember spouse, and the other spouse became active.

# 16

## Marriages and Baptisms

Prior to my going to Niuatoputapu, the mission president told me that I could not baptize anyone who was living with a member of the opposite sex but was not legally married (meaning registered with the government). He told me that as a missionary he had listed me as one with authority to perform marriages. He doubted I would use it much but wanted me to know I had the authority.

As we started teaching a few people, we found that many who had been married by local customs for years, and even had large families, had never had that marriage registered. Some of them said the papers had been lost, but usually they simply couldn't afford it. The registration fee wasn't so much, but the fee to the ministers in pigs, food, and similar fare was very high.

When we were ready to baptize one couple, we found that they were not legally married. They wanted desperately to be baptized, but couldn't afford the fee their minister required, which was higher than normal as they were threatening to leave his church. I was wondering how to help them when I remembered that the mission president had said I could marry people. There was some skepticism, but we checked with the chief magistrate, and he reaffirmed that I was registered and fully authorized to perform marriages.

The couple was anxious to get officially married and then get baptized, but now I had a new problem because I had no idea how to perform a marriage. I had only been to one wedding in my life—my sister's wedding in the temple the day before I left on my mission. I didn't think I should use the same words used there, but the ideas were good. Feki and I talked to several people, and between our investigations and what I remembered from the temple, we pieced together what we thought was a good wedding ceremony.

With the proper government authority, I married this couple and then we baptized them. When others found out that I could perform marriages and that I didn't charge anything for the service, I received many inquiries. I told them I would marry them if they would listen to at least one discussion. I guess some complained to the magistrate, and he explained to me that I was acting as a government agent and therefore could not impose extra requirements.

I guess some of the ministers complained also, so Feki worked out an agreement that was acceptable to them. While I didn't perform a lot of marriages, I did perform more marriages than baptisms on Niuatoputapu. I felt good about helping people become "officially" married, even though outwardly nothing much changed in their lives.

Our first baptism was the wife of a less-active member in another village. He wasn't interested in coming to church, but when we found he was a member and his wife was not, we instinctively knew what to do. Through much friendshipping and lots of discussions, progress was made and soon she was baptized and he became active.

There were other families brought together in similar manner, as well as some single people, and others who joined the Church later. It is good to sow seeds and it is good to harvest also—so good that no one who has been an instrument to teach another the truth, and who has seen the light go on in their life, and watched them come up out of the waters of baptism, can ever fail to appreciate the sacredness of that beautiful ordinance.

It is wonderful how well the Lord repays honest effort, no matter how unproductive it may seem at the time. We tried to reach everyone and felt we were pretty good friends with nearly everybody, including the chief magistrate (the highest government official on the island), who was always kind and helpful to us. In reality, however, most of the people whom we were able to talk to and who would listen to our message and accept us without reservation were those considered to be on the fringes of society. I thought of Alma turning from the wealthy Zoramites and speaking to those who were poor and cast out from among the rich (see Alma 32:4–8).

There were times when I wondered if we would ever get a good nonmember family to honestly listen to us. However, after some of the people from the fringes joined the Church and improved their lives dramatically, others started to take notice, and little by little a few good families began to show some interest.

I want to acknowledge how good some of the nonmember families were. They lived honest Christian lives. I learned to admire the teachings of John Wesley and others who tried hard to teach the truth as they understood it from the scriptures and who tried diligently to instill in their followers a discipline in life and a dedication to God that was impressive. Some of the ministers were very strict in adhering to their interpretation of Bible teachings. In many respects, there was not a lot of difference in the way some of the members of these churches lived from the way our members were supposed to live. Of course, these ministers had no priesthood authorized by God, but their lives of kindness, helpfulness, and trying to live according to God's laws from the Bible were wonderful, even inspirational, to me.

I often saw men and women sitting for hours reading and studying the Bible, trying to absorb its teachings and make them a part of their lives. Many people were trying hard to live good, Christian lives, so what we had to offer from a life-style point of view was not that different.

Of course there were many doctrinal differences that I constantly tried to point out, but it was still hard to get them to listen. I learned that to show any real difference, I needed to explain about Joseph Smith, priesthood authority, and modern prophets and Apostles. This was the only way I found to substantiate a viable reason for them to investigate the Church.

I became very tolerant of the efforts of other churches and very appreciative of the good things they do. I am convinced the world is a much better place to live in than it would be were it not for the efforts of many who try so hard to teach people to be loving and kind and to live good moral lives. I learned that God blesses good people everywhere as they try to do His will to the best of their knowledge.

Years later, when I returned to Tonga as mission president, I found it much easier to get people to listen to our message than before. It was not so much that our method or message had changed as it was that a generation of solid old-fashioned preachers had passed away and a new generation of much more liberal preachers had arisen.

This new group tended to move away from definitively denouncing sin and asserting the need for living disciplined lives. On the other hand, our doctrine and preaching remained the same as always: sin was sin and was not to be tolerated in any degree. It was not that we were any better than before, but the modern preachers in other churches were generally washing away the footings that had been so solid when I first met their fathers.

I am convinced the world will largely continue that way, with eventually only a few groups being willing or able to hold the line against sin, as it seems easier to sink into sin than to rise above it. I hope we can always be in the forefront of teaching the truth and holding the proper line. I am sure we can. It is our destiny!

I always felt our baptisms were wonderful, spiritual experiences. I loved the idyllic setting of our baptisms. Let me explain.

At one end of Niuatoputapu a small stream meandered peacefully down to the ocean. The source of the stream was a natural artesian well, which bubbled from some shaded rocks in a heavily forested area. As the stream moved along, it was turned at one point by a large boulder, which created a beautiful pool large enough and deep enough to be perfect for baptisms. The pool was close to town, yet secluded by heavy, verdant foliage. Since there was only one trail to the pool, there was total privacy, and the dense growth all around absorbed the sounds of ordinary life and made the pool a place of peace and beauty.

Each time we went for a baptism, my thoughts turned to the description of the waters of Mormon in Mosiah 18. I don't know how anyone could experience more peace, beauty, love, and unity than we felt there.

I can still hear the singing of colorful birds blending their songs with the quiet rippling of the water as it flowed to the sea. I can still see the sunlight filtering through the tall fern leaves and hear the silence of those beautiful, green palms as they moved slowly in the calm breeze. I can still smell the freshness of everything and feel the joy that permeated everyone as beautiful, faithful people made eternal covenants of baptism in that sacred place. The pureness of the white clothing they wore was equaled only by the depth of joy that shone from their beautiful brown faces as they rose from those sacred waters, having buried the natural man or woman and become new creatures raised by His authority to the hope of eternal life in Christ. Heavenly smiles filled all in attendance as the covenant-makers were given the gift of the Holy Ghost, and everyone knew that something eternally good had been done.

I marveled at the symbolism of the pure, clear waters springing from the solid rocks and flowing freely from a source made not by hands, yet giving life to all it touched. I thought of the living waters offered by Jesus—pure, free, and life-giving.

While our baptisms were few and far between, each one was a wonderful experience. How I wanted to baptize everyone and have them feel the joy and peace that came from that sacred ordinance! We tried very hard, but very few would listen to us. Still, we continued to hope and work.

# 17

## *Girl Troubles*

Nothing made us happier than to find a good family to teach. After working with one such family for a while, they seemed willing to listen to the lessons. We taught them several times and seemed to be making progress. I felt wonderful about the prospects of baptizing the whole family, but one thing bothered me.

For some time I had sensed that their eighteen-year-old daughter was "making eyes" at me and that her family was encouraging it. There were little comments and unexplained entrances and sudden exits that would leave us temporarily alone. I dismissed these as my imagination, and we continued visiting the family and giving the discussions.

One day, on what missionaries would now call preparation day, we agreed to go to the back side of the island for a *kai tunu* (cookout) with this family. Such an event is always exciting, and Feki and I were up early to help get the wood, the food, and the mats ready. With our investigator family, we started for the picnic area.

It was a long way to the back of the island. The sun was hot, the trail was narrow, and over time the eight of us became somewhat separated. Occasionally those in the lead would stop and wait for the rest of us to catch up. Often they would have green coconuts for us to drink. Nothing can be sweeter on a hot day than the cool taste of coconut juice under the shade of a banana leaf on a small island in the South Pacific.

Feki was among the fastest and was usually far ahead. I was among the slowest and was toward the rear. We had been walking for quite a while and had been separated and back together many times. There was a lot of high vegetation and as I rounded one turn, I could just see the back of the person ahead of me going around another bend. I started to hurry to catch up, when I heard a cry for help from behind me. Because of the many turns in the trail, I couldn't see anyone. But I knew someone was there, so I went back to see if I could help. I called out, "What's the problem?"

A female voice called back, "Help me! I twisted my ankle." I came around the bend and sure enough, there was the eighteen-year-old daughter. She had put down her load and was in the process of undressing.

"What's wrong?" I said. She quickly looked up. As her beautiful brown eyes caught mine, she replied, "*Ta hola ki he vao*," which is literally "Let's run away together in the bush," but really means "Let's make love."

I couldn't believe I had gotten myself separated from the others, though as I look back now I assume that there probably was some complicity on the part of at least some of the group. I realized I was caught in a bad situation. The question was, "What do I do? How do I get out of this?"

Almost immediately an impression came to me. I said, "Listen, put your clothes back on. Let's hurry and catch up with the others. While they cook the meal, I promise I'll talk to you about marriage, family, and what love really means." Her eyes brightened. I turned and started down the trail. She put her clothes back on and followed without a word.

Within a few minutes, we caught up to the others. They asked what had happened. She said she had hurt her foot but was fine now. Since only a couple of minutes had passed, nothing more was said. We soon arrived at the back side of the island.

There were some rocky ridges and a gradual drop to the beach. Everyone knew it was against the rules for missionaries to swim, so that wasn't a problem. We played some games and had a good time with the family. Then while the others began cooking the meal, I sat by this girl, within sight of everyone but far enough away for a private conversation. For an hour or so we talked about love, marriage, and family, as I had promised her. I had no preconceived plan of what to say, but just started talking and followed the promptings of the Spirit.

I explained that we are all spirit children of our Father in Heaven and that He gives us our physical bodies as a marvelous gift, a beautiful temple created by Him, which houses the equally marvelous spirit that gives life to the body. I told her that since our bodies were created by God, they really belonged to Him and He just loans them to us. The real "us" is our spirit, and since we are using His gift of a body, we need to use it according to His desires and not defile it or deliberately hurt it. Since He created our body, He knows the most about how to use it so we can get the greatest joy and happiness from it. His instructions on how to use it are given in the scriptures and through His prophets.

I told her that each body contains within it seeds put there by God, who made it; that part of the potential for godhood is to share in the creation of additional physical bodies as earthly homes for more of His spirit children; and that this is done through marriage and family.

I explained about the priesthood, temples, and the eternal marriage covenant. I remembered my sister's wedding that took place just before I left Idaho Falls and explained parts of it to her. I told her it is God's will for all men and women to be married in the temple so their families can be together forever. I explained that it is His will that the act of procreation take place only after marriage in the temple. In this way He can ensure the greatest joy and fulfillment possible to those who obey Him, for He is then a full partner in the sacred triangle of man, woman, and God. I said that others not married in the temple could experience happiness, but the greatest joy and happiness possible could only come with a temple marriage.

She looked up incredulously and asked, "Are you saying it is God's will that we remain virgins until we marry?"

"Yes," I answered, "and then remain true to your spouse after marriage for your whole life."

"Wow!" She shook her head. "How can you possibly do that?"

"You may not be able to if you try to do it alone," I responded. "But with God's help we can do anything, no matter how hard it seems. Remember, God was talking about the process of having children when He told Sarah, 'Is any thing too hard for the Lord?' (see Genesis 18:14).

She thought for a long time and then said quietly, "And what if you've already blown it?"

"Then join the Need Help Club," I answered.

"The what?"

"The Need Help Club. Join it along with the rest of mankind. You wouldn't be so different. All of us have made mistakes of some type or another. Everyone is lost unless they turn to the Savior. If you turn to Him and have faith in Him by doing what He says, He will help you through the gift of repentance and get you going on the right course again. That's the basic reason I'm out here on a mission, to teach and testify of these things, especially faith and repentance, and also to baptize people who believe these principles and are willing to follow them."

To my knowledge, I had never talked to anyone about these things, or even thought much about them, at least not in that way. But as I spoke, my understanding was opened and I was able to explain about love, marriage, temples, bodies, spirits, God's will, and His love for us, in a way that made me want more than anything to someday worthily marry in the temple. I knew if I married someone who had those same desires, we could feel God's love and power and help in our marriage and family. I knew we needed Him as a full partner to be truly happy. I knew that all people needed the same things and that no one could have a fulness of joy in any other way.

The conversation seemed to have a profound effect on me and on this girl. She asked several questions about how you know who the right person is, when the right time is, and why God gives us such strong drives if we are not to use them until we go to the temple.

I didn't have many answers other than to bear my testimony that what I had explained was God's will and that the closer we are to doing His will, the happier He *and we* will be.

She asked about the priesthood power to seal for time and all eternity, who holds that power, where temples are and how you get there, and many other things.

I explained that there would soon be a temple in New Zealand and that God would not withhold his blessings from anyone if his or her desires were right. I promised her that if she would listen to the missionary discussions, pray, read the Book of Mormon, gain a testimony of the gospel, repent, and get baptized, and follow the leaders of the Church, she would be able to go to the temple and have all of these blessings in her life.

Just then the call *Taimi kai* (time to eat) came. It had the effect of bursting the spiritual bubble I was in; instantly I found myself on some hard rocks above a small beach on a tiny South Pacific island. It took me a few minutes to remember where I was and what I was doing. Then I remembered and realized we needed to join the others for the meal. It had been a good conversation.

*Picture Jean sent John on Niuatoputapu*
*that helped solve a problem.*

*John's missionary passport picture*
*sent to Jean about the same time.*

I left those rocks with a solid determination to follow God's will and eventually get married in the temple. The spirit of peace, assurance, and certainty I had felt was tremendous. Some of those feelings must have been felt by this girl also, for she later joined the Church, married a faithful man, and was sealed in the temple. She became a good mother of several children and a faithful wife and supporter of her husband, who served in many positions. She also became a good leader in the various auxiliaries and has truly spent her life trying to follow God's will and build His kingdom.

How grateful I am to God for his help in allowing His truths to be taught and understood, and also in giving needed protection from evil that could have been so destructive.

I still marvel at the wonderful blessings that have come from following the spirit of that discussion while sitting on some ordinary rocks on an obscure island overlooking the endless Pacific Ocean. How good God is!

There were no further problems with that girl.

# 18

## "Seilo, Seilo"

After the last few problems, I instinctively listened more and stayed closer to Feki. I was happy that word about our requirements as missionaries, especially the "no fooling around" part, was now pretty well understood by everyone. This seemed to be accepted by most people, but I sensed that the girl's mother was still quite disturbed.

She was always nice to us, fixed meals, and helped us in many ways, but I felt a distance and a coolness from her that bothered me. I tried to talk to her about some of the principles I had spoken to her daughter about, but she would not listen.

Finally, on one occasion when just the two of us were visiting, I asked her, "What's wrong? What's bothering you?" When she realized no one else was close, she poured out her feelings.

"You say you love us and are trying to help us, but you don't like my daughter. Are you too good for her? Isn't she pretty enough for you? What do you want, anyway? My husband has offered you hundreds of acres of the best land if you would just marry our daughter and stay here. But you turn your nose up at us. What more do you want? I'll make you an even better offer. You don't even need to marry her or stay here. Just give us a half-white baby through our daughter and we'll not say any more. Surely you can't be so selfish as to not do that for us!"

I tried as hard as I could to explain that it was God's will to *not* do that and that as a missionary I was duty bound to follow His will. She refused to accept that and continued to accuse me and my companion of selfishness, of not feeling for their plight. "All we want is a half-white baby," she said. (At that time, some of the islanders still subscribed to the myth that white people were smarter or more powerful or superior in some way.)

I did not want to offend her, nor have her feel we did not care, but I could not offend God or go against His will. How to reconcile these different feelings was beyond me. I prayed and asked Heavenly Father to please soften her heart and help her understand so she would not be angry with me, but it seemed the more I tried to explain, the angrier she became. The atmosphere was such that bearing testimony did not seem appropriate. I determined the only thing I could do was leave, so as to not make things worse. I didn't want to leave with those bad feelings but could see no alternative.

As I stood to say good-bye, a thought struck me. I turned to the mother and said, "I know I haven't explained things very well. But if you will be patient, I'll come back tomorrow. We'll talk again, and I'll have something new to say." She accepted that, I suppose, with the faint hope that I might change my mind by the next day. I felt somewhat perplexed, for I didn't know what I could say tomorrow that I hadn't already said, but I had followed a prompting—and by now I knew that was always the best thing to do.

Later that day I heard that most welcome sound, the haunting cry from high on the mountain, "*Seilo, seilo*" ("A boat is coming").

It is difficult to describe the feelings of a boat day or the activity that takes place on the infrequent occasion when a boat comes to a small, isolated island. Normally, a boat came about once per month, but because there was no real schedule, sometimes there would be two boats per month and other times it would be two months or more between boats.

Boat day is an event that can only be appreciated by those who have been isolated for long periods of time. It is almost impossible to describe the all-pervading stir of a boat's arrival. People drop what they are doing as eyes widen with delight; and whispers of anticipation are heard and felt everywhere. Horses, dogs, and pigs lift their heads and start sniffing and moving as they also know something is happening. Slow-paced life becomes more animated, and, almost by herd instinct, everyone and everything starts moving toward the boat landing.

That cry, "*Seilo, seilo*," seemed to stir every type of emotion known to man. There was anticipation and apprehension (who, among family and friends on other islands, had been born or married, died or become ill?), joy and sadness (who would arrive and who would depart?), and happiness and fear (what good news and what bad news would come?). It was like a microcosm of that grander event of spirits shuttling back and forth from this small planet, earth.

It took several hours from when the boat was first sighted until it arrived. It took another few hours to unload the cargo and carry the mailbag to the post office in Hihifo. Everyone gathered around the post office and waited as the sorting began and names were called—"letter for Samu," "package for Mele," and so on.

We went to Hihifo, mingled with the people, and listened to the news: the Queen's birthday was lovely; the rugby team lost in Fiji, but the referees were prejudiced; Joe caught twenty-five fish in one night; Mele had twins. No one cared much or said anything about world events or the economy, as such things had no relevancy to them—or to me at that time.

We comforted those who had received bad news, shared the joy of those who had received good news, and encouraged those who had received no news. This total sharing of happenings and feelings by everyone, together with the small, communal interdependency of the island, produced a feeling of unity that was at the same time frustrating (because everyone knows everything about everyone else, and nothing goes unnoticed) and wonderful (because everyone cares about everyone else, and nothing goes unnoticed). With the present rapid increase in communication and transportation, boat days on small, isolated islands are a dying institution. I wonder if heaven won't be more like boat day on Niuatoputapu in the 1950s than the hectic days and hurried schedules of a busy city in the 1990s.

On nearly every boat day I received a few letters. This day was no exception. I received letters from home and from friends, including a letter from Jean. Feki received some letters also. We put the letters we had written in the return mail bag, took our mail, and walked back to our home in Vaipoa.

It was always good to receive mail from home. The bonds of love and family ties are strengthened on both ends. I was happy to receive a letter from Jean. It had been mailed from California over two months before but seemed as fresh and encouraging as though it were written yesterday. She was in her senior year at Brigham Young University and graduating soon. To my surprise, she had sent a small but lovely photo.

As my eyes fell on that picture, a thought formed in the back of my mind. It was not a dramatic revelation or an absolute, certain instruction, but rather a sort of happy feeling about a direction to take. By the time we finished reading the mail, it was late, so after prayer and scripture study we retired for the night. As I woke early the next morning, that previously nebulous feeling had become very clear. I knew what to do.

I told Feki I needed to go to Hihifo but would be back shortly. It was very early and hardly anyone was up and about. I ran most of the way and arrived at the mother's house almost out of breath. Sure enough, she was sitting in the *peito* (separate cooking house) stirring coals and starting to boil water.

She rolled out a mat away from the smoke and fire and motioned for me to sit down. Her attitude was still quite sullen, but somewhat anticipatory and better than it had been the day before. We sat for quite a while saying nothing. I was trying to clear my thoughts and praying in my heart that I could say what God would have me say and that He would soften her heart and help her understand.

Finally I began, "Look at this picture." Tongans love photos. She looked at Jean's picture long and admiringly. "That is my girlfriend. Her name is Jean. I love her, and she loves me." I hoped I was telling the truth. I felt I was. "We want to get married in the temple when I return, so we promised each other that until we were married, I would not have sex with anyone and neither would she." I felt I needed to be very clear to her. "See how beautiful she is? She is keeping her promise to me. You don't want me to break my promise to her, do you?"

She continued to look at the picture. I could sense a little softening in her posture, then a tiny shaking, then some semi-sobbing sounds as she inhaled deeply and began to breathe out with a light moan. Tears came to her eyes as she finally looked up at me.

"You promised each other?"

"Yes."

"You love her?"

"Yes."

"You're going to marry her?"

"Yes."

"She's true to her promise?"

"Yes."

"*Kolipoki* (Elder Groberg), you must keep your promise." (In Tongan there is no G, R, or B sound, and each consonant is followed by a vowel. Therefore, the closest the Tongans could come to *Groberg* was *Kolipoki*.)

Tears were coursing down her face and falling on her lap as she handed the picture back to me. "Go now. Thank you for telling me. It's okay. I won't bother you anymore." And she didn't.

# 19

## "One . . . , Two . . ."

After much effort, another strong, prominent family finally agreed to listen to us. What a thrill that was! The family seemed sincere and invited us back several times. I suppose this upset their minister as they were probably good contributors to his church. When we gave this family the fourth discussion, they had lots of questions, so we stayed and talked late into the night. As we concluded, the father said, "We'd like you to stay here tonight." I had noticed the family getting a little fidgety towards the end of our discussion. I wondered why but thought they were just pondering our message.

"Thank you," I responded, "but we must go to our home." I was still concerned about sleeping in other people's homes. Our home was about two miles away on the other side of the forest, or jungle, between the two villages. Their house was right on the edge of this large, forested area, and the small trail that led through it to our house was right behind their home. We had been down this trail many times in the past, and I felt confident we would be just fine.

The father persisted, "We'd really like you to stay tonight. I think you should." I could even see my companion nodding in approval. I had been giving the lesson and was sort of in charge, so being a little stubborn, I insisted, "No. We must go. It's against mission policy to stay." I wasn't sure whether it was but thought it sounded like a good way to end the discussion.

They appealed to us several times to stay, and I sensed that maybe something was wrong. However, since nothing was definite, I didn't think more about it and we left. Even though I felt a bit uncomfortable, I felt sure God would protect us if there were any problems. As soon as we got outside and started home, I sensed that something wasn't right. It wasn't anything I heard, but rather a spooky feeling. I wanted to go back to the house we had just left, but as impetuous youth often do, I determined to go on as we had said we would. How foolish we are at times!

We had gone about a hundred yards when from the trees behind us emerged a group of eight tough, young men. They were partly drunk and had stones, sticks, broken bottles, and rocks. They formed a semicircle and started to tighten it, moving closer to us. We could see we were in trouble, for they were obviously bent on hurting us. As they moved closer, my companion, like a mother hen, pushed me behind him and said, "Now, here's what we'll do. I'm going to count to three. When I say, 'three,' I'll yell as loud as I can and charge right into the middle of them. The second I do that, you turn and run as fast as you can down the trail and through the bush toward home. It's dark and they won't know what's happening for a while because I'll be swinging both fists and yelling as loud as I can. By the time they find out it is just me, you'll be halfway to Vaipoa. You'll make it safely home, I'm sure."

"I can't do that," I said (even though I wanted to).

He replied, "Look, I'm older and more experienced. You do what I say. There is no sense in both of us getting hurt. You didn't listen to me in the house, but you'd better listen now." He started counting, "One . . . , two . . ." I froze with fear and uncertainty. *What should I do?* Just at that instant, out of the bush behind us, where the trail began, came crashing the man whom everyone on the island feared more than anyone else. He was the toughest of them all.

My first impression was, "We've had it now—sealed off from in front and from behind."

This big, tough fellow walked right past us and stopped halfway between us and our attackers. He was a little tipsy himself. He glared at those eight young men and said, "The Mormons are mine. I'll take care of them. If anyone touches them without talking to me first, they will answer to me!"

Like a cube of butter put into a hot frying pan, that crowd of young men quickly melted away. They simply vanished into the darkness as quickly and as quietly as they had appeared.

As soon as they were gone, the tough man told us to start down the trail leading to our village. He was right behind us. I could hear and smell him. I thought, "When he gets us to some deserted spot he'll surely 'take care of us,' all right." I knew he was big enough and tough enough to do so. We kept walking, and he stayed right behind us. I was scared and wondered when the blow might come. I didn't dare run nor did I dare look back. I had a fervent prayer in my heart, which counterbalanced my fear a little. Each step we took brought us closer to Vaipoa; finally we emerged from the bush onto the open edge of our village. Nothing had happened yet. My heart was still racing, but I summoned the courage to turn around and face our fearful friend. He just grunted and indicated we should head to our home.

I was breathing a little easier now. As we came to our home, I finally realized we were safe. It had been a long two miles, but how relieved I was! The walk had worn off some of the effects of the alcohol on our friend, and he seemed more willing to talk. We were alone and a big part of the night was gone, but we summoned the courage to ask, "Why did you do that? Why did you protect us and help us?"

"Well," he explained, "someone who wanted you out of here called us together and gave us some free home brew. He suggested that we take care of the Mormon missionaries and see that they don't come back to town. He said, 'Mormons are bad people.' When I heard that, something started to stir deep down inside me. I was pretty drunk but I wasn't completely under, and something kept bothering me. I thought, 'Mormons—bad people? No, they are good people. Something's wrong.'"

Our friend then told the following story: "I never knew my real parents. I was raised by some relatives on Niuatoputapu, but when I was about ten, I was sent to Vava'u [another island in Tonga]. I'm sure I was a problem there because I was picked on a lot and fought back a lot. It seemed that no one wanted me. I hadn't been to school so I couldn't read or write.

"On Vava'u, I kicked around from place to place. One day I was loafing on the street when two young men wearing white shirts and ties came by. They asked why I wasn't in school. I told them I didn't really live here and my family couldn't afford to send me to school. They asked if I would like to come to their school. I told them I had no money. They said that was all right, come anyway. So I went with them. They taught me some English. They even let me stay by their place and gave me food. They taught me to write my name and read a little and were very kind to me. Everyone else kicked me around, but they didn't. They had a feeling of love and concern for me, something I hadn't felt much in my life.

"After I had gone to school for a few weeks, they took me out in the ocean, put me under the water, and said, 'Now you are a Mormon.' I didn't know exactly what that meant, but I felt good about it. I liked those two young men, and they seemed to like me.

"Shortly after that, I had to return to Niuatoputapu. When I got back here, I had no further association with the Church because there weren't any missionaries here, nor were there any members that I knew of. So, over a period of years, I forgot about it. People started picking on me again, and soon I became a real fighter. But tonight when someone said, 'Mormons are bad people. Go take care of the Mormon missionaries and see that they don't return,' it all came back to me: 'I am a Mormon. Mormon missionaries aren't bad people; they are good people. They loved me. They helped me.' I wondered what to do. Then I thought, 'I'll just sit by the house and protect them. I'll help them, just like those two young men in white shirts and ties helped me.' And that's what I did."

How grateful I was for those two Elders serving in Vava'u twenty years earlier! And how grateful I was to God for bringing those good feelings to our protector's remembrance. I wish I could say he became active, but he didn't. He kept drinking and doing other bad things. However, we had no further problems with any of those young men or others, because they knew we were under his protection.

As time went on, we became more and more accepted by everyone. Even though our protector died in a freak accident a few months later, we had by then become such an integral part of the island community that we experienced no further problems of that nature.

I often wonder what would have happened had those two missionaries twenty years earlier not shown love to that young boy. I don't even know their names or anything about them other than that they showed love and kindness to a little orphan boy who was kicked around by others. I am confident the love and kindness they showed him went into some type of an eternal kindness bank to come out twenty years later, with rich interest, to help us and save us from harm, and, without too much stretch of the imagination, possibly save our lives.

I learned how important it is to constantly make deposits into this eternal kindness bank, not only for ourselves but also for others. No kindness shown is ever lost. It is always deposited and available, with added interest, to be drawn on in time of need by us or others. I wondered if the whole universe isn't balanced by depositing and withdrawing acts of kindness. Maybe the total amount of kindness available to draw on and bless our lives is the total amount of kindness deposited by all of us as we bless others' lives. It made some sense, especially as I realized that the greatest depositor of all is the Savior. Maybe His deposits outweigh everything, but still I feel He wants us to be partners with Him in this great kindness depository program. I don't understand much, but I do know we need to be more kind.

As I began working on developing this quality of kindness, I soon found it imperative to take anger, evil, and bad thinking of any nature from my life. I found that as I did, there flowed into my life a peace and joy that was worth everything.

It was hard, but I eventually learned that wherever we are, whatever our background, whatever the situation, if we desire to be kind, the Savior will help us act and feel as He would under similar circumstances. What a great blessing!

As I thought of these things, I determined to try to be kinder to everyone. I thought I should start with those eight young men who were bent on hurting us and also the people who put them up to it. It was hard, as they were embarrassed and I was somewhat angry, but little by little we developed a good friendship. One of the eight later joined the Church. I learned that it pays to be kind, not only for what it does to others, but also for what it does to us.

# 20

## *Of Pigs and Irons*

We continued about our daily activities. At times I thought nothing new ever happened. I felt that life was pretty slow and that each day seemed the same as the one before. It would either rain or be sunny; the wind would either blow or it would be calm. We followed the same routine day after day: Get up, shower, study scriptures, eat, decide on places to visit, go out, try to share the gospel, get rejected by most everyone, return home, eat, pray, and finally retire for the night.

When it was damp and cold, I didn't feel like going out. When it was hot and humid, I didn't feel like going out. Since it was usually one or the other, and since people generally wouldn't listen to us anyway, it often seemed easier to just stay home. If it weren't for Feki, I'm not sure how much I would have gone out. But Feki made going out and visiting a regular part of each day, so that's what we did.

I soon realized that every day and every situation was less than ideal, and if I let circumstances or conditions govern my actions, I would just sit and rot. We had to decide ahead what we should do and then move forward and do it regardless of the weather, apathy, or opposition. Feki always encouraged me with a big smile, but never forced. How grateful I was for him!

Spending month after month among seven hundred people, I soon learned everyone's name and their relationship to everyone else. I learned to not talk bad about anyone because he or she was invariably related to everyone else, including the person you were talking to. They fought a lot among themselves but always came together on important matters. I not only recognized every person but could also tell most of the animals apart. Horses, dogs, pigs, goats, and even chickens have their own personalities and looks, just like people. If you constantly live with them, you soon learn these different characteristics. Anyone with a pet knows that.

There were lots of pigs on Niuatoputapu. They were a sign of wealth, and everyone knew which pigs belonged to whom. Stealing a pig was almost as serious there as stealing a horse was in early western America. They fenced the pigs inside the village so they wouldn't get out and mess up their gardens, which were outside the village.

Some of the major events in village life were the feasts for special occasions, such as births, deaths, marriages, birthdays, and commemorative days. For these feasts, certain families were required to furnish pigs. The day before the feast they would open the gate and let a few pigs run into the bush, then a few minutes later a group of men and boys armed with sticks, rocks, and machetes would go chasing after them. They had no guns. It was a big event to go pig hunting. Everyone knew which family was to furnish the pig, and had to be careful not to kill a pig belonging to someone else, although the other pigs had to be captured and returned to the inner village.

I was aware of these hunting parties but had never participated for lots of reasons. As time went on, the hunters kept working on me to come with them. Finally they said, "If you're going to eat the pig, you need to do your part in getting it." That made sense, so I finally said, "Okay, I'll go with you once." They gave me a couple of nice rocks as we went to the gate.

The gate was opened and several selected pigs went running into the bush. A few minutes later the hunters, with loud whooping and hollering, started through the gate, and the pigs knew the chase was on. There were about fifteen men and boys in the hunting party. Eventually someone found the pig we were after, and almost like magic the hunters moved into position and got the pig semisurrounded. They ignored all the other pigs and concentrated on getting this one.

The hunters gradually tightened the circle until the pig bolted and ran. They tried to hit it with a rock or a stick. The first time, they missed and the pig ran off unharmed. During the hunt you had to be careful not to hit someone else coming from the other direction when surrounding and throwing at the pig.

They eventually found the same pig again and started moving in very quietly. The man next to me pointed at the pig. Suddenly the pig jumped out and headed down a small trail immediately ahead of us. There was a small log on the trail, and just as the pig jumped over the log, both of us threw our rocks.

While the pig was still in midair, one of the rocks hit him square in the head. He crumpled over and fell to the ground, stunned and unable to do much but kick. The cry of victory went up, and almost instantly the whole party was on the scene with clubs and machetes to finish him off. I never quite got over seeing a desperate pig flying freely through the air, then seeing a rock crash into his head, and watch him crumple to the ground helpless while men and boys swarmed around yelling and hitting, then watching his neck get cut and seeing the blood squirting from his body and draining away his life. Fortunately, the pig died quickly. They tied it to a long pole, and we were soon on our way back to the village. Everyone was laughing, shouting triumphantly, and having a great time—except me. I didn't feel very good.

The man with me kept saying what a good shot I was and how my rock had hit the pig in midair. I suspect my rock missed completely and this man's rock found the mark, but he kept insisting it was mine. It started a legend of how accurate the Mormon missionary was in throwing rocks.

We ate the pig the next day at the big feast. The villagers made sure I got the two main delicacies: The ears and the roll of meat along the backbone. Both tasted great.

They put a lot of pressure on me to go hunting again, but I steadfastly refused. In effect, I retired as the rock-throwing champion. I suppose I knew I could never equal that feat (if in fact it had been my rock), but mainly I didn't feel good about being involved in hunting. Feki was a very good hunter, and he contributed our share of the work on future expeditions. I never went hunting again.

As time went on, I found myself caught up more and more in people's feelings (of which they had many) rather than people's possessions (of which they had little). I learned that people everywhere, regardless of their circumstances, have deep feelings. I also learned that a certain number of "things" can be helpful, but too many can be harmful. I'm not sure where the right balance is, but I suppose the statement "sufficient for our needs" is the best guideline.

Once I visited a member lady shortly after a boat had arrived. She looked very concerned and asked that I come in. Her problem was that her husband's family from Tongatapu had bought her a newfangled iron that had just arrived on the boat. It had a small gas tank on the back that you could light like a Coleman lantern, and the flames went down between two metal pieces and kept the iron hot.

Her question to me was what to do. If she kept it for her ironing, she could use it for a long time, but then people would call her selfish and she would not have friends. If she loaned it to others, they would soon ruin it and neither she nor they would have a good iron.

I asked her how she ironed now. She showed me her old cast-iron model. It was partially hollow, so she would drop hot coals or embers into the open chamber and try to iron without burning her hand, since about as much heat went up as down.

I told her I didn't know what she should do. I thought the family intended the iron for her use, but she would have to do what she felt best. She seemed very perplexed. I was sorry I couldn't help her more, but I had no definite feelings.

A few weeks later I saw her again. She seemed happy. I asked what had happened. She said she was miserable for a while because she tried to keep the iron to herself and use it. Then she decided ironing was only a small part of her life, but family and friends were a much more important part, so she loaned the iron around and sure enough it was quickly broken and became *ta'eaonga* (useless).

She pointed to it on the floor. It was being used as a weight to hold some mats down. She explained, "A rock would do the job just as well, but the iron is here and I can tell my in-laws it is useful. I'm glad it's broken and I can do things the same way others do. We're all good friends again."

I wondered about the correlation between physical progress and selfishness. I came to no conclusion.

# 21

## *Lockjaw*

We had many good friends, particularly among the young men about our age. One of these young men, named Finau, showed interest in listening to us. He was in his midtwenties and very strong. His parents were opposed to us and would not allow us in their home. Even though he still lived with his parents, he was old enough to be on his own, so he came often to our house to hear the lessons. He was reverent and thoughtful and seemed to accept the principles we taught.

One day, after a lesson, he invited us to go fishing with him, but we explained we were not to do that as missionaries. This surprised him, as basically everyone fished or did some type of *fangota* (fishing or digging for small crabs or shellfish in the reef area).

A popular fishing method on a calm night is to take a lantern and a machete into the lagoon and hold very still. The light attracts fish, and if you are fast you can slice through the water with the knife and get one. On the next calm night, Finau went fishing with a lantern and a knife. A large fish came to his light, and he carefully raised his knife. Apparently just as he was ready to strike, some slight movement caused the fish to flee, but Finau was so intent on getting the fish, he sliced through the water behind him as the fish darted away. He must have lifted his foot, for he missed the fish and sliced off his heel!

Others who were fishing nearby responded to his yells of pain and got him to his home. With next to no medical facilities on the island, there wasn't much they could do. I suppose a tetanus shot would have helped, but they didn't have any. They did the best they could, but within a short while, lockjaw (tetanus) set in.

At first his parents tried to blame us and told him, "That's what you get for listening to those Mormon missionaries!" He kept calling for us, but they wouldn't let us see him. They called their own religious leader to help. Finau continued to get worse and continued calling for us. When the parents realized he was going to die anyway, they finally asked us to come and visit as he desired. They refused to let us give him a blessing, but said we could pray for him, which we did.

I had never seen anything like this before. Lockjaw is a terrible disease, and I thought, "No one should ever choose to die in this way!" Finau was having convulsions and was rigid and shaking terribly when we got there. It was a pathetic situation. I tried to hold him and talk to him. Occasionally I thought there may have been some meaningful eye contact, but I wasn't sure. I felt compassion for him and could tell he was in great pain as he shook with spasms and convulsions. Trying to hold him was like trying to hold a raging, twisting bull. I tried to calm him, but to no avail as he was very strong.

I watched him as he went through that final stage and died. My testimony that there is a spirit in our body was made doubly sure at that time. One moment there was a young man with a strong body; the next second there was nothing. You could almost feel something leave him as his body went limp. I knew his spirit had left his body, and I knew that spirit gives life. In fact, I knew that spirit is life and there is no life without it, literally or figuratively.

As his spirit left, I had a distinct feeling that he appreciated what we had done. It was as though his spirit, now free, was expressing appreciation to us for teaching him and for coming and comforting him. I felt an impression from him that went something like this: "Don't be angry with my parents. They don't understand. Help them. Help the other people. Thanks for being my friend. Thanks for wanting to help me; thanks for trying to help me. I'm just fine. Thanks for everything."

His way of dying seemed so cruel to me, but his spirit didn't seem to mind. I wondered why some struggle so hard to die and others slip away so quietly. I didn't know the reasons then, nor do I now, but I am convinced that in the eternal scheme of our lives, there are little chinks filled in or rough edges smoothed over or understandings gained that have something to do with the way we pass to the other side.

When the parents realized he was gone, they began to cry and howl and tear their clothes. Fortunately they were no longer angry with us. I'm sure his spiritual influence helped them. They knew their son was gone, and they also knew he had wanted us to be there, so they were grateful we had come and had done what we could. Through their mourning and howling at his death, they thanked us for trying to help and even asked us to come to his funeral.

We held the funeral early that afternoon. I was not asked to speak but was asked to sit in a place of prominence. The family had been pressured to not have us come to the funeral at all, but they knew of their son's kind feelings towards us and invited us anyway.

During one of the lulls in the funeral, I heard a few old men sitting by me talking. They were asking each other, "How come he's so lucky to die so young, and we still have to live and work and sweat and hurt? It doesn't seem fair. What does God have against us?"

It was a new thought to me. I realized how different our Western attitude toward life is as compared to many places in the world. For many, life is tough, and to continue to live is to continue to sweat, hurt, and wonder when and how the end will come. I realized as forcefully as ever that all people everywhere need the gospel and the true understanding of life and why we are here. They need to know that life is precious and comes from God and that we are here to learn to obey God, to love Him, and to show this love by helping others.

How I wanted to explain these things to those people, but in that setting they wouldn't let me. They were good people, more "blinded by the craftiness of men," I suppose, than anything (see D&C 76:75).

This whole experience had not been very pleasant, but I learned a lot. I had a sure knowledge of the true nature of body and spirit. I knew that the body has no power without the spirit and that the spirit can express feelings or convey ideas, even after leaving the body.

The Lord has ways of teaching us truths that many of us miss by refusing to go through some of the required "unpleasant" prerequisites. How grateful I was for Finau and his parents and the great lessons the Lord taught me through them! We continued to teach gospel truths whenever, however, and to whomever we could. Unfortunately, Finau's parents were not among those willing to listen.

While Finau's death and other similar experiences were tough to go through, to a degree I began to feel sorry for those who don't experience them. Birth and death are part of life. Aging and sickness are part of life. In our modern society we tend to isolate ourselves and our children from these things. Some of these situations are difficult to handle, and often we don't know what to do. I remember trying more than once to get out of uncomfortable situations.

One time a family called me to come quickly because a lady was having terrible complications with a birth. I went over, but with all the screaming, the blood, and the very personal nature of the birth process—and my knowing absolutely nothing about what to do—I took one look and asked if it would be all right if I stayed outside and prayed for her. They could see I was scared, so they said that would be all right.

And did I ever pray! I wanted everything to be in order, not only for them but also so I wouldn't need to get more involved with the lady and her baby, who was having such a difficult time getting here. The screams seemed to last a long time, but eventually the baby was born and things were then satisfactory with both mother and daughter. How grateful I was!

Again, I received a strong testimony of prayer. If we pray with all of our heart for that which is *right*, that which is according to God's will, it will be granted as the scriptures promise. The key, of course, is to be willing to accept His will and ask only for those things that are according to His will. In fact, I don't believe you can pray in faith except for those things that are according to His will.

I remember thinking about God's plan for this earth. Here I was a young man not knowing much about life and yet being involved in births, deaths, and sickness—in what we sometimes term "raw life." I thought again how we tend to isolate ourselves and our children from some of those fundamental parts of this earth's experience. When someone gets sick, we turn them over to a doctor or to a hospital. People generally die in a hospital or a rest home or under professional care. Too often family members do not experience the feelings that come from being part of the whole experience.

I quickly add that I do not advocate a return to primitive conditions. I am grateful for the health professionals, the morticians, and other helpers in our modern society. I am convinced, however, that there is something missing from our mortal experience when we do not participate to some degree in some of these basic life experiences firsthand. Sometimes we, or our children, see a person getting sick, and the next time we see them they are in a beautiful casket all nice and pretty. We don't realize the trauma and pain that has occurred in the interim, nor the reality of the physical and spiritual separation that has taken place.

To understand that spirit is life and to be able to feel gratitude coming from someone's spirit who appreciates what you are trying to do for them often gives you more incentive to do good and help people than any number of sermons might do. I doubt we want to go back to the way it was on Niuatoputapu, but I think good would come from more involvement by more people in more of these things.

Maybe we are too removed in our society from some of the basics of life. Tongans generally put more importance on how people feel, act, or even smell, than we do. They seem to be able to read more in our eyes and in our sighs than we can.

I remember once while going along a trail, Feki suddenly stopped, put his finger to his mouth while pointing with his other hand to a tree some distance ahead. I whispered, "What's the matter?"

He whispered back, "There is someone behind that tree. Let us approach it carefully."

"How can you tell?" I asked.

"Oh, you wouldn't understand, but let's be careful." As we got closer, sure enough there was a man resting behind the tree. He obviously meant us no harm, and we continued on our way. I guess this ability comes from living closer to nature than we do.

I remember people often saying to us, "You look hungry or tired. We'll give you something to eat. Sit down and rest." Soon we would hear the final death cackle of a chicken, and a while later, there it would be, ready for us to eat. When people just go to the store and buy a clean piece of meat all wrapped in plastic or buy a bottle of milk, they often have no idea of what went into getting it there. Maybe that is the way it should be. I am just glad I was able to feel and understand a little of the other side as well.

I learned a lot from Finau and his family. Expressions of true tenderness and love, under all circumstances, then as now, are very real and very needed. Finau's family never joined the Church, but from then on they were friendly to us, fed us, and helped us.

# 22

## "For Good and Evil"

Niuatoputapu is relatively small, but by now I had learned there was always plenty to do. Sometimes missionaries get the idea they have "tracted out" an area. I doubt that is possible. Spending a year with seven hundred people in a seven-square-mile area—and with only one companion—could be considered boring, but there was always more to do than I could get done. I honestly felt I had as much to do and learn in my last month as I did in my first month.

If missionaries ever get discouraged by thinking they are assigned to one place with too few people for too long a period of time, they should realize that others have been through it before and grown thereby. I know there are always lessons to learn, as well as blessings to gain, if we are only willing to pay the price for them. I am convinced that there is more potential in the smallest area, or in the seemingly least significant calling, than any of us will be able to achieve.

Shortly after Finau's funeral, we decided to go to the nearby island of Tafahi. Probably eight miles away, it is the only island within reasonable sailing distance of Niuatoputapu. Beyond Tafahi, the closest islands are Samoa, Vava'u, and Fiji, which are several hundred miles away.

Tafahi is a high volcanic island and very steep. About eighty people lived there. Since there was no naturally level place on the island, the inhabitants had literally hacked the side of the mountain away in one place to have a level area to build a few houses and raise crops.

While there was nothing mechanical on Niuatoputapu, and the people lived close to nature, with no running water or electricity, and very little contact with the outside world, the people on Tafahi were even more isolated and, if possible, lived closer to nature and had less contact with civilization as they had no telegraph and no scheduled boats.

When we sailed to Tafahi, the seas were very choppy. We got as close as we could to shore, waited for the bigger waves to recede, quickly jumped in, and swam and waded to shore. I was impressed with the strength of the people who lived there. Some of the young women put a yoke on their necks, attached a large *kape* (big tuberous plants weighing up to eighty pounds apiece) to each end of the yoke, and carried them up the hill, almost running. I could hardly lift one, let alone two!

Shortly after arriving, we started tracting. We visited every home (eighteen in all), leaving a tract at each one and inviting the people to a meeting that evening. At the last home, a strange thought occurred to me, "Why don't you test the prophecy that the name of Joseph Smith should be known for good and evil throughout the world?" I don't know why the thought came, but it did.

We gathered the family of six around, invited them to come to our *po malanga* (cottage meeting) that evening, and handed them a tract. I then asked, "Have you ever heard of President Eisenhower?"

"Who's he?"

I explained that he was the president of the United States.

"Where's the United States?"

I tried to explain where it was, but they couldn't understand. They asked how big an island it was. I replied that it was a very big island, thousands of miles away with millions of people living on it. I told them that many people there had never even seen the ocean and that many people didn't know one another. They couldn't comprehend that. I then asked, "Have you ever heard of a man by the name of Kruschev?"

"Who's he?"

"Well, he's the leader of Russia."

"What's Russia?"

"Russia is a country." I tried to explain that it was a great big island, even bigger than the United States, and there were millions of people there. They had no way of comprehending that.

I then asked, "Have you ever heard of a person by the name of Charles DeGaulle?"

"No, who's he?"

"Well, he's the president of a country called France."

"Where's France?"

I again explained and then asked about other countries and leaders, but they had no comprehension of these famous political figures of the day.

Next I asked about some sports figures, some movie stars, famous business people, about the Depression, the Korean War, and other things. It was an exercise in futility because they had no comprehension of any of these people or events.

There was not a member of the Church living on this island, although there were two other churches there. I took a deep breath and said, "Have you ever heard of Joseph Smith?"

Immediately their faces lit up. Everyone looked at me, and the father said, "Don't talk to us about that false prophet! Not in our home! We know all about him. Our minister has told us!" I could hardly believe what I was hearing. The scripture from the Pearl of Great Price sounded in my mind that Joseph's name should be had for good and evil among all nations" (JS—H 1:33). To me this was a direct fulfillment of prophecy.

I am convinced that you could hardly get a place more remote, more out of touch with modern civilization, than the little island of Tafahi. The people there knew nothing of the great leaders of the day—political, economic, or otherwise—but they knew the name *Joseph Smith*. In this case they knew it for ill, at least to begin with. I spent the next few days explaining more of the mission of the Prophet Joseph Smith, and before we left, a few of them knew his name for good.

We made some friends on Tafahi, and several of us hiked to the top of the mountain. We went up through clouds and mists, bamboo forests, and thick junglelike vegetation until we finally came to the top. What a sight! It seemed like we could see forever. The ocean was everywhere. The only land you could see was Niuatoputapu, which seemed so small and far away. I was impressed at what different perspectives we have from different vantage points. I guess that to God this earth seems pretty small.

During my stay on Tafahi, several of the older men, who claimed they had the authority, went through a ceremony and made me a *matapule* (chief) and gave me an official name, *Ngalu 'o Tafahi* (The Wave of Tafahi). Other than writing it in my journal, I never used the name or made further reference to it. I preferred the title of missionary.

*Sailboat taken to Tafahi (in background).*
*The only way to get to shore was to swim.*

When we finally left Tafahi, I had a greater love for the Prophet Joseph Smith and a firmer testimony of his divine calling. A few people from Tafahi eventually joined the Church. I never visited there again, but I have not forgotten the people, the climb to the top of the mountain, the spectacular view, the ceremony, and particularly the deepened testimony I received in the last home as I asked about the Prophet Joseph Smith.

# 23

## *The Hurricane*

After returning from Tafahi, we continued tracting and trying to visit people on Niuatoputapu. For some reason, they seemed even less receptive than before. We asked the Lord to soften their hearts and to bless us with understanding of how we could better teach them. I'm not sure of the exact correlation of all these things, but shortly after, an interesting event took place.

Niuatoputapu is generally flat but has a relatively large mountain that rises rather abruptly from the flatlands about two-thirds of the way through the island and falls away just as abruptly to the ocean on what we called the "back side." The prevailing winds come from the south, or the back side, where the waves crash against the coral that rises sharply from the ocean. The wind-whipped sea is stopped by the mountain, which acts as a barrier and protects the front side of the island from the deadly salt spray.

Going north over the mountain, you drop quickly onto a large fertile plain that is quite flat and runs to a lagoon, with its smaller reef, that further protects the level cropland. Generally life goes on smoothly, with the mountain absorbing the salt spray and the protected side growing all the food needed for a suitably sized population.

Once in a while, however, nature plays a mean trick in the form of a hurricane. Most people are familiar with the devastating winds and terrifying waves, heaving themselves beyond their bounds, that mark a hurricane. But for small islands, one of the most destructive elements is the winds that reverse themselves and bring the waves and salt spray from the opposite direction onto the unprotected side.

There was no official warning, for at that time and in that remote location, forecasting or weather tracking was not available. The old-timers said they could feel it coming, though. I'm not sure whether I actually felt it or just believed others. There was something about the oppressive heaviness of the air that made all the animals and humans sense that something was wrong. There was a subtle, almost indiscernible, feeling of uneasiness as the wind started coming from the wrong direction. The sky was dark, the air was heavy; even without a lot of wind and rain, the people's disposition became dark and pensive. Everyone instinctively looked for shelter.

Suddenly that oppressive feeling burst in indescribable fury onto the defenseless little island. The winds shrieked, the waves crashed, and salt spray and sea came roaring across the fertile garden land and through the homes all the way to the front side of the mountain before being stopped.

Trees were uprooted, houses were toppled, roofs went flying, and people and animals tried to hide wherever they could. The flying debris was dangerous. A vacuum effect occurred sometime during the hurricane, causing pieces of reed and blades of grass to become like tiny spears that buried themselves in trees and even killed small animals. I saw pieces of flying tin roofing cut small trees in half and become deeply imbedded in the thick trunks of other trees. I tried to act excited or curious but must admit I was also scared. The fury of nature and the sights and sounds of destruction, especially when compared to the normally placid days and nights, were unnerving.

I don't know exactly how long the hurricane lasted. It struck during the afternoon and continued on through the night and into the next day, or at least it seemed to.

It was a long, terrifying afternoon and night. When you are closer to nature and not so protected by concrete buildings or prepared ahead by forecasts, you feel things in a different way. I can better understand the prophecy from the Book of Mormon telling of the storms at the time of Christ's crucifixion, "Many of the kings of the isles of the sea shall be wrought upon by the Spirit of God to exclaim: The God of nature suffers" (1 Nephi 19:12). That's just how it felt.

Hurricanes don't start with a single blow or end with a final whimper, but they do eventually stop. As we felt the winds lessening and the storm passing, we came from our hiding places with a feeling of awe and a look of unbelief at the terrible destruction we beheld. Trees were uprooted, roofs were gone, houses torn apart, fences missing, debris from everywhere was deposited everywhere else. Nearly all the big mango trees were down, the breadfruit trees were down, other trees were down, the wells were fouled with seawater, but worst of all, the crops were ruined, mostly by the destructive salt water.

Several animals had died, but as far as I knew no person was killed, although several were hurt in one way or another. What a pitiful sight we looked on! People began looking for family members, friends, animals, and other possessions. Men came from their gardens with tears in their eyes as they told of the loss of the year's labors and the looming specter of hunger.

The government magistrate called a special meeting for all adults. He tried to reassure everyone by saying, "We've been through this before, we can make it again. Let's all help one another. Gather the breadfruit from the fallen trees, and get as many tuber crops out as you can before they spoil. Start cleaning up and rebuilding. Don't hoard. See that the old, the young, and the sick are taken care of. Be glad no one was killed. Eat sparingly. Let's ration what food we have to last about four weeks. A boat should be here within three or four weeks so we'll be okay." He called on someone to pray and give thanks that we had been spared and ask God to guide and protect us, especially over the next few weeks. What a wonderful official government meeting! Belief in God and keeping the Sabbath holy are major parts of the Tongan constitution and culture.

We began cleaning up, and everyone made sure everyone else had something to eat. There was a beautiful feeling of cooperation. It's strange how disasters bring out the best (and occasionally the worst) in us.

Even though most of the fruit trees were blown down, there was lots of fruit on them, so we gathered it and used as much as possible. Many of the root crops were newly planted, so there was not much to salvage there. People generally did not seem overly concerned as the situation appeared to be mostly a matter of rebuilding and waiting for the next boat. So life slowly got back to a semblance of normality. I suppose most people were glad they didn't have much in the way of worldly possessions, because nature or others couldn't take away what they didn't have.

The storm ruined the telegraph, so we couldn't send a message for help. The boat normally came about every four weeks, so food allocations were made to last about five weeks "just in case." On those rations you'd never be full, but you wouldn't starve, either.

We started eating breadfruit, which would be our main staple. We also ate mangoes, oranges, and other fruits that wouldn't last long once picked. They tasted good, except the green ones, but they weren't very filling.

Everyone hoped the boat would come in about three weeks, since it had left Niuatoputapu for Nuku'alofa several days before the hurricane struck. The first two weeks passed rather uneventfully. The third week came and went with no boat. The hopes for a boat during the fourth week were very high, so when it passed with no boat, we could sense a different feel everywhere. It was somewhat like a cloudy day: the normal optimistic attitudes were more subdued, and people began telling stories of hard times that they had heard as children.

I remember some of the old men talking about whole islands being wiped out because of drought or storms that ruined the crops. Some talked about the earthen pits they used to make for storing food. Apparently in earlier times they practiced food storage through some type of fermenting process. They would wrap certain food in leaves and bury a huge mass of it, enough to feed many people for a long time. According to the old-timers, it kept well for years and years and had been the means of saving many island populations when natural disasters struck. They lamented that there was no such storage now. "We rely too much on the outside world, such as boats and telegraphs," they told me. "We should be more self-sufficient."

By the end of the fifth week, the food supply was low and there was still no boat. Things started to look and feel rather grim. I learned that attitude determined a lot. As people began to think pessimistically, things did get worse for them. The facts did not lend themselves to much optimism, but some on the island remained optimistic. I noticed a marked division among the people: some slid into negativism and defeat while others kept their optimism and faith intact and kept moving. Those who maintained their optimism seemed better off, physically and mentally.

The sixth week began on a very somber note. I suspect some people had stashed a little food away here and there, but even that was now mostly gone. Feki and I had each been eating the equivalent of about half a breadfruit per day. Now we cut that to a half between us per day. Then a quarter, then a sliver as the days dragged on. Liquid was a big problem too, as there had been very little rain after the hurricane. The wells were still brackish, and we had used most of the coconuts.

It is strange what our bodies do as we begin to cope with hunger. At one time we went into the swamp where we had previously cut ironwood for our house. In just a few seconds my forehead was full of mosquitoes. I quickly clapped my hand on my forehead, removed it, and licked off the dead mosquitoes. I never would have thought to do that, but someone mentioned it, and someway my body told me there might be a bit of protein in those mosquitoes, so I tried it. It wasn't very filling, so I only went to the swamp once.

Another interesting signal my body sent was to be quiet, don't move much—just sit, wait, relax. I found myself not going far and not doing much. No one told me to act that way, I just started to slow down automatically.

At the end of the sixth week things were serious. There was some light rain, which helped, but generally people were hurting badly, as they had been on very limited rations for a long time. The seventh week saw some genuine despair, as well as more fervent prayers. We stayed close to home and I spent a lot of time reading the scriptures. Helaman chapter 11 was especially meaningful to me. I felt I could understand Nephi's request in verse 4: "O Lord, . . . let there be a famine in the land, to stir [this people] up in remembrance of the Lord their God, and perhaps they will repent and turn unto thee."

I could see the reality of verse 7: "And it came to pass that the people saw that they were about to perish by famine, and they began to remember the Lord their God." I sensed that the people *were* more humble.

I wondered if we would live to see the same thing as recorded in verses 17 and 18: "And it came to pass that . . . the Lord did turn away his anger from the people, and caused that rain should fall upon the earth, insomuch that it did bring forth her fruit in the season of her fruit. And it came to pass that it did bring forth her grain in the season of her grain. And behold, the people did rejoice and glorify God, and the whole face of the land was filled with rejoicing."

During the seventh week there was more light rain, so although not plentiful, water was available in limited amounts. The eighth week began with deep foreboding. No one moved much. The sun was hot, and everyone stayed in the shade. I was aware of people dying, but it was generally the very old or the very young or those who had previously been ill and whose bodies just finally gave up. I don't think anyone died from what we technically call starvation, although some must have come close. Seeing the looks of hunger in the children was the hardest thing. Mothers had difficulty nursing babies, and there was generally a lot of suffering and despair.

I could understand Jeremiah's feelings as expressed in Lamentations 4:8–9: "Their visage is blacker than a coal; they are not known in the streets: their skin cleaveth to their bones; it is withered, it is become like a stick. They that be slain with the sword are better than they that be slain with hunger: for these pine away, stricken through for want of the fruits of the field."

During the eighth week I could almost hear my body say, "Don't move. Don't do anything." It wasn't really painful, I just didn't feel much. I remember sitting on the ground with my back resting on the trunk of a tree that had blown over. Some of its roots were still in the ground and a few branches had leaves that gave shade. The tree was at a rather odd angle but perfect for me. I sat there for several days and pondered, prayed, and read the scriptures. When you don't have much food or water, your body seems to absorb about everything so you don't have to move a lot.

It was a good time for pondering. The Lord really gets our attention at times like this. Just sitting in a weakened condition for several days makes a deep impression. I wondered if that may have been one of the reasons that the Lord allowed Joseph Smith to sit in jail for several months. I reflected on the Prophet's statement, "The things of God are of deep import; and time, and experience, and careful and ponderous and solemn thoughts can only find them out" (*Teachings of the Prophet Joseph Smith*, p. 137).

I learned that we need to take time to ponder. Sometimes the situations that compel us to do so, such as illness or disasters, are seen as cursings rather than the blessings they can be if properly used. Is it possible that in our busy, work-a-day world, one of the great blessings the Lord gives us is to put us in a situation where we must be quiet, without a lot of outside disturbance and pressures? Maybe then we will study, ponder, and think of Him, His ways, and His purposes.

I reflected on the scripture, "Be still and know that I am God" (D&C 101:16; Psalm 46:10). I had always thought of that scripture as a statement to watch for His salvation after we had done all we could. Now I looked upon it more as a commandment, or better, an invitation and explanation of truth: "Be still (sit quietly, get rid of outside pressures—go to the temple, for example—don't worry about this world) and know that I am God." Or: "Be still *so* you can know that I am God and so you can learn of Me and My ways." If we aren't willing to be still, it's harder to know that He is God. If the purpose of life is to know and love God, then maybe one of Satan's best weapons to keep us from that knowledge is to keep us so busy, even doing good things, and so occupied with commitments and pressures that we don't allow ourselves to be still so we can know that God is God!

The ninth week began with little outward change. There was, however, a great inward change. I started talking, or at least thinking to myself, saying, "Well, maybe my mortal life will end here." It was not a panicky feeling at all—I was past that stage. It was a calm feeling, an assured feeling, a feeling that it really didn't matter, because I knew all would be right.

I remember thinking, "If I do die here, my folks may feel kind of sad for a while. They sent me on a mission and hoped I would return to their home." These feelings were more sorrowful for them than for me. But I also remember thinking, "They have great faith. They can handle any problem."

I was pretty much skin and bones by now. I remember being aware of my ribs sticking out, of sensing my heart beating and my lungs breathing, and feeling a great wonderment for the miracle of the human body. What a marvelous mechanism the Lord has put together to house our equally marvelous spirit! The thought of a permanent union of these two elements, made possible through the Savior's love, suffering, and resurrection, was so inspiring and satisfying that any small physical discomfort faded into nothingness. What a great blessing to know that things will be right! What a tremendous blessing faith is! Faith is the opposite of fear. We fear what we don't understand. When we understand who God is, who we are, how He loves us, and what His plan for us is, fear evaporates.

At times I wasn't sure which side of the veil I would end up on, but it didn't matter. All that mattered was that God was in His heaven, and He knew me and my situation; He would see that what was right was done, for as far as I knew, I had done all I could.

I remember jotting down a little phrase, which undoubtedly is not original but which came at that time with the power of firsthand knowledge: "The only thing that is important is your standing in the sight of your Father in Heaven. If that is as it should be, nothing else matters. If that is not as it should be, nothing else counts." I am amazed how hard it is to learn that simple lesson and even more amazed at how hard it is to remember it!

As I sat there, I realized more and more how much I had to learn.

I was genuinely excited about getting on with that learning—on whichever side of the veil the Lord deemed most appropriate. I wish I could always have that zest for learning spiritual things. I understood clearly that the spiritual is more important and more powerful than the physical and, in fact, controls all physical things. I understood that both physical and spiritual elements are necessary and are in effect one when fully comprehended and perfected.

The next day as I sat under the tree, almost trancelike in my thinking, I felt a hand on my shoulder. I barely moved. An old man tapped me again, and I slowly turned.

"Here," he said, "I want you to have this can of jam. You're young. You're a missionary. You can live and do good. I am an old man. I will probably die. I am evil and bad. I have no right to live. Take this jam. It will help you."

The old man was gaunt and pale but very sincere and very determined, so I thanked him and took the can. There seemed to be a certain aura of light about him. I felt he had given his life to me. The jam would only help sustain life for a little while, but by now each little while was critical. It may be farfetched to say he gave his life to me, but not beyond the realm of possibility.

He turned and walked away. I looked again. I thought I recognized him. I vaguely remembered some past conversations with him and some feelings I had had.

Yes, I remembered now, he was one of the "bad guys," at least in my former way of thinking. I was aware of some things he had done that were wrong by almost any definition, yet here he was giving his last precious can of jam to me, me who in some respects was his enemy—at least to his life-style.

I experienced an overwhelming feeling about the importance of not judging (see D&C 64:8–11). We must leave judgment to the Lord. He alone knows all the facts. We may have had some experiences with some people at some time, but only God comprehends all experiences with all people at all times. Only he can weigh everything in its proper context.

It is interesting how the Lord orchestrates things. Feki and I ate that jam on tiny slivers of breadfruit for the rest of that day and part of the next. One could say the Lord sent the man with the jam to preserve our lives in a physical sense, and to a degree that is true. But in a more important sense he may have sent him to preserve our spiritual lives in helping us not judge. That jam and the man's willingness to give it to us was a blessing not only to us but also to him. He didn't die of starvation, but he did die a few months later of other causes. I am sure he was even happier than we were that he had given us the jam.

The next day started as another hot, humid set of hours slowly passing. We continued to waste away physically but grow in the more important spiritual sense. Feki was much stronger than I was. I guess he was more used to going without. I read the scriptures a lot, but even that got to be somewhat taxing. I pondered things and tried to understand relationships. I often dozed and at times wasn't entirely certain where I was. There is sometimes a very fine line between "here" and "there."

Many of the things I experienced cannot and should not be elaborated on. But during those days of sitting quietly, studying, praying, and pondering, I learned much about who God is, what the plan of salvation is, who the Savior is, and what His part in that great plan is. I learned something about why and how the world was created, a little about the love our Father in Heaven and Jesus have for us, and why God allows supposedly evil things to happen. In effect, I learned that the world was created to accomplish certain purposes and that everything, including our being here and having moral agency, is planned to accomplish those purposes.

I learned a lot about relationships: our relationship to our Father in Heaven and to the Savior, Their relationship to us, our relationship to each other as children of God, and the all-important role of the Holy Ghost in conveying and confirming the correct understanding of these relationships. I learned a little about our relationship to this earth, the earth's relationship to this solar system, its relationship to the universe, and the relationship between systems, universes, stars, and also something about how they are governed. I didn't understand much, but I could sense the grand design.

I sensed that I was learning more and more about less and less, but also felt that that was all right. I realized there aren't many things we *must* know to fulfill our purpose here, but the few vital things we must know *must* be known deeply and well.

I read and reread, with increasing appreciation, the accounts of Abraham and Moses. My soul resonated to the words of Moses, "which thing I never had supposed" (Moses 1:10). All I can say is that these are important things to understand, and they simply cannot be understood fully in a worldly or engineering or mathematical sense, although those disciplines are undoubtedly valid and can and should be used in their proper context.

I became convinced that just as we must break the bands of the gravitational pull of this earth in order to explore the farther universe, so we must break the bands of the gravitational pull of the cares of the world before we can begin to see the realities of some of these eternal relationships. When we begin to understand the relationship of opposition to growth and start to sense the type of growth God has designed for us and is trying to help us achieve, we tend to give thanks rather than complain about obstacles to overcome. People unchallenged are largely people undeveloped, be it physically, mentally, or spiritually.

I thought that just as rockets must overcome the pull of gravity in order to roar into space, so we must overcome the pull of the world in order to soar into the eternal realms of understanding. That is where God is, and that is important!

I realized that as we get the tiniest glimpse of these things, our concern over physical or worldly things becomes almost comical. To think that we actually fall for Satan's lie that things like worldly power, fame, or wealth are important is truly laughable, or would be were it not so sad.

As these thoughts were rolling around in my soul, I gradually became aware of some excited voices. I heard people yelling that a boat was coming. The sleepy, languid atmosphere that had oppressed the island for so long seemed to fade as everyone started to "wake up." With the renewed energy that comes from anticipation, most everyone began to move almost as a body to the shore where the sighted boat would soon arrive.

Feki's eyes were dancing once again as he came over and asked if I wanted to go to the boat with him. I was mostly awake, I think, but I said, "Thanks, but I'll wait here. I'll be fine until you come back." Several others asked if I wanted to go, and I gave them the same response. I was very comfortable leaning against my tree.

I remember realizing that things were going to change. A certain chapter was closing and another opening. I thought about some of the things I had learned: If you die, you die, and it doesn't matter so long as you've done what is right, and the only thing that really matters is your standing in God's sight. When you feel God's love and have the confidence and assurance that He is there, then other things aren't important. You understand that what we're doing down here on earth all evolves around learning to love and serve God and our fellowman. Life here is but a little blip in eternity. Mortal life and its environment, while important in terms of growth, is really the abnormal rather than the normal state of things. I suppose seeing things in their true relationships is among the greatest gifts we can receive.

Everyone about me left for the boat, and I soon found myself alone again. I recognized the yard, the well, the houses. They were not displeasing—in fact, they were lovely. But I found myself wanting to close my eyes, wanting to go back, wanting to understand those eternal relationships better. However, I felt myself being pulled away from them and returning rather grudgingly to the reality of skies, trees, shade, water, jam, and other people. I don't know how long I struggled with these two realities before I heard Feki excitedly telling me, "The boat's in, and it's full of food: flour, sugar, taro, and hard biscuits. I have some. Aren't you excited?"

I had to honestly say it didn't really make much difference to me. Since the boat had come, that must be the Lord's answer, so I was happy. Feki handed me a piece of hard-baked bread with the last touch of jam on it. "Here, eat it," he said.

I hesitated. I looked at the bread. I looked at him. I looked into the sky. I closed my eyes and heard Feki say, "Oh, yes, we should have a blessing first. I'll say it."

He thanked God for the food, for the boat, for preserving our lives, and for all the other blessings we had received. I added my own heartfelt thanks for new understandings, especially of eternal relationships. I also asked for help to remember these things and to act accordingly.

Others were returning from the boat now with sounds of joy. I remember taking that first bite of *ma pakupaku* (dried biscuits), closing my eyes, and crying. When I opened my eyes, those about me were crying as well. Some said how good it was to eat again and to feel this great gratitude to God for saving our lives. But I felt something deeper. I would never say I was unhappy with being able to eat again, and I was happy that life here would go on as before. But there was a wistful feeling—a subtle sense of postponement, as when darkness finally closes the brilliant colors of a perfect sunset and you realize you must wait for another evening to enjoy such beauty again. Fortunately, life can be colored by the memory of that brilliance which, while not always discernible, is always available and can be drawn upon, especially in times of great need.

I am convinced that everyone can feel this who will take the time to reflect on who they are and whose they are, where they are and where they came from, why they came here and where they can go, and what kind of help they can receive along the way. I am certain that that understanding can influence our lives, just as that perfect sunset, though long since faded, never quite leaves our consciousness and is available for us to draw on as we come face to face with the sordidness and unpleasantness of this earth's challenges.

When we have these special feelings, we often say, "I'll never be the same again," but the fact of the matter is, we often are. The pull of this world is strong, and too often we revert to former attitudes and behaviors. Thank goodness for repentance.

By this time, quite a group of friends and members had gathered around. How excited they were to bring me plates of steaming food! We had another prayer of thanksgiving, and everyone joined in eating. One older man said we should not eat too much for a day or two. Most everyone ignored him, but I felt he spoke the truth. I ate a little but did not fully share in the obvious joy of the main group as they relished the now-abundant food.

Evening came. I looked at Feki. I think he knew something of what I was feeling. I took another bite of food. I raised my head and slowly chewed a few times. I sensed it was growing darker. I looked over the heads of the circled crowd and caught the last rays of the most beautiful sunset I had ever seen. I could eat no more.

# 24

## Mail and
## Other Messages

The relief boat stayed overnight and was to leave the next day. In the morning I felt like moving around some, so Feki and I slowly walked to the government building in Hihifo to see about mail. When we got there, we were told that the boat had not brought mail, only food and supplies. They explained that the same storm that hit us had moved south and crippled the boat; because of repairs, this was the first they were able to come. They were taking mail back to Nuku'alofa, however, so I sent a few letters that covered about ten weeks, assuring my folks and others that I was fine.

After this boat left, the next one did not come for another six weeks, so in total it was nearly four months before I received any mail. That wasn't too bad for me, but it had been over three months since my folks had heard from me and I suppose they were worried. I felt sorry for them but I assumed that since the Lord had let me know they were all right, He would also let them know I was all right.

When this second boat after the storm arrived, the effects of the hurricane were largely over, and we were busy tracting and teaching wherever and whenever possible. On the second boat, I got about four months' worth of mail. It was great! I probably shouldn't have done it, but I told Feki I was going to take the afternoon off and read letters. I put them in chronological order in piles: family, Jean, mission office, and friends. I started reading mission items first, then letters from friends, then from Jean, and finally those from family. It was almost like reading a book, as a letter would talk about a problem, then the next letter would tell of another happening, and by the last letter a resolution had been reached. It was fascinating. At times I wondered why they spent so much time worrying about things which generally turned out fine anyway.

I could tell I was getting more and more removed from the life at home because many of the things they talked about held no special interest for me.

For several weeks after the hurricane, I was blessed with a series of special feelings or understandings, most of which I will not mention. These came mostly in the early mornings. I will mention but two examples.

I awoke early one Sunday morning with one of the most beautiful, calm feelings a person could imagine. I don't remember if it was a voice or whether I just instinctively knew that my father had been ordained a patriarch in our stake in Idaho Falls. I remember that when I said my prayers that morning I said, "I'm glad to know that Dad is worthy to be a patriarch, and I am grateful thou didst give me this understanding." Three months later I got a letter from home, saying, "Guess what happened? Elder Mark E. Petersen interviewed your dad and set him apart as a patriarch." It had happened at the time I felt the impression.

I don't know why that message came, but I felt a deep reverence for the calling of a patriarch and sensed there is a stronger link between patriarchs and heaven than we now understand. I had the feeling that we will have a much deeper appreciation for our patriarchal blessings at a later time as we see things more clearly. I also felt we should try to follow our blessings better and be more appreciative of them.

These feelings, each a little different, usually came early in the morning just as I awoke, but some were in the evening. They were all glorious, and each carried a feeling of love and peace and beauty that is hard to describe. I suppose they cannot be described in mortal terms as they have to be spiritually experienced, and that, in a way, is beyond mortal description.

The second example occurred again in the early morning. I saw myself in a farm setting with fields and cows and with a long pasture leading up to a beautiful house. I was aware that some very special people were visiting the house, where my folks and some of my family from some other generation were living. There was an aura of light and a feeling of love that can't be described, only felt.

I heard someone calling, "Johnny, I want you to come up here and meet someone." I walked up that long pasture and went into the house. They introduced me to somebody I had never met before, yet he seemed familiar. There were three other people there. I felt sure they were relatives. The spokesman was an old man, kind of grizzled but with the kindest expression you can imagine. He smiled and spoke to me, saying, "I'm sure you have enjoyed your farm work and the other work you have done. That's wonderful work. But there is another work to do, and you will enjoy that just as much." He sat me down and put his hands on my head and blessed me. There were some other people around. I didn't hear any words, but felt the whole scene evaporate into an aura of joy and beauty that cannot be described.

The main message I received was, "Wherever you go or whatever you do, under proper assignment, put your whole heart and soul into it and you will be happy and have joy therein. It doesn't matter whether it be family, work, missions, or other callings, joy comes from hard work and proper attitude, not location or type of work or calling." I knew I could enjoy any assignment, or any place, if I made up my mind to do so. I determined that I would.

I was glad for this period of special feelings and experiences, which were mostly family oriented. I sensed firmly that families are *the* important thing. I understood this was not necessarily the nuclear family we tend to think of—such as mother, father, and children—but the broader family, which we call multigenerational, extended family, clan, kin, tribe, or whatever. I knew for sure that all of us—married or single, male or female, old or young, light or dark—are part of this larger family unit and we need to understand it and appreciate it even more than we do now. Here again I felt that the Tongans may have a better understanding of the true eternal nature of family than Westerners do.

As I thought of many in our society putting other things ahead of family, such as their own convenience, schooling, friends, or other conditions, I almost gasped with disbelief. One reason we are here is to do things for others that they cannot do for themselves, such as vicarious temple ordinances and having children. I remember thinking, "If we, as Church members, delay or refuse to have children, where will God send them?"

As I thought of the eternal consequences of putting worldly things ahead of God and family, I literally shuddered. I realized that everyone has moral agency and no one but God can see the whole picture, but I also knew that we will answer to him for our actions. If those actions have been motivated by selfishness, it will be a sorry time for us. On the other hand, if we have been motivated by a sincere desire to help others, it will be a happy time for us no matter what inconveniences we have experienced.

I became firmly convinced that we should always look at the eternal perspective in all we do and say, for only by acting according to that perspective can we find safety and joy. It was a happy, peaceful few weeks, for which I was most grateful.

# 25

## The Delegation

On the third boat after the hurricane, my mission president came to visit us on Niuatoputapu. The boat stayed overnight. How happy I was to see my mission president! He was a great man, and I had the feeling he could do anything. For instance, he met a member just returning from his garden. The member's hands were dirty, so he didn't want to shake hands with the mission president. The mission president looked at him and said, "I don't care how dirty your hands are, so long as your heart is clean," and they shook hands. How that impressed me!

We held meetings with the mission president and the Saints, and I was able to talk to him for a long time about many things. He asked about the hurricane and about how things were going. I told him they were going great, and Feki and I loved it here and had plenty to do. He said he had a meeting that evening with the chief magistrate and several other important island leaders. I was impressed. I was not aware of what the meeting was about.

Feki and I had no appointments that evening because of the mission president's visit, but for some reason the president asked Feki to be at the meeting, but not me. I wasn't sure what to do, so Feki made arrangements for me to visit an investigator family on the other edge of Vaipoa. It felt strange visiting them alone, but they were happy to see me, and we talked for a long time about important principles. They had many questions, and it was late when we finished and I started walking home. I had no idea what time it was.

We were entering the hot months again; since the people didn't use watches or go by outward schedules, the general flow of activity just naturally tilted away from the hot daytime towards the somewhat cooler nighttime.

It was a beautiful moonlit night and a soft breeze caressed the palms and enveloped me in a hint of coolness. How lovely everything seemed! I thought I could see and feel and hear everything as I walked towards home.

There were small flickering glows of light from kerosene lanterns coming from a few houses where friends were gathered for *kava* parties. I heard the quiet tap-tap-tapping of rocks carefully pounding the *kava* root and could even hear the muffled swish of the *fau* as it filled the coconut cups with *kava*.

As I continued homeward, I heard a beautiful sound coming from a distant *fale*. I instinctively moved in that direction. As I came closer, I heard the plaintive sounds of a heartfelt love song filling the air, and I thought, "What a beautiful voice"; the young man sang with great feeling. I listened to his perfect, clear voice and the soft guitar accompaniment and thought, *"How could anything be lovelier?"* I listened for a long time, transfixed by the beauty of it all. In a sense, I felt he was singing just for me. I was glad there were no talent scouts around that evening, for surely they would have gobbled up that young man with the crystal voice and mellow guitar.

I felt that the song, the evening, the moonlight were all made just for me. I knew then I was in love with Tonga and the Tongans, their language, singing, character, and faith. I could hardly keep myself from crying. I listened, watched, and drank in everything for a long time. I thought of my family, of Jean, and of God. I wondered if this is what true love felt like. If it was, I wanted to be in love forever.

I finally returned home, quietly said my prayers, and carefully slipped into bed. Feki was already asleep. The next morning we went with the mission president to the boat and saw him off. Nothing more was said, and when the boat left, we went back to work.

Years later I learned that the mission president had originally planned on keeping me on Niuatoputapu for just a few months, then transferring me back to the main island and returning Feki to the building program. It seems the Lord had different plans, though, for the hurricane hit, then the famine followed, and nearly three months went by with no boat. I guess the three months my folks went without mail from me created a concern, and the mission president came to Niuatoputapu with the intention of bringing us back.

The local leaders must have guessed his intentions, and a delegation of leaders (mostly nonmembers) came and pleaded with him to let me stay. It was probably the trumpet they wanted more than anything. The mission president considered their request overnight, and the next morning canceled the transfer so that we could stay. I knew nothing about any of this, and he said nothing to me except that he was happy with my work and that I should keep on working hard. I was happy and anxious to do whatever my mission president told me. He gave me no new instructions, so we just kept doing what we had been doing.

As I look back, some of the greatest lessons I learned came during those last several months on Niuatoputapu. It was during this time, when the language and the setting were no longer a major challenge, that I learned to feel how the Tongans felt. That is very important. How grateful I am for inspired leaders who listen to the promptings of the Spirit and are willing to make changes when that is the right thing to do, rather than paying attention only to logic or predetermined reason.

I never had the opportunity of seeing my first mission president in Tonga again, as he was released a few months later. However, his influence on my life was, and still is, incalculable. His having the courage to do what he did has been a constant inspiration to me.

# 26

## *The Third Testimony*

After the mission president left, I felt a renewed desire to work even harder. We kept trying different ways to reach people and tell them about the gospel. Some ways worked, and others didn't. One day as we were planning, I said to Feki, "We really should bear our testimony to everyone on the island." Feki agreed. We didn't know how much longer we would be there, but we set a goal to bear our testimony to a minimum of three people per day. While it wasn't a very big goal, it was better than we had been doing; more important, if we did it, in a few months everyone on the island would have heard our testimony.

For several weeks we met that goal, but then one evening as we were returning home from Hihifo along the coast road a realization hit me. "Feki," I said, "we've only borne our testimonies to two people today and we agreed to three." He replied, "Well, it's too late now. We can't go back, and by the time we get to Vaipoa, everyone will be asleep."

Even though we were tired and had worked hard all day, I still felt bad at not keeping our agreement. I wondered if there was some way we could talk to one more person. "Forget it. It's too late," Feki said. "We'll only be able to do two today; maybe we can do four tomorrow."

I said, "Look, Feki, we agreed to bear our testimonies to three people. The Lord will provide someone."

"Who?" he said. "They'll all be asleep," so we kept on walking.

Along this road was a graveyard. Tongans were very superstitious about graveyards. Some believed they were inhabited by spirits and devils who could do them much harm. I noticed as we got closer to the graveyard that Feki, as usual, started to leave the road and go into the water to get farther from the graveyard.

Tongans bury their dead under the ground just like we do, but they also mound sand up several feet high on top of the grave. They decorate the mound beautifully, with colored rocks, flowers, mats, old bottles, and other things. Over time, the wind and rain smooth the mounds down so they become just a series of small rises, almost like pillows.

As we got to the graveyard, Feki was well out in the water. "What's the matter?" I chided. "Are you afraid of those devils?" Then the thought struck me, "I'll show him there are no devils in the cemetery." So I said, "Hey, look." And I turned off the road and went straight into the middle of the graveyard. There was a bright moon that night and I said, "Let me show you there are no devils here."

I recalled Feki's earlier words, "They'll all be asleep," and for a moment I thought I should bear my testimony for the third time that day to those asleep under the ground! However, upon reflection I decided that was bordering on the sacrilegious, so I dropped the idea. A sudden weariness hit me and I decided to lay down for a moment, using one of the gentle rises as a pillow.

I could tell Feki was scared for himself and worried for me, but I still laid down and rested for a few moments. I was just ready to get up when I heard a clippity-clop, clippity-clop, and knew a horse was coming. I heard the horse speed up as it got closer to the graveyard— the rider obviously wanted to get past the graveyard as fast as he could.

Suddenly the thought occurred to me, "Here's someone to talk to," so I jumped up and said, "Wait a minute, I want to talk to you!" You can imagine the effect my rising up out of the graveyard had on that poor man! He pulled the rope bridle in fright. The horse reared and the man tumbled off. His feet were churning even before they hit the ground. The horse ran on down the road. Even though all I wanted to do was talk to him, I could tell I had made quite a mess of things, as he probably thought spirits from beyond were coming out of the graveyard to get him!

I called after him and said, "Hey, it's just me. Come back!" By now I was acquainted with everyone on the island, and they all knew who I was, so when the man heard my voice and realized it was only me and not a spirit coming after him, he stopped running.

As I came up to him, I could tell he was partly scared and partly angry. "What did you do that for?" he demanded. "What were you doing in the graveyard anyway?" I told him I was sorry and tried to explain that I just wasn't thinking. I asked Feki to go and get his horse while I talked to him. "Look," I said, "Feki and I made a commitment that we would talk to three people each day about the Church. You are our third person today and I need to talk to you." He was still scared enough to not talk back or run, so he listened. I told him I had come several thousand miles to give him and others the most important message there is: that God has appeared again to man, raised up living prophets, and begun the final dispensation of the gospel. I basically told him the Joseph Smith story and explained about the Book of Mormon.

By the time I finished, Feki had returned with the horse, and the man had calmed down. As we gave him his horse, he seemed a little more angry than scared, but he got on his horse and rode away without saying much. I wondered if I had made an enemy. We continued walking home in silence. Feki was upset with me, but for some reason I felt better. We had agreed to bear our testimony to three people, and we had. The third one was a bit unusual, but it was done.

A few weeks later we were in Falehau, the smallest village on the island. We had worked all day with no success. We were discouraged and had just started back to Vaipoa when we heard a man calling us. We turned and saw it was the man who had been on the horse that night. I thought, "Uh-oh, this could be bad!" He asked us to come into his home. It was the first time we had been invited into any home in that village that I could remember. We hesitated, thinking he might have some revenge in mind, but since he seemed sincere, we went in.

He was quiet for a while and then said, "You know I haven't been able to sleep very well these past few weeks. I keep thinking about what you said about modern prophets with authority like Moses. Please tell me more about this prophet, Joseph Smith."

What an invitation! We eventually gave him and his family all of the discussions. He did not join right then, but did a while later. He moved to a different island and served in many important callings. He and his family have been sealed in the temple and have been faithful in the Church.

I learned that when we do things according to the Spirit, the Spirit and power of God take over. The Spirit justifies what we have done. The Lord then orchestrates future events so that what was started spiritually is brought to fruition downstream in a marvelous way.

*At the grave of the infant daughter of one of our investigators*
*(Elder Groberg in middle with tie). Burial is beneath the ground,*
*then sand and coral are piled on top and decorated to mark the grave.*

I learned that if we try hard, make good commitments, and do all in our power to keep those commitments, the Lord will help us keep them. Sometimes He does things in a way we would never think of, but if we are humble and obedient, good will always result. Truth *can* be, and often is, stranger than fiction. I know He helps us. I know He adds His increase to our feeble efforts, and this makes all the difference.

# 27

## "I Feel Sorry for Him"

As time passed and I became more and more acquainted with the islanders and their language, food, and customs, I also became more aware of the physical poverty in which they lived. I thought of all the conveniences we had at home and wondered why we should have so much in America and they have so little here. It seemed irreconcilable. I still didn't fully perceive the great spiritual blessings they had.

As memories of deaths, illnesses, and hurricanes faded, the monotony of living out the daily routine of a small island returned. One long, uneventful day gave way to another with very little change in village life. It would rain fiercely, then the sun would shine intensely. The diet of fish and breadfruit was almost unchanged from day to day. The oneness of the sun and the sea, the lagoon, and the soft laughter of those beautiful, brown-skinned people seemed to melt into a covering of peace and quiet.

Then, one day, new excitement! A strange boat was working its way into the harbor. Hurray for something different! The whole island was soon down to the seashore looking at one of the most beautiful sailing yachts I have ever seen.

Quietly, as if in slow motion, a crewman threw an anchor into the waiting lagoon. It did not even appear to make a splash, as though to refrain from disturbing the beauty of the scene. It was nearly dusk. The light from the setting sun silhouetted the yacht's sleek shape, its sails furled against the backdrop of deep blue waters and emerald green islets. Golden shafts of light painted everything in unbelievably vivid hues, as though framing the whole picture for eternity.

Silently the crew rolled out deep red carpets on the freshly scrubbed deck, and then the master emerged in his crisp white "tropics" to survey the situation. By now there were canoes all around as curious islanders wanted to be a part of this experience, this change.

Our members were caught up in the excitement. They soon brought back reports, and even though I was young and inexperienced, it did not take long to realize what was happening.

The man was a millionaire from overseas, cruising the world. He wanted to trade for food and water, and he wanted girls. There was liquor on board and a real "swinging time" for those who would accept his invitation.

I counseled the members to stay away. Most did, but some did not. The wealthy adventurer stayed for a few days until he filled his wants. Then he announced he would leave before noon the following day. Some of the faithful members pleaded, "Can we go out before he leaves, just to see the boat?" I agreed that at ten o'clock the next morning we would briefly look at the yacht.

When we got there, it was even more elegant than I had pictured. Evidence of the previous night's activities was still being cleared away, and preparations were being made to raise anchor and take sail. We spent a few moments in wonder and awe, astonished at the beauty of the deep mahogany paneling, the rich bronze fittings, the luster of the freshly painted surfaces, and the gleaming white of the hull as it lapped quietly at the deep blue lagoon.

We got in our canoes. The owner, nearly sober, waved good-bye, and we returned to shore. As we pulled our dugouts onto the sandy beach, I turned again to see that sleek, white form move toward the horizon. I thought of the millionaire in his white "tropics," having had his fill, comfortable with his well-stocked cupboards and expert crew, with his money and power. He seemed to have everything he wanted.

Then I looked at the men who had brought me to shore: no shoes, shirts of rags, tattered *valas* (skirts) tied with coconut sennit around their waists. I looked past them to the village. I saw the smoke from the morning's cooking twisting lazily into the air, heard the monotonous sound of *tapa* being beaten, and felt the heaviness of the overhead sun as it filtered through the palm trees. I watched the men slowly walk to their gardens and heard the laughter of naked children as they chased scrawny dogs.

Suddenly the oppressiveness of island life, with so little opportunity for change, struck me as being grossly unfair. I turned again to

*This scene, representing the story "I Feel Sorry for Him,"*
*shows the shore of Niuatoputapu with Tafahi in the background.*
*Painting by Clark Kelley Price, a missionary who served in Tonga.*

gaze at the yacht, now receding into the distance. The contrast was so great as to be almost unbelievable. My heart cried out, "Unfair! Unfair! These poor people—look at them. And you—look at you!"

I returned to the group, and we trudged up the shore to the village. Then one of the older men turned to me and said softly in his native tongue, "I am very sad. I feel very sorry."

"Well," I interrupted, "I am very sad, and I feel very sorry, too. It just isn't fair, is it?"

"No," he continued, "it really isn't fair. I feel so sorry for him, for he will never be happy."

I stopped dead in my tracks.

"*You* feel sorry for *him? He* won't be happy? What are you talking about?"

My mind was groping to come to an understanding of what he had just said. This man with nothing was saying he was sorry for that man with everything! My immature mind was spinning, trying to interpret words, feelings, and relationships.

The islander continued: "I feel sorry for him. He will never be happy, for he seeks only his own pleasure, not to help others. Yet we know that happiness comes from helping others. All he will do is sail around the world seeking happiness, hoping others will bring it to him, but they cannot. He will never find it, for he has not learned to help others. He has too much money, too many luxuries, too much power. Oh, I feel so sorry for him."

I looked at the wrinkled brown body of the old man. His teeth were gone, his hair was white, and his skin was leather. But his eyes were soft, his voice quiet, and his countenance immaculate. His powerful words had taught me a great lesson.

Years have passed, but occasionally as I see proud people traveling in their sleek, new cars or sense my own unwillingness to help others, I close my eyes and see a beautiful yacht moving toward the horizon, then see an old man with a wrinkled, brown body, white hair, and skin of leather. I listen as his soft eyes penetrate mine. His toothless mouth moves and his spirit explains: "I feel sorry for him. He will never be happy. He hasn't learned to help others."

# 28

## *"My Island"*

By now I was so thoroughly enmeshed in island life that I truly felt I belonged. There were those who still fought against the Church and us, but I felt I understood them. They were more open now and talked as friends, even though we saw things differently.

Feki and I were invited to attend almost every major function including government meetings, funerals, and similar events. You learn something about cultures, customs, and people when you sit among them and visit for hours on end. I had many opportunities to do so.

Some of the major occasions for large gatherings and feasts in Tonga were funerals, marriages, holidays, and some birthdays. Much has changed now, but back then actual births were not celebrated much. If a child lived a year, however, it was cause for celebration—then it was considered his birthday. From birth to one year a baby was somewhat of a nonperson, like a test to see if he or she could survive a year.

It was also considered a big event if a child lasted to around twenty-one. Not many people knew their actual birthday, but they generally had an idea of approximately when they were born by reference to some event—a hurricane, a drought, a boat sinking, someone catching a big fish, a celebration, or something similar.

A funeral was a big event. On small islands, there are not too many things to do. You work, you fish, you sleep. To have something unusual happen is a welcomed change, and a funeral is a major break from the norm.

At this time there was no embalming in Tonga. The rule was that if you die in the afternoon, you are to be buried before noon the next day. If you die before noon, you are to be buried before the sun goes down that day. It was so hot and humid, the body starts decaying within hours of death and the smell became really bad after several hours.

Even though a person was buried quickly, the funeral often lasted several weeks. Family and friends came from all over, to be with the family. This placed a big burden on the family of the deceased to furnish meals and lodging. Visitors would cry and mourn and comfort in their own way, which was usually loud and long. I wondered if it was healthier emotionally to "let it all out" than to try to act controlled as we so often do in our Western culture.

During the last few months I was asked to speak at several funerals and found it was an excellent time to explain some of the most important doctrines of the Church. At first some people were critical about my preaching "my doctrine," but the truth is so comforting that eventually no one complained, not even the ministers. In fact, many people accepted those truths, for I was told that several of the preachers modified their sermons about what happens when we die, especially their teachings pertaining to infants.

Even though I generally controlled my emotions, there were times, such as at the funeral of the infant daughter of one of our investigators, when I felt I could join with the family in venting my grief and sorrow—not for the infant daughter, who was fine, but rather for the parents, who as yet didn't understand. As I watched them, I thought of their Israelite background and wondered how they felt as they read Micah 1:8, "Therefore I will wail and howl, I will go stripped and naked: I will make a wailing like the dragons, and mourning as the owls."

Sometimes I cried in a way that would not be acceptable in our society but which was fully acceptable and even expected among them. As I became closer to the people, I found myself crying more often. I could see how they were related to the Book of Mormon people, particularly as mentioned in 3 Nephi, "Behold, they began to weep and howl again because of the loss of their kindred and friends" (3 Nephi 10:8).

I also found myself relating much more to the way they felt about "mother earth" and "father sun," and plants, and fish, and nature in general. They truly saw God's handiwork for what it was. They sensed the spiritual element of temporal things and felt they were entrusted as caretakers rather than exploiters of all that lived and breathed, including the earth, the sea, the plants, the animals. Most important, they felt that way about one another.

I remembered hearing how the early Native American Indians felt about these things and realized that there was a closeness that was more than coincidental.

Generally, the people were very healthy, with straight, white teeth, clear complexions, beautiful hair, and strong bodies. I enjoyed excellent health most of the time as well. Very rarely was there flour, sugar, or any kind of processed foods. There was no refrigeration, and all cooking was done with fire.

Unfortunately there was quite a bit of drinking (mostly home brew), and people who could get cigarettes certainly used them. There was a sort of unofficial contest between a certain element of older boys and young men to see who could stay drunk for the whole week between Christmas and New Year's Day. Sadly, there were several cochampions.

The culture and the people of Tonga seemed ingenious in devising elaborate ceremonies that took up lots of time. At nearly all major events, such as the coronation of a king or welcoming of a visitor, there was a *kava* ceremony that went on for hours, even days. Speeches were given that went on and on, with lots of flowery words but no particular progress toward a conclusion. To me, at the time, it seemed ridiculous—just a lot of talking back and forth with no change in the predetermined outcome.

Once I was helping at such a ceremony that seemed to go on forever. In frustration, I asked one of the old men sitting by me, "Why do you take so long? Why take hours or days to accomplish something that could be done in thirty minutes?"

He thought and thought, then said, "Well, it's something to do. It is very orderly and very long. When we finish this, we'll just have to think of something else to do, so why not do this?" I thought that was silly. But the more I thought about it, the more I realized that we are not so different in our culture. Men and women play bridge for hours, watch soap operas, or do other things that do not really accomplish much but are just something to do. I wondered how much of our lives are spent in this way. The more I thought about it, the more I realized we were indeed the same as the Tongans, if not worse. I penned these words at the time about our society:

*Most of what we buy isn't necessary*
*Most of what we eat is not very good for us*
*Most of what we do is not very important*
*Most of what we store should be given or thrown away*
*Most of what we talk about is trite*
*Why don't we spend our time and means better?*
*Why don't we concentrate more on loving and helping others?*

I didn't have a good answer then, nor do I now, but at least I thought about it.

I suppose I was getting to a point where the language, customs, and activities on Niuatoputapu seemed proper and normal; by contrast, my old *palangi* words and ways seemed strange, contrived, and in many ways hypocritical and meaningless.

There were still adjustments to make, but often as I walked to another village, and passed a familiar tree or rock, met a familiar horse or person, saw a familiar house, or heard a familiar sound or voice, I had the feeling, *This is my language; these are my people; this is my island.*

*Niuatoputapu (in foreground) and Tafahi (in background).*
*Painting by Clark Kelley Price.*

# 29

# Leaving
# Niuatoputapu

We were busy and happy and continued to work hard. We were teaching several families with hopes of more baptisms, when one day I received this telegram from a new mission president: *Elder Groberg—Niuatoputapu—If you are there, please reply*. It was my first notice that we had a new mission president.

I replied that I was there, and he sent another telegram back: *New assignment for you—Take the next boat to Nuku'alofa with Feki.*

What a shock that was! A new mission president, a new assignment, and leaving Niuatoputapu—all in one telegram! I wasn't sure I could cope with it all, but knew I had to. *Leaving Niuatoputapu?* I couldn't believe it. And worse, the boat was scheduled to arrive in just a few weeks. How could I ever get all the things done I felt I needed to do before I left?

As the reality of it all sank in, I became quite philosophical. I knew I couldn't finish everything, so I would just do everything I could and leave the rest to others. I reflected on what had happened over the past year.

I had come not knowing the language or any of the people on Niuatoputapu. I was now leaving, able to speak the language and recognize everyone. When I first came I was scared and felt the locals had bad motives. Now I felt at home and knew the people had good intentions and were wonderfully helpful. I had come to a small branch with lots of problems, now I was leaving a relatively strong branch with at least a few less problems.

We had baptized only seven people in a year's time, but we had worked hard and tried the best we knew how. It was very satisfying to know that all seven were still active members and were powerful additions to the Church. Generally those who join the Church despite heavy opposition tend to remain active.

Years later, I did a quick calculation and found that those seven baptisms eventually formed six families with over fifty members, including spouses and children, in those immediate families, or an average-sized branch. They all had large and faithful families. For example, one family we baptized ended up with twelve children: nine boys and three girls. All twelve served missions. Using average baptisms per missionary for Tonga, the family members of these six families who served missions accounted for over 450 new members, or a good-sized ward. These children then got married, and many of them went on another mission as couples. Nearly all of their children served missions as well. Again, using average figures, this group of missionaries would have baptized over three thousand new members, or an average-sized stake.

With no stretch of the imagination, there could be well over three thousand additional members brought into the gospel from those original seven baptisms who remained faithful, even to the third generation and beyond.

When we do things according to the Spirit, the power of God takes over, the Spirit justifies what we have done, and the Lord orchestrates future events so that what was started spiritually is brought to fruition downstream—both temporally and spiritually. When the Apostle Paul wrote, "The letter killeth, but the spirit giveth life" (2 Corinthians 3:6), he wrote the truth. Seven isn't very much, but the Spirit brought life; eventually branches, wards, and stakes came into existence, and the end is not yet. If we do our part, if we make and keep commitments under the influence of the Spirit, what marvelous things happen! I am convinced that all we have to do is try our hardest by putting forth effort and having great faith in God, and He indeed will cause the increase.

Those last few weeks rushed by like a fleeting cloud. Suddenly the boat arrived on which I was to leave. The time of departure was here! I can't explain the depth of emotion I felt as I realized this was my last day on Niuatoputapu. The boat was in, the passage had been purchased, and we were going back to Tongatapu in the morning and leaving Niuatoputapu and its wonderful people behind.

I could hardly believe it, yet I knew it was true. I had become so accustomed to the island and its people, I didn't want to leave. A year doesn't seem like a long time, but from an emotional and spiritual point of view, the months on Niuatoputapu seemed more significant than the last twenty years of my life. I had learned much. I knew Niuatoputapu would always be a sacred place to me, a place where I had seen the power of God manifest among his children.

I had learned the greatest lessons anyone can learn in this life, namely that God lives, that He is our Father, that He loves us and is involved in our lives and cares what happens to us; that Jesus is His son, our Brother, our Friend, our Redeemer, who because of His infinite love for us paid a terrible price that we might return to our real home with Heavenly Father with joy, love, opportunities to serve, and increased capacities that are indescribable. I learned that Joseph Smith is a prophet of God and through him the Book of Mormon, other scriptures, and the priesthood of God and the holy ordinances thereof are again on the earth; that the kingdom of God, with living prophets, is real and here and now, with the power to seal for all eternity and bind on earth and in heaven. I had seen and felt its power and knew of its efficacy.

I knew all of these things and felt them deeply, but strangely enough, my thoughts that day were not so much on those things as they were upon the people. I wanted to see and talk to everyone. I knew everyone, or at least thought I did. I was sure I could call all seven hundred by name and tell who they were related to and what house they lived in and how many pigs they had and how often they had fed us. It was a heart-tugging experience to move around and visit everyone.

Even though we didn't sleep the whole night, the next morning came too quickly. We slowly walked toward the boat, where a large crowd was gathered to see everyone off. This boat was scheduled to arrive in Nuku'alofa just before school started, so it was full of students—mostly high school age—going away to school on the "big" (twenty-one miles long) island on Tongatapu.

Feki and I said our farewells and embraced almost everyone. We loved our little flock and hoped that we left them better than when we found them. We loved those we had baptized and those we had not. We had great hopes for all of them. Everyone expressed their love, member and nonmember alike. The chief magistrate gave us a warm farewell. He was a wonderful man and a great friend.

As we got on the boat, the Saints gathered together and sang the beautiful parting hymn *"Oka Tau Ka Mavae"* ("When We Part"), sung as only Tongans can sing. Talk about heart tugs! Tears flowed freely and emotions were hard to control. I suspect most missionaries feel the same way as they leave the area and the people they have served and come to love. For me, it was a day of wonderment and fulfillment. My first mission president had asked me to learn the language and build the kingdom. I felt both had been accomplished, at least to some degree—and oh what I had learned in the process!

# 30

## Warning in the Night

The boat finally got under way. We were actually leaving Niua-toputapu! I still couldn't believe it. I realized that physically we were leaving, but a big part of my emotional and spiritual being was staying and would stay there forever. I stood by the rail and looked longingly at the people and the island for hours until it sank below the horizon.

Would I ever return? Would I ever forget? Would I ever be the same? Could God's love and goodness and man's kindness ever be found in such rich abundance again? I felt they could somewhere, sometime—at least in the celestial kingdom. I was glad for that hope, but I sensed a loss as I knew it would be difficult to duplicate those feelings anywhere soon. Once you have felt these feelings of deep love, you want nothing less. I hoped I could endure faithfully to the end and feel that indescribable love eternally.

The promise of new adventures seemed a little hollow when compared to the loss of known love and acceptance and the certainty of being needed and wanted. The assurance that I was following the directions of an inspired, albeit new, mission president gave me the strength to move on.

The day was beautiful and the ocean mild. There were a few whitecaps and some choppiness, but nothing unusual. It only took three days to go directly to Nuku'alofa as the boat was much larger than the one I came on. We slept on the deck along with many others, mostly students. We talked, sang, and enjoyed the voyage. We drank coconuts and ate crackers, *taro,* and *ufi* that some of the Saints had given us. I remember trying to recall how large and what shape plates and glasses might be and wondering what it would be like to use a knife, fork, and spoon again, as I had eaten only with fingers the last twelve months.

It seemed strange to be on a large boat with crowded decks, but Feki and I staked out a nice area for our mats, baskets, and *tapa* cloth (used for warmth, like blankets) on the higher deck. Everyone helped everyone else and enjoyed each other's company. Not many got seasick. It was wonderful to visit with good friends, and the days passed pleasantly.

We came to the last evening of the voyage and were told we would be in Nuku'alofa the next morning. It was a beautiful evening as we swayed to the gentle, undulating motion of the boat. I marveled at the bright stars above and wondered at the clouds playing hide-and-seek with the moon. I felt the caress of the warm sea breeze and listened to the quiet murmur of peaceful conversations. I was enraptured by the beautiful strumming of guitars and the melodious singing of some of the best voices on earth. It was almost intoxicating. All this and more combined to lull me into a state of wonderment at God's goodness to us all. I finally fell asleep with these beautiful feelings on my mind. Feki was close by, and tomorrow a new adventure would begin.

I soon learned we should never get too complacent. As I slept, my hand was lying outside my covering of *tapa* cloth. Sometime during the night, I felt something moving my hand slightly. I stirred a little but thought nothing of it. A moment later I felt something rub across my hand. I stirred again slightly. Part of me said, Just relax. But another part said, *There is danger here, wake up!* I wrestled between the two for a moment, then felt a surge of strength and sureness of what to do.

I woke and sat up with a start. The moon was bright and I could see fairly well. I looked around. Where was Feki? Where was everyone else? I was in the same place where, with many others, I had gone to sleep, but now there was only one young girl nearby, who had moved her mat next to mine. As I sat up and began looking around, I heard a few snickers from behind a large metal stack and noticed this girl putting her shirt back on. Where had the others gone?

I asked where Feki was. The young girl said he was visiting someone "over there," but didn't I want to stay where I was? "Lie down and go back to sleep. It's okay." I was fully awake now and it was pretty easy to see what was going on. I simply said I needed to be with my companion. There was some whispering, and soon Feki returned. I asked him where he had been. He said he had been asked by several people to come over and tell them more about the Church. Since there were lots of people sleeping by me, he went. He was surprised when he returned to see so few people there. I asked him not to leave again. He agreed. The girl and some other students moved away, and Feki and I went back to sleep.

The next morning this same girl asked me, "*Koeha na'a ke hola ai anepo?*" ("Why did you run away last night?") I knew what she meant. I told her I was a missionary, and that missionaries don't get involved in that way. I was not so much angry as factual. I felt great compassion for her and for the vast multitude of mankind who have been deceived by the evil one as they continue to seek pleasure or joy in places and ways it cannot be found.

I thought of the lessons I had learned, particularly that in physical things our imagination or anticipation is much kinder than reality, whereas in spiritual things, no matter what our imagination or anticipation, the reality is always greater and deeper and more fulfilling. How grateful I felt to God for His protection and for the gospel of Jesus Christ and for its teachings and for His laws that bring eternal joy when followed.

I have often reflected on that night. It was warm, beautiful, and full of feelings. The rolling motion of the boat, together with a long voyage, a tropical breeze, beautiful music, and tender feelings, combined to bring out emotions that are deep and basic and that may be closer to the surface under these circumstances than in some other climates. I was grateful for the help the Lord gave me that night and grateful for the feeling that warned me of danger. I never saw that girl again.

Later in the morning, someone called and pointed to the south, where we could barely make out the faint outlines of the big island of Tongatapu. In a few hours a new phase of my mission would begin. *What will it be like?* I wondered. *Where will I be going, and what will I be doing? What will the new mission president look like and be like?* I felt nothing could be better than my time on Niuatoputapu, but I also felt good about going wherever and doing whatever the new mission president wanted me to do. I was sure he would be inspired, as my first mission president had been. I knew that with God's help, any assignment could be accomplished. I also knew there would be trials and challenges, as that is part of missionary assignments. However, I knew that filling assignments with God's help, no matter what the challenges, brought happiness and joy and deep fulfillment.

I hoped I would never forget Niuatoputapu. I also hoped I was ready for the next step.

# 31

## Soft Beds

Shortly before noon we arrived at Nuku'alofa on the island of Tongatapu. The island *did* seem big—and very different from Niuatoputapu! There were two wharves, roads, cars, stores, electric lights, and people everywhere. All these things! All this noise! All these people! My mind was a blur. I had left from here a year ago, but in contrast to Niuatoputapu it seemed so different now.

I didn't know what the new mission president looked like, but soon I spotted a kindly looking American couple who were obviously looking for us. As we met, I introduced myself and Feki to them and they asked about our suitcases. I told them we had none, but my possessions were folded in a mat, as were Feki's. The mission president had two helpers who put my mat in his car and Feki's mat in another car. I wanted to visit a bit and get an idea of what was going to happen, but almost immediately they whisked Feki back to the building missionary quarters at Liahona, and I hardly had a chance to say good-bye. It did not seem right to me, as I wanted to be with Feki, but there wasn't much I could do about it.

The mission president and his wife were kind. She reminded me of my mother—a warm, loving woman. I remember her putting her arms around me, crying, and saying, "Oh you poor thing, how could they leave you up there for so long?" As far as I was concerned, there wasn't anything poor about it at all. It was great! I didn't know what to say. In fact I could hardly say anything in English. She may have taken my silence for agreement. We got in the car and drove to the mission home. The cars, roads, wooden houses, stores, and power lines—all seemed so strange. We arrived at the mission home and went in. It was noontime.

The mission president's wife seemed very excited. She asked me to sit down as she spread the table. She had a meal of steak, potatoes, gravy, bread, milk, butter, and jam. "It's ready now," she smiled, "I know how much you'll enjoy these foods you haven't had for so long. Let's eat!"

A prayer was offered. I tried to appear happy and grateful, but I missed Feki terribly. It was the first time we had been apart for over a year. I missed the Tongan language. English seemed so foreign to me. I missed sitting on the floor and eating with my fingers. I missed the familiar smells and sounds and people I was accustomed to. I felt awkward sitting on a chair by a table and trying to use a knife, fork, and spoon. Plates and cups seemed so out of place with eating. And this strange food tasted weird!

It was difficult to converse. They spoke of things I did not understand, such as how sorry they felt for me and how I was now back in civilization. I'm sure they were sincere, but it did not ring true with me. That wasn't the way things were in my life. I had been happy on Niuatoputapu and was beginning to feel uncomfortable, even miserable, here.

They could see I was somewhat melancholy, so they said, "Why don't you rest for a while? You must be terribly tired after all you've been through. We'll leave you alone for a few hours." The mission president said he was going to some meetings at Liahona but would be back for supper.

They took me to a room. It had a wooden door with hinges, a door knob, windows, and curtains. It also had a bed with a mattress, a pillow, and clean sheets. They showed me an inside bathroom with a shower that turned on with a tap, a basin with running water, and a mirror. There was a toilet that flushed by pulling a chain, and I noticed there were even curtains on the bathroom window as the breeze rustled them slightly.

They left me and told me to rest and relax and assured me everything would be fine. I suppose they wondered about my mental state because I was quiet and stared at all these strange things for a long time. In a way they seemed familiar, yet I wasn't quite sure. I was grappling with trying to put two worlds back together. I remembered

steak and potatoes; mattresses, toilets, and running water; even curtains and English words; but they seemed to have little relevance now.
I was having a difficult time seeing exactly where everything fit.

I wondered what I would be doing and what my new assignment
would be. It was hard to be alone, and it was hard to think and feel
comfortable in this foreign atmosphere. I tried to rest, but couldn't, so
I sat on the floor and started to read the Book of Mormon in Tongan. I
came to a verse where Jacob lamented, "For we [are] a lonesome and a
solemn people, wanderers, cast out from Jerusalem" (Jacob 7:26). I
started to cry. I knew how he felt.

That evening we had supper and talked for a while, and then I
took a shower and went to bed. I do not think I slept at all that night
as my stomach hurt from the strange food, my mind hurt from the
strange language, my back hurt from the soft bed, and I hurt all over
from missing Niuatoputapu and Feki.

The next morning my mission president called me in for an interview. He assigned me to be the district president in Ha'apai, a group of
about seventeen islands one or two days north of mission headquarters. He said, "They have lots of problems there. There are several fac-
tions and much discord and disharmony. I want you to go up and
straighten it out. You will be in charge of all the missionaries and the
missionary work, and also in charge of all the members and the
branches. You will need to choose two good counselors. Pray about it,
and when you feel right, set them apart and go to work. We are short
of missionaries, so I don't think I can spare a companion for you, but if
you have good counselors, you'll be all right. You can use your counselors and other members who are willing to help you as companions. I
would suggest you choose two men who are married as counselors.

"I also want you to start a school there. Schools have proven to be
helpful in the work. I won't get there very often, but you will be fine.
The Lord will bless you. Get rid of the discord up there. Do whatever
is necessary to get the people united. Teach the gospel. Build up the
Church. Baptize those who believe. Strengthen the branches and follow the directions of the Spirit."

He asked if I had any questions. I shook my head negatively. He
then said, "The boat for Ha'apai leaves in a couple of days. We are
having a conference at Liahona now, and I would like you to come
and participate." I agreed.

We got ready to go to conference, but before we left, his wife
asked if I had any special request for supper, as she was anxious to

make my stay as pleasant as possible. I suspect she sensed I was miserable. "If there is anything at all we can do to make your stay more comfortable, just let us know," they both said.

It was hard for me to do, but they had asked so I gently said, "If I really have a choice, I do have a request."

"What is it?" they replied in unison.

"Could I take my things with me and stay with Feki at Liahona until the boat goes to Ha'apai?"

The mission president was surprised, and his wife began to cry. "You mean you don't like us?" she sobbed. I tried to explain the best I could that it had nothing to do with them. It was just that I couldn't sleep on the soft mattress, I couldn't eat the food, I was uncomfortable with English, and I missed being with Feki and the Tongans. They told me there were only little thatched huts for the labor missionaries, and the conditions were pretty primitive. I said that would be fine. I am sure they felt bad, but they were very nice and said they would think about it.

I could tell they were concerned about my health and about me. They communicated that well. I assured them that I had never had better health or been happier than while on Niuatoputapu. They had heard of the famine and other problems and were a little questioning, but in the end they believed me and let me take my things, and we all went to the conference together.

The conference meetings lasted all day, but in the evening I walked to the labor missionaries' huts, found Feki, and excitedly told him I had been given permission to stay with him for a couple of days until I went to Ha'apai. The huts were really only thatched roofs lifted up on one side so you could crawl in. I couldn't stand up, but, oh, how good it felt to take a piece of boiled *taro* in my hand and savor it and lick my fingers! How fresh and familiar the smell of the dried coconut fronds was, and how wonderful it was to sleep on a nice, woven mat on the ground! It rained hard the next night and everything got wet. Despite this I felt much better, as my body and mind were used to this.

I enjoyed the conference meetings and was asked to speak several times. I enjoyed getting acquainted with other people. The evening before my boat left, someone came with a message for Feki saying his mother had passed away. She had been ill, and Feki and I had visited her the day before. Feki left immediately. I wanted to come, but he said, "No, you stay here."

He was back before sunup and ready to go to work. I asked about going to the funeral to be held about noon that day. He said, "No, I will do my regular building missionary work, and you will go to town and take the boat to Ha'apai. That's the way Mom would like it." I never questioned him. His attitude of total commitment always made a great impression on me. Feki thanked me for coming and staying with him at the school. He assured me all would be well in Ha'apai if I worked hard and was humble. I thanked him for his help. This was the last time I saw Feki on my first mission.

I found out years later that the little act of moving in with the labor missionaries, which I did because I felt more comfortable, is one of the things that solidified my acceptance among the members on the main island of Tongatapu. When they saw I truly preferred to eat Tongan food and sleep on the floor and be with Tongan people, rather than staying in the big house with the fancy food and the soft beds, they felt my love for them came from my heart and that I did what I did because I wanted to, not because I had to. I certainly had no lofty motives but rather came because I felt better—physically and emotionally. In a sense, those few days closed the circuit with the local members as they said, "He understands us. He can feel the way we do."

I learned that unless we feel the way others feel, we cannot be too effective in meeting their needs. I have often said we must feel another's needs before we can fill them. Sometimes we learn another language or culture and are able to feel the way they feel, but not always. Feelings go far beyond mere language or knowledge. To feel how others feel is a great blessing and is accomplished as we hurt with them, laugh with them, mourn with them, rejoice with them, cry with them, suffer with them, wonder with them, pray with them, experience miracles with them, and become reconciled to die with them if necessary.

I think the Savior truly felt how others felt. The scriptures tell us that "I, the Lord, will feel after them" (D&C 112:13). He went below all things so that He might rise above all things and draw *all* people to Him. I think this means not only physically but also emotionally, as He actually understands them and knows how they feel—each one. I don't think we can feel what we haven't experienced, at least to some degree.

I wonder if some of our so-called trials with wayward children, poor health, or financial reverses may be to help us feel things we otherwise might not be able to feel. I am confident that we can best understand and help people when we have felt the way they have felt. God has lots of children, some of whom do some pretty strange things, but His love is still universal.

Sometimes when we tell others, "I know how you feel," they say in their hearts, "Sure. You're just saying that. No one knows how I feel, especially not you, for I am the only one who has ever felt this way." It takes a great deal of trust to open up and bare our true feelings to one another, but it can be done. Feki and I could share feelings. My wife and I can do so also, and there are others with whom I can share how I feel. I know that the Savior understands how we feel. We can share fully with Him and be helped fully by Him.

As I prepared for a new assignment in Ha'apai, I prayed I could understand the people there as I had tried to understand the people on Niuatoputapu. If I did, maybe I could accomplish what the president had asked me to do.

# 32

## Ha'apai Veu

I rode from Liahona into town with my mission president. The boat was almost ready to leave for Ha'apai, but we still had awhile to visit. I asked again about a companion because it seemed strange to be without one. He told me that since there was a government restriction on foreign proselyting Elders in Tonga (four, counting the mission president) and since they needed most of the able-bodied young Tongan men as builders, I would have to work alone. He assured me I would be just fine and reminded me again that my counselors could help and be like companions.

He also explained a little more about my new area. He said there were about thirty local missionaries (mostly couples) on the various islands of Ha'apai, but he wasn't sure where they were or what their names were. He suggested that as soon as I got counselors, we should go around to the various islands and see what missionaries were where and how they were doing. He suggested that I call as many local member missionaries as I could; if I needed more, I should let him know and he would try to do what he could, but he wasn't sure how much he could help. "If you're smart," he said, "you'll get your own help locally."

I asked about the present district presidency. "Just tell them they are released and you are taking over," he said. "They are in a state of disarray anyway, so you shouldn't have any problem. But if you do, send me a telegram and I'll verify that you are in charge." (I had no problem. The members were anxious to have someone new take over.)

He basically told me that I would be on my own and that I

shouldn't bother him unless absolutely necessary, because he had lots to do on Tongatapu, such as running the main Church school, coordinating the building projects, and handling various official matters there.

He gave me a couple of lists and said to look at them later. I got on the boat and just as it pulled away, he said, "Work hard. The Lord will bless you. You'll have plenty to do." Truer words were never spoken.

I felt the mission president trusted me. I hoped I could live up to his expectations. The lists he had given me were the most current lists of the twelve branches and branch presidents and approximately two thousand members in Ha'apai. I looked at the lists and wondered who they were, where they were, and what they would be like. I felt a thrill of excitement pass through me. I looked forward to this assignment.

When I arrived in Pangai, the capital of Ha'apai, I was met by a large group of members and missionaries. The telegraph worked and besides, some of them had been to the conference in Liahona and heard that I would be coming as district president. The former district president was nowhere around. The members showed me the chapel and the missionary home next to the chapel. The chapel was a rectangular building about twenty feet wide by forty feet long. It had no rooms or offices, just one large central area filled with benches. It seemed to be in fair shape.

The missionary home was a different story. It was a white, frame plantation home, smaller than the chapel, with a red roof of corrugated tin and a front veranda. It had one central living room with two walls that divided each side into separate rooms. The right side was for sleeping and the left side for cooking (although I never cooked meals because the members always brought food to me). The house was built about 1910 and had fallen into a terrible state of disrepair. Large sections of the roof were rusted out and big parts of the walls and floors did not exist because of termites.

It did not take long to realize that feelings among the members were in about the same condition as the missionary house. The members were angry with one another. There were a lot of personal and family conflicts. The phrase "Ha'apai Veu" basically means "Ha'apai in turmoil," and it was!

By way of explanation, the people in Ha'apai live on seventeen scattered islands. Some islands are relatively close to each other, and some much farther away. One must travel long distances by sailboat to get anywhere in Ha'apai and just the process of staying alive there required a lot of effort. Generally, the people of Ha'apai are the most aggressive of the Tongan people. Many leaders, both Church and political, have come from Ha'apai, even though many have now moved to Tongatapu or other places. Ha'apai people represent the same syndrome as people moving to cities from small farming communities: They come to the larger areas with a strong work ethic, which almost automatically propels them forward.

Many strong-willed men and women lived in Ha'apai. Several men had taken turns being district president. When someone from one family was installed as district president, many of the others would not participate. Later when someone from another family was installed as district president the first group would stay home. It was a mess.

The Church was not growing much because there were too many personality conflicts and very little unity. The members were good people—they just couldn't stand one another! Under the circumstances I guess it made sense to have an outsider as district president. I knew very little about Church administration and didn't know what being a district president was all about, but I was willing to try.

I reviewed in my mind what the mission president had asked me to do: (1) set the Church in order; (2) get missionary work going; and (3) start a school. I wasn't sure where to begin but remembered that he had suggested I get two good counselors as soon as possible. Over the next few days I met most of the members close to where I lived and felt pretty good about some of them.

When I asked how we visited the members on the other islands, I was told there was a twenty-eight-foot mission sailboat (a former whaleboat), but the ropes and canvas were rotten, the hull was full of holes, and the boat was on the beach right now. When I heard this, the thought came very clearly to me, "To visit other members and missionaries, you have to use a boat. Therefore, at least one counselor must be a good captain, who can fix the boat as well as sail it." That narrowed my choices some.

After a few days and lots of prayers, I knew who my counselors should be. I approached both of them and their wives and told them of the call. They knew by the Spirit ahead of time and willingly accepted.

When I first met with my counselors, I asked them, "What are the problems?" They looked at me and said, "You name it, we've got it." At that time, the district president was over all the members and the mis-

*Missionary house (in foreground) and chapel (in background)
in Pangai, Ha'apai, Tonga. School was held on front veranda, which
was later extended considerably as the number of students increased.*

sionaries. My counselors were married and had families, so they
needed to be home quite a bit and to work to support their families.
They were both strong, faithful men with great wives and families and
both had been in presidencies before. We talked about how to get the
boat repaired, how to put the Church in order, how to help the missionaries get going, and how to start a school, as the mission president
had requested.

We felt we should start officially, so we called a district conference,
which was fairly well attended. I told the members that I had been
asked by the mission president to be the new district president and
that I would like these two men to be my counselors. I asked if the
members would sustain that action. They all did. We were proceeding
with the meeting when someone asked if we shouldn't release the former district presidency. I wasn't sure how you did that or even who
the counselors were, so I got up and said, "All in favor of releasing the
former district presidency, show by raising your hands." They all
stood up and raised both hands. I hoped it was official. Whether it
was or not didn't seem to be the most pressing matter at the time, for I
knew we had lots to do and we were now irreversibly on our way.

# 33

## "The Spirit Giveth Life"

For the first little while, I spent nearly every evening with my counselors trying to figure out how to fulfill the mission president's charge to bring unity to the district, as that seemed to be the overriding problem. Since my counselors worked, I had to find others to help me during the day. I did this by asking around and watching who came to church regularly. I soon had a list of several men who would go visiting with me during the day. Between them and my counselors, we visited the nearby branches and noted many problems. Nothing was going very well, mainly because the members were arguing so much. The missionaries seemed to be working hard but getting virtually no results, and, of course, we hadn't done anything with the school yet. I wasn't sure how to proceed or what to give priority to, but felt I should work with the members and missionaries first, and then work on the school later.

I was unable to visit the missionaries or branches on the outer islands, because the boat was still in disrepair. No one seemed willing to help repair the sailboat. Since I didn't know anything about boats, I told one of my counselors that we were going to visit the outer islands in two weeks and would be taking the Church boat, so he was responsible to have it seaworthy by then. He accepted the assignment and got a few others to help him with the needed repairs; in two weeks the boat was able to go.

I felt an urgent desire to visit the rest of the missionaries first. I knew we had one other *palangi* Elder in Ha'apai, and I knew where he and his companion were, but I did not know how many local missionaries there were, or where they were. I hadn't been given a list of names but instead was simply told there were quite a few missionaries, especially couples with families, in Ha'apai. Who the other branch presidents were and where the other chapels were was still a mystery to me.

With the severe limits on missionaries from America, the only way missionary work could go forward was to call local missionaries. Married couples were the most trusted group. When a man and woman got married and showed a desire to be active, they were usually called on a mission for a couple of years. They always responded to the call, and they always came back happier and stronger in the faith. At that time the leaders weren't too sure about calling local young men and women on missions. I couldn't understand why, as Feki was as good a missionary as it is possible to be. They did call quite a few young men as labor missionaries. However, within a few years they began to call many local young men and women to serve regular full-time proselyting missions, and they did very well.

I marveled at how the Lord makes strengths out of supposed weaknesses. I suppose the enemies of the Church felt they would seriously hurt our efforts by curtailing American missionaries from coming into Tonga. As it turned out, they couldn't have helped us more. Since the local people couldn't rely on Americans to do missionary work, they had to do it themselves. What strength came as they grew under the burden of carrying the whole program themselves!

With the boat now somewhat seaworthy, we began to visit the outer islands. I was not pleased with what I found there. If anything, the disunity was worse than in Pangai. I learned that when the members are in disarray, the missionaries tend to be in disarray also. There was arguing between members and missionaries, between missionaries and missionaries, and between members and members.

I tried to settle differences as best I could, but after a few weeks I began to wonder if the Church in Ha'apai would ever come together. It seems that the three charges we had been given: (1) the members, (2) the missionaries, and (3) the school, were going backward instead of forward. Everything, including the house and the boat, seemed to be falling apart. I couldn't think of anything else to do but keep trying to hold things together the best I could.

I was most surprised and discouraged by the poor attitude of the missionaries. My previous experience on Niuatoputapu with Feki was very positive, with a marvelous attitude of hard work, unity, and dedication. I had been aware of some personal bitterness between people, but remembered it as generally short-lived and resolved by gospel forgiveness. But here I found anger that seemed exaggerated and long lasting. I couldn't understand it.

When I found companions fighting with each other, couples not getting along, and missionaries arguing with branch presidents, my heart sank. With the school not yet started, my counselors questioning some of the things I was doing and telling me I just didn't understand, and the boat not fixed very well, I knew I needed major help from above. I did not know how to proceed, so I fasted and prayed a lot—but seemed to make precious little progress.

I remember one particular evening very clearly. I was out alone walking and pondering what to do. It was a clear, balmy evening with a fresh sea breeze. Everything in Ha'apai is close to the ocean. It was later than usual for me to take such a walk. I noticed the sister of one of our good leaders riding a bike with one of the wealthier men in town, even though she was married to someone else. I could hardly believe my eyes, as she was obviously enamored with this fellow.

The next day I asked that leader about his sister. He hesitatingly said, "Yes, she has been going with him. In fact, she's pregnant with his baby. It's a bit of a problem because she is married to someone else, and that man is married to someone else, but it's best to just leave it alone."

"A bit of a problem!" I exploded. "In this Church, that can't be!"

He replied, "Well, that's the way it is, and there's not much you can do about it."

"You bet there is something I can do about it!" I shot back.

I went to visit this lady's widowed mother, and did I ever get a shock! While she wasn't for the affair, she wasn't really against it either, as the man was one of the wealthiest men on the island and she was getting some nice benefits from it. Life was tough in Ha'apai, and because she was getting some help, this widow was looking the other way! It shocked me, even though I felt for her situation. Here was a supposedly good Church leader, a mother who had been a Relief Society president, who in effect was going along with this affair because of personal benefit. We talked about it, and she and her daughter said I shouldn't pick on them—lots of people were doing the same thing. They told me of another prominent Church leader who had a daughter in the same kind of situation: not married and having children out of wedlock. I checked and found it to be true.

I immediately called a special meeting with my counselors, explained the situation, and said, "This has got to stop."

They condescendingly nodded their heads and replied, "Well, after you have been here a while, you'll understand. You'd better just leave it alone." It was one of those times, especially as I look back, when I felt the hand of the Lord very clearly.

I replied, "I've been here long enough. What they are doing is wrong. I'm going to talk to them again and tell them either they leave these men or they are out of the Church."

My counselors replied, "You can't do that! They are very prominent families and you will wreck the Church!"

"Their evil will wreck the Church if we don't," I replied.

Still, I had to consider their counsel. I knew there was a risk, but I knew what was right. After prayer, I still felt strongly so I told my counselors we should go and talk to the two women and their families and give them the choice. They shook their heads and would not come, so I went alone.

I told the women, "You either drop this, quit it completely, or you are out of the Church."

Each in turn said, in essence, "You can't do that. My dad is So-and-So," or "My brother is So-and-So."

I said, "I not only can, but I will."

I told my counselors what I had done and they both said the same thing, "You just can't do that. You've got to be more understanding; you've got to be more loving and kind."

I replied, "I have been. I've given them both two chances, and they won't respond."

When they could see I was determined to do something, one of them said, "Well, you still can't do it. You don't have the authority. You've got to go according to the handbook. Have you read the *General Handbook of Instructions?*"

I had to admit that I had not read the handbook. In fact, I didn't even know such a book existed. But I knew what was right and I didn't have to have a handbook to tell me that. I gave the two women a third warning and explained what they had to do. They refused to do it, so I said, "Okay then, you are out of the Church." They replied, "Does that mean we are excommunicated?"

I replied, "I don't know exactly what that word means. All I know is that you are no longer members of the Church." They repeated that I couldn't do that, and I told them I already had. I told my counselors of my action, and they both shook their heads. I announced in the next leadership meeting that these two were no longer members of the Church. There were many looks of disbelief.

To begin with, there was anger and bitterness. It seemed I had made an already bad situation worse, but soon a very interesting thing began to happen. Several people quietly and almost unbelievingly whispered, "Is it true that So-and-So are no longer members of the Church?"

"That's right," I replied. "They are no longer members."

Everyone knew what the girls had been doing, so when they were actually cut off from the Church, other members started to shape up. The dire prediction that people would quit coming to church proved wrong. In fact, the opposite occurred. People started coming back to church, confessing their sins, and asking for forgiveness. Within a few weeks, things were not only better, they were markedly better—and the Spirit was stronger! A remarkable transition began taking place, and everything started to improve.

The missionaries started being more cooperative with the local leaders and more helpful to one another. The members not only came to meetings but also started to smile and speak nicely to one another. We were still not making much progress with the school, but we were at least talking about it more. There continued to be a lot of opposition, but it did not seem to have the same effect as it did before. We felt we were finally moving ahead.

One of the strong testimonies I have of doing what is right regardless of opposition is that over a period of not many weeks, order started to come into the Ha'apai District. I began to learn a great lesson: The scriptures say, "The letter killeth, but the spirit giveth life" (2 Corinthians 3:6). Maybe I didn't follow the letter in that I did not have a handbook, but I knew what the Spirit was directing me to do; I was sure the handbook would have directed me to do what I did, for the handbook is written under the direction of the Spirit. I learned that if you follow the direction of the Spirit and do what is right, you turn the responsibility over to the Spirit—and it gives life.

In effect, the Spirit said, "You did what I asked you to do, now I will do my part," and it did. It breathed life into the district; it breathed life into the members; it energized the missionaries; and it softened the hearts of our enemies. I didn't work any harder, nor did I do anything very different, but things just started to change for the better.

We had a fair number of disciplinary actions during the first few months, but after that not so many. We didn't try to find problems, but we did quickly handle those we became aware of. For many years some district members had gotten away with bad things simply because they were related to important people. This followed the Tongan tradition that if you are of high birth, you can pretty much do as you wish. But when the members and the leaders understood that the priesthood and principle took precedence over high birth and that they could not get away with violating God's laws, no matter who they were, things started to improve.

After the excommunications and the general "tightening up," missionary work started to move strongly forward. We had many baptisms. Ha'apai was the smallest of the seven Tongan mission districts, but for the next couple of years, we accounted for the majority of the baptisms in Tonga. I do not think we were any better or smarter, we were just more united. That made all the difference.

Leaders from other areas often asked what program we followed to get such results. I couldn't tell them, for I didn't know. We had no program. We just tried to do what was right and were very united.

We did lots of training with the members and the missionaries, and everyone worked together. Often the missionaries were the branch presidents, so that was easy. The scriptures were our lesson materials, as that was all we had translated into Tongan, except the pamphlet series, *Rays of Living Light,* by Charles W. Penrose. The missionaries and members read and studied the scriptures, memorized many of them, and tried to follow them. That was our program, and those were our principles. Everyone tried, and little by little unity came; before long, there was a great outpouring of unity.

I learned that unity is peace and that lack of unity is pain. If you have once experienced the peace that comes from unity, it is always a goal you seek to achieve. I gained renewed appreciation for the Lord's plea to "be one," and if "ye are not one ye are not mine" (D&C 38:27). I know the principle is true. You can't be one if you are doing evil or winking at evil in others. I have experienced the miracle that being united can bring. It is wonderful. I learned that you cannot compromise principle to achieve unity. Peace and unity only come from living God's principles. There is no other way.

Some thirty-five years later, I was at a conference in Ha'apai. I noticed in the congregation these two ladies who had been excommunicated years before, and I wanted to find out what their status was.

Even though I had been to Tonga many times since my mission, for some reason I had never learned what had happened to them. We had a full day of feasts and meetings, but that evening, after we had all retired, I couldn't sleep. I wondered about those ladies, so I got up and went out. It was about 2:00 A.M., but in Ha'apai, two o'clock in the morning is just about as good a time to visit as two o'clock in the afternoon. People don't care. To them, the important thing is the visit. Also, I knew a person was as apt to find them asleep at two in the afternoon as at two in the morning.

Since there was always someone up and about, I asked a few people and soon found where the ladies lived. Even though nothing had been said, I think they felt I might visit them. At least they seemed to be expecting me. One lady introduced me to her husband and several of her eight children. Six of the children were returned missionaries, and all had been married in the temple.

She told me that being excommunicated had caused her to realize for the first time, "I can't rely on my brother. I really *can* lose my membership in the Church if I don't do what I ought to." She eventually quit her sinning, sincerely repented, was rebaptized, and later married in the temple. She was very active in the Church.

Basically, the same thing was true with the other lady. She had had more problems with her marriage, but someway they worked it out. She was active, and her children were active. One of her children was serving as a bishop. In fact, he was one of the illegitimate children fathered during the affair, but he had been "adopted" by her and her husband when they got back together.

It was a great lesson to me: if we repent and return from our evil ways, the Lord can take most any situation and make it right. I thought of Ezekiel's promises. I thought of David and Bathsheba. As terrible as their sin was and as much as David lost, apparently there was enough repentance that through that union came the ancestry of the Savior. In one sense the Lord tries to tell us, "Don't do wrong things, for there is a terrible price to pay." But he also says, "If you do wrong things, repent as fast as you can and as completely as you can, and I'll take the sin away."

I thought of that bishop, the offspring of an affair. You can't hold the fact that he was born out of wedlock against him. You have to follow the Spirit. There does have to be discipline in the Church, and in our lives. There is a place for excommunication. Both of these women told me the same thing, "Excommunication was one of the greatest blessings in my life." I know they didn't feel that way at the time, but looking back they realized how necessary it was and what a great blessing it turned out to be for them and their families.

As I returned home that night, I was almost walking on air for joy. I noticed the same clouds, the same breeze, the same balmy evening of over thirty years before. And as I floated home, I seemed to hear those words again, "The letter killeth, but the spirit giveth life." Then the understanding of what that "life" was came to me. The Spirit not only had brought life to the district thirty-five years ago but also continued to work with those ladies through the years so that they and their families were now enjoying the sweet fruits of the gospel. They too had been given "life."

# 34

## *The School*

Things were starting to move in the right direction with the members and the missionaries, so I felt I should direct my attention to getting the school started. This was a major challenge as it was new ground for me. The members were excited about helping until they found how little I knew about a school. It must have been hard on them, for if they took their children out of their present schools and sent them to "my" school, and I left or the school failed, what would they do?

Despite all the problems and reservations, many members said they had faith in the mission president (not necessarily in me); if he had said I should start a school, they would send their children to it.

On Niuatoputapu I had taught a little school in the chapel for a while, but it was mostly for member children after their regular school. My understanding from the mission president was that he wanted me to start a full-fledged school in Haʻapai. Even though I didn't know how to start a school, nor did my counselors, we felt we must do something, as the mission president had sent a telegram asking how the school was coming.

The only places large enough to hold a school were the chapel or the front veranda of our home. Some of the members had been to the Church school at Liahona and knew that the Mormon school colors were green and white. We announced that we would hold a meeting on our front porch Monday morning for all those who were interested in attending our school and who could afford green skirts with white stripes (or the reverse). To our surprise, about twenty children came with their parents.

Now the questions started: What was the tuition? What subjects would be taught? When? By whom? What time did school begin and end? How long would classes be? What was the syllabus? When were holidays? Did we have government approval? Did we pay our teachers? Were our teachers qualified?

Unfortunately, we had no answers and no official government approval, as I had thought the mission president's permission was all I needed. We had no teachers, at least none who knew what they were doing. To say the least, we were off to a rocky start.

The other schools in the area were opposed to our efforts and obtained a local government order barring us from holding classes until we got official Ministry of Education approval from Nuku'alofa, which required certified teachers. Some of our members started arguing with the local government officials, and others began questioning if I knew what I was doing, which I really didn't. It was a mess, but at least we were making an effort.

As I look back now, I was incredibly naive. Starting a school required all sorts of government approvals, and neither the mission president nor I had communicated well on where to start or how to get the needed permission. I guess I was naive enough to think the authority I had received from my mission president exceeded all other authority.

Since at least twenty children showed an interest, I just bulled ahead and announced that we would start holding classes the next day. I spent the rest of the day and all that night desperately trying to get some experienced help and figuring out what to do.

Despite our best efforts, when we actually started holding classes there was great confusion. We were not well prepared, and opposition to the school was intense. Several times the Ha'apai director of education came and said I had to close the school down until he got word from his superior in Nuku'alofa that it was approved. I said, "You tell the children they can't come anymore. I'm not going to." He wouldn't either, so we kept going. The battle went on for several weeks as telegrams flew back and forth between myself and the mission president, and between the local education official and the head government office in Nuku'alofa.

After a few weeks, we were still not doing very well and it appeared we might not get the needed government permission. At the height of all this, the mission president wired that he thought the officials in Nuku'alofa were dragging their feet and suggested I should close the school for a while and come down to Nuku'alofa to see if we couldn't work things out.

The telegram was a bitter blow to me and my counselors. They pleaded with me, "Let's call a special fast before we tell the members, as they have sacrificed so much. We feel it would be better if we didn't close down. We think the Lord will see it our way, but we have to get through to Him first."

The next day we all fasted and prayed—and we all felt impressed to keep the school going. I wired the mission president and told him we felt we should try to keep the school open, and I asked if it would be all right if I stayed in Ha'apai and didn't come to Nuku'alofa. I received no reply, so I stayed and we kept the school going. A few days later, the local director of education came up the road to the school waving a telegram in his hand.

He had come many times before with telegrams from his superiors. But by the strange way he was smiling, I thought he might have some bad news. He asked to see me alone. My heart was heavy. I still hadn't been able to absorb Tongan faith fully. When we were alone, he opened the telegram and with that same strange smile read:

> Today we have granted official permission to the Mormon Church to hold a school in Pangai, Ha'apai, with Mr. John H. Groberg as headmaster. See that they follow the prescribed government syllabus and have adequate quarters.
>
> Director of Education
> Nuku'alofa, Tonga

He informed me I would need to meet with him immediately and review the syllabus. He also said he would inspect our facilities and classes weekly. He let me know if we didn't meet the standards he would close us down. He didn't seem to be so much angry as resigned, but I suppose there was a touch of annoyance at having "lost round one." I could tell there were more rounds to come.

I was so happy I could have shouted for joy and probably did. I ran to my counselors and told them the good news. They nodded knowingly. I asked if they weren't excited. They said they were, but I had the distinct feeling that they wondered about me with a sort of a "what-else-did-you-expect?" attitude.

The school, which we named Deseret, started with 20 students, but began growing, especially after we got official government approval. It went from 20 to 30 to 40, 50, up to 120, then 150, and finally close to 200. Naturally this created jealousies and problems among the other schools.

*Some of the students at the LDS school in Pangai, Ha'apai, in front of the veranda
where classes were held. Elder Groberg is about four rows back on the right.
Also note several missionary teachers in the group. Official school uniform
was green with white stripes or the reverse.*

I wrote to the mission president and said I had to have more help. To be district president and do all that entailed; then to go tracting, visit the outer islands, and work with the missionaries; and to try to teach school—all at the same time—was more than I could physically accomplish. He was glad for our success and sent me three local lady missionaries and two local Elders, all of whom were certified schoolteachers. With those five, and myself, and two others I had recruited locally, we had a good staff.

The five new teachers lived with the members, as did all the missionaries. They taught school during the day, then tracted and taught discussions in the evening. They were good teachers, brought discipline and order to the school, and helped make it very successful.

By the time I left Ha'apai, there was so much unity and such a feeling of oneness among the schoolteacher missionaries that it had to resemble very closely the society described in 4 Nephi, where the people were of one heart and had no contention among them (see 4 Nephi 1:17). What a blessed experience the school was! I can't say this same oneness was true of all the members, because they were a little more individualistic, but they were building good unity as well.

# 35

## *Riding the Circuit*

With things starting to move in the right direction with the members in Pangai, and with the school under way, I turned my attention to proselyting.

We traveled between islands by sailboat and either walked or rode horses while on land. There were very few motorboats and no airplanes. We had no cars or bikes, no telephones or electricity, no running water or indoor plumbing, no use for money or day planners, but lots of desire to preach, testify, and baptize.

While our methods of traveling, preaching, and proselyting were a little different from what is common today, the process was about the same as it has been throughout the ages: we took our testimonies to the people and tried to preach and testify to them of what we knew to be true. Our challenges were basically the same as all missionaries: (1) travel from where we were to where the people were; (2) encourage them to listen to us; (3) help them study and pray about what we taught; (4) help them see the importance of baptism, then baptize them; and (5) help them stay active in the Church. It wasn't easy, but it was wonderfully worth the effort!

We spent a lot of time in the sailboat. I estimate that I spent at least six months actually on the surface of the ocean going from island to island. I was seasick much of that time, especially in the beginning. I often wondered, "Since the Lord knew how much time I was going to spend on small boats in rough water, why didn't He bless me with a stronger stomach?"

It took a while to see His wisdom in this. I finally realized that if the only physical challenges to overcome had been the weather and the dangers of reefs, rotten sails, and leaky boats, then getting out and going to where the people were wouldn't be overpoweringly difficult. But when I added to that the personal discomfort that comes from seasickness on each voyage, I had to develop a strong enough desire to share the gospel to overcome that personal discomfort.

How grateful I am that God gave me the needed desire, as I know I could not have done it on my own. There may be a principle here somewhat akin to mothers who must not only overcome the discomforts and dangers of childbirth but also long periods of personal sickness to allow a new spirit to receive a body. I *know* they will be doubly blessed.

On the first several voyages in Ha'apai, I was terribly sick, but as time went on I became a little less sick, or at least more used to it. On rough voyages I was very sick, but occasionally I would have a voyage during which I didn't feel sick at all. What a blessing that was! Being ill during most of those trips made my joy and thanksgiving very meaningful when I had a voyage that was relatively smooth and I didn't feel very sick. Once in a while my happiness became almost ecstasy as I realized I was in the midst of a heavy storm with the boat twisting and jerking and bouncing all over creation—and I was not ill! Maybe the joy of feeling well helped me to not worry about other dangers. I'm not sure about that, but I do know I was very grateful when I wasn't ill.

As I look back now, I should have been frightened to death to go out on that unpredictable sea in a tiny sailboat with holes in the hull, old sails that often ripped, and ropes that were largely rotten. But concerns about safety or danger never entered my mind, because this was God's work and I knew He would protect me. I knew that going to those islands was part of my duty, because that was where the people were for whom I was responsible, and the boat was the only way to get there. Having been raised in a farming community with the Depression and World War II as a backdrop taught me that you did whatever you needed to do to get things done.

One of the problems with all of the safety consciousness we have today is that it tends to cause us to hesitate to do things that we might otherwise do. I'm sure it's good to have better information, such as weather reports, forecasting, safety inspections, and audits, but I sometimes wonder if we don't get so filled with facts and figures and possible dangers that we do less than we should. I suppose we could all find legitimate reasons to hardly do anything because of the potential dangers involved, all the way from not going someplace because of a possible storm to not making a business decision because of a possible loss or lawsuit, to not getting married or not having children because of the possible physical, mental, social, or financial problems.

As I see it, all of life is a risk, which is where faith comes in. We do what is right, and let the chips fall where they may. God will help us— I know that for sure! We will have problems with health or accidents, finances or family—at least we will have the ones God knows we need for the growth He wants us to have. If we protect ourselves from too many things, I have a feeling we may protect ourselves right out of the celestial kingdom!

I know we shouldn't do foolish or rash things, as there is enough evil and danger around without our seeking it out. I tried not to do dumb things; however, I knew we needed to be moving and accomplishing many things, much of which would be done in the face of potential dangers. I understood that life was risky, and trying to do good things makes it even riskier. But I knew that God understood all of that and still wanted us to move forward. I remembered something about a plan and then a counterplan that supposedly removed the risk, but at the terrible price of no progress. I knew which one God chose. Even in troubled waters we make more progress if we are trying than if we wait until the dangers and discomforts are removed.

I suppose the Savior was aware of the danger that awaited Him as He entered Jerusalem that last time, but He went anyway. He may not have known the full extent of what lay ahead or exactly how He would handle it (witness His prayer in Matthew 26:39 that "*if* it be possible, let this cup pass" [italics added]), but His faith in His Father and His love for all mankind propelled Him forward as He willingly "finished [His] preparations unto the children of men" (D&C 19:19).

I didn't look on these voyages as acts of faith so much as a performance of duty. I'm sure I didn't understand all the dangers involved, which was probably just as well. Many times on those voyages things got pretty rough, and a few times life and death at sea hung on very tenuous threads, but that was just the way things were. What a great blessing it was to know that God was there! It was always comforting to remember Him calming the turbulent seas.

As we visited the islands, we learned that we had missionaries on about half of them. Most of these missionaries were married couples— normally young couples with small children. We also had a few young local Elders and sisters serving. During those days, if the mission president saw someone he felt should go on a mission, he just called them and assigned them. He always checked with me before moving someone into or out of my district. Virtually everyone I dealt with was local, and what good workers they were!

The mission president authorized me to call missionaries also. When we called a couple, we assigned them to a particular island to become the branch president or a counselor in the branch presidency and to live and raise their family there for a few years. On most islands, we had a *ngoue fakafaifekau* (a piece of land given either to the Church or to the missionaries) to grow food on. Generally, it was not deeded to the Church, but everyone understood it belonged to the missionary family while they served there.

If there wasn't already a missionary house, the branch got together and built one for the missionary family. Generally the house and the chapel were on the same property, and sometimes the house doubled as the chapel or vice versa. The missionary family was expected to plant and tend the garden for their family. When they were transferred and a new missionary family came, the garden would be ready for them. It was like the pioneers going west as they planted crops for those who followed. This system was supposed to provide a continuous cycle, with each successive family living in the same home and planting and harvesting from the same garden. It worked most of the time.

When we decided to open new islands, the missionaries started from scratch. Sometimes they had a difficult time getting established, so we tried to call only the strongest families to the new islands.

There was no monetary cost to missions then. Each missionary family furnished their own clothes, grew their own food, and lived in a house built by the branch. There were a few costs for stamps and such, but local members helped or the missionaries would work for others to get these things. These couples experienced many difficulties but thrived spiritually; consequently, they became some of the strongest members I have ever known. Eventually we had forty missionaries, including the schoolteachers, in the Ha'apai District. Most of them were couples with families.

I taught school as much as I could, but being responsible for the members, the missionaries, and the school, my time commitment to teaching became a real conflict.

The official government registration had me as the headmaster of the school, so I needed to be there some of the time, but I basically turned the school over to the newly called teachers sent by the mission president. They did a much better job than I could anyway. I continued to teach a few classes in English, music, geography, and history on an irregular basis, but assigned nearly all other classes to them. In this way, I could visit the branches and the missionaries on the outer islands nearly every week on preaching circuits. Usually we were gone four or five days, but sometimes we were away for several weeks; even the government officials understood when I couldn't get back to school because of weather or boat problems.

We tried to have a regular schedule of visiting the various branches and missionaries. I understood well the early ministerial labor of riding (or preaching) the circuit. It sounds somewhat romantic, but it was a lot of work.

# 36

## *Wind in My Face*

On a typical week, we would leave whenever I could get away from the school to visit two or three outlying islands. I would ask one of my counselors or some other experienced member to captain the boat. We would then ask a few other members to come along and help. Most of the time there were from three to five of us in the boat. The boat had one center mast and required at least three people to keep it going properly: one person at the rudder, one to work the main sail, and one to work the jib sail.

I became fairly experienced in each position, but I always preferred to have three Tongans working the boat. I don't think I was lazy, I just felt better about the way they did things—as they had much more experience. I think I only got knocked into the ocean once when I wasn't quite quick enough to get out of the way of the boom as it swung from one side to the other during a *fakahua* (tacking maneuver).

I enjoyed working the jib sail the most because it was smaller. It also had its dangers, for as you moved it by hand to change the course of the boat, you had to overcome the strong pull of the wind from the other side. If you were not careful or didn't have the rope well secured, it could pull you right out of the boat. Everyone learned to work hard and work together. After all, their very lives depended on it. When there were good winds, the helmsman could handle the rudder and the main sail ropes together.

There is hardly a more exhilarating feeling than to have a nice tail wind with the main sail extended (sometimes close to 90 degrees) and feel the power of God as His wind fills the sail and propels you across

His ocean. At times I could almost see Him smile through the clear blue sky. It was great to feel His power and protection as the tiny boat raced to its destination over the deep blue sea.

Once in a while, when the wind was right and I had some sea legs, wobbly as they were, I would climb the mast (twelve to fifteen feet), hook my leg around the rings and ropes, get into a fairly comfortable position on the small block of wood that kept the top arm of the sail from going any higher, and think, listen, and ponder. The mast would sway back and forth and almost lull me to sleep. The wind would whistle around me and pull at my clothes. At times the deep blue of the ocean and the bright white of the spray would almost merge with the blue of the sky and the white of the clouds, making it hard to tell where I actually was. It was like being suspended in space.

Being on God's errand and sensing His power and approbation in the wind and the sea and the sky put me in such a mood as to understand more how the ancient shepherds felt as they watched their flocks at night, studied the stars, and communed with God. As I watched the prow slice through the water, felt the wind power us forward, and sensed the undulating motion of the mast, I felt very close to God. I doubt anyone could deny Him and His power under those circumstances.

I realized why so many of our early Church hymns had as their theme ocean travel. I feel sorry for those who have little idea what the songs are talking about when they sing: "Master the Tempest Is Raging"; "Jesus, Savior, Pilot Me"; "Jesus, Lover of My Soul"; "Brightly Beams Our Father's Mercy"; or any number of other beautiful and meaningful hymns. There is a lot of emotion involved with the ocean and ocean travel.

I have heard of how some of the astronauts feel when they see the earth as a tiny sphere and sense the majesty and power of God. Maybe if we develop enough technology and get enough people into space, we can eventually get back to some of the important feelings of faith the ancients had as they studied the stars and relied on God's help upon His mighty ocean. I could relate to the scripture: "Sing unto the Lord a new song, and his praise from the end of the earth, ye that go down to the sea, and all that is therein; the isles, and the inhabitants thereof. . . . Let them give glory unto the Lord, and declare his praise in the islands." (Isaiah 42:10, 12.)

Sometimes we were gone for ten days or two weeks. We tried to return by Saturday and never traveled on Sunday. I remember several lessons I was taught by those faithful people. We would always pray for protection, success, and good seas and wind to take us to our destination. Once I asked the Lord to bless us with a good tail wind so we could get to Foa quickly. As we got under way, one of the older men said, "Elder Groberg, you need to modify your prayers a little."

"How's that?" I replied.

"You asked the Lord for a tail wind to take us rapidly to Foa. If you pray for a tail wind to Foa, what about the people who are trying to come from Foa to Pangai? They are good people, and you are praying against them. Just pray for a good wind, not a tail wind."

That taught me something important. Sometimes we pray for things that will benefit us but may hurt others. We may pray for a particular type of weather, or to preserve someone's life, when that answer to our prayer may hurt someone else. That's why we must always pray in faith, because we can't have true, God-given faith in something that is not according to His will. If it's according to His will, all parties will benefit. I learned to pray for a good wind and the ability to get there safely, not necessarily a tail wind.

I learned another lesson in patience once on a trip to Uiha. We had left Pangai about noon with very favorable winds and made it to Uiha in just a few hours. We spent the afternoon and evening working with the missionaries and had some preaching engagements that evening, so we stayed overnight on Uiha.

Early the next morning, I was anxious to get back to Pangai for some important school meetings. We left Uiha just as the sun was rising, and I felt sure we would be back to Pangai by early afternoon. I had been up late and was tired, so after helping get us started, I lay down in the boat and went to sleep.

I slept soundly. A few hours later when I awoke, I could see an island not too far away. I assumed it was our home island and felt we had made good time, as the sun was still high in the sky. I told the others how happy I was to be so close to Pangai. The captain looked at me and said, "That's not Lifuka [the island Pangai is on], but Uiha [the island we had just left]."

I was very surprised, even upset, and said, "How come? We've been going for several hours. What have you been doing? We must be closer to Pangai than that!"

The captain just replied that that is the way things are. I then showed my *palangi* background by saying that we needed to do something because I had to be in Pangai soon to attend an important meeting.

When I had finished, the captain looked at me and patiently said, "The winds have been against us. Who are you going to blame for that? Are you going to curse God? Or tell Him He doesn't know what He's doing? He controls the winds and the currents, and we are in His hands. You had better calm down and learn to live within the framework He has set, and not try to force your schedule on Him."

Rather than causing me to become angry, his quiet, correct reasoning had a profound effect on me. I spent the rest of the day thinking about the implications of the truths he had spoken.

Sometime later I wrote home: "It's Friday evening here and there is a big harvest moon out. The wind is a soft South Pacific breeze. I walked down to the seashore, about one-half block away, and could hardly help but be stirred by the beauty of everything. With such a soft breeze and beautiful moon, several ships gliding into the harbor, and the beautiful coconut palms, it really does make a beautiful picture. I do like it here in Ha'apai. I have learned to enjoy sea travel. The breeze is so refreshing and the sea air is so clean. You meet all types of different circumstances on the sea. Sometimes the sea is fairly calm with a good wind, and it thrills me inside to stand on the brow of the ship, raise the sails, and watch the wind fill the white canvas and see the keel begin to cut the water. Man moving under the power of nature. It thrills me as our big sails billow with the power of nature, and we literally glide through the ocean. I never appreciated the romance of the sea before. The reason so many stories, movies, and music are based on the sea is it is a romantic thing, mysterious, unpredictable, gentle, beautiful, harsh, angry, and often a monster stirred by some power that man cannot know. Then the wind—a factor long questioned—its currents, its sudden comings and goings, its strength, its weakness, its unpredictability. Sometimes a good wind and a good sea will take us quickly to our destination. Then with a disagreeable wind and contrary sea, it could take hours, even days. We went to a little town today. We had a fair wind to begin with, but out in the deep it suddenly died, the sail sagged, then motionlessly announced the end of the breeze. Nature rules. No machine to challenge its supremacy.

"We sat leisurely rocking in the deep blue of the warm Pacific. Songs were sung, stories told, a deeper appreciation of why Tongan customs are as they are. If we lived under similar circumstances, we would be the same. Every once in a while a wandering breeze would give the sails a small tug, raise our eyes, then laughingly flitter away and be lost somewhere across the big ocean. The day wore on, the sun became low in the evening sky. Suddenly, a small, rushing sound and all our eyes were on the sails. A wind, first faintly caressing the sails, then straightening the creases, then pushing. All hands on deck— *Fakahua* (shift sails)! The calm water begins to froth at the sharp nose of the vessel.

"Then there is the day when the wind is a lion, whipping the ship at quite an angle for a quick arrival. It fills you with pride as you feel the power of the elements under your control, but you soon realize it isn't our power when the wind decides to stop.

"I do love it here. I have wondered how much it would change our culture if we had no machines, but had to depend on nature to go to the office, sometimes in forty-five minutes, sometimes in several hours, and sometimes taking days—never predictable. This would make quite a difference in our thinking and acting. Maybe we would learn a few more songs and be a little more talkative and friendly. There's something to learn from everyone and everything."

# 37

## *Preaching the Circuit*

The purpose for riding the circuit was to preach. Many of the islands were six to eight hours apart, depending on the weather, so by leaving early in the morning we could arrive at the next island by midafternoon. We would then anchor the boat, go ashore, and tract the island using the *Rays of Living Light* series and *Joseph Smith's Testimony*. They were the only tracts translated into Tongan. Most of the islands had fifty to one hundred families, with a few having several hundred families. We delivered a tract to every home, asked them to read it, and invited them to a meeting that evening. Usually most of the population would show up for our *po malanga*. At first, because so many came, I thought people were interested in the Church, but eventually I realized that most of them came because there wasn't anything else to do, and hearing a *palangi* speak their language was something different. Some of the islands hadn't seen a *palangi* for a long time, and many of the children had never seen a *palangi,* though most of the parents had.

Nearly always we met outside under the trees or in the town square. If it was raining, we met in a schoolhouse or another church, depending on the schoolmaster or the minister. When the people were gathered, we sang a song and had a prayer and I started talking. We had good attention and those who came were quite respectful.

Since I wasn't sure when I would get back to this particular island, I felt I had a responsibility to let the assembled Tongans understand how I felt about the gospel. We normally gave seven or eight discussions, but on these occasions I tried to cover the main points of all of them in one evening as we would leave for another island the next day.

I often talked for two or three hours straight. Often my voice got tired and hoarse from talking so loud for so long. Sometimes my throat hurt so much that tears streamed down my face. At times the audience was in tears as well. My tears usually came from a hurting throat; hopefully theirs came from testimonies borne and truths received and felt.

Sometimes when my throat got too sore, I called on those who accompanied me to say something while I drank a coconut. One reason I couldn't turn the meeting over to them completely, or even use them heavily, was that the audience had come to hear a *palangi* speak (for some reason they preferred to listen to a *palangi*). Another reason was that while my companions were great scripturalists and preachers, their method of preaching was to knock the people and their beliefs down. No matter how much I explained to them about not offending people but rather explaining the truth simply and clearly and lovingly, they just couldn't do it. They seemed impelled to knock others down and vigorously call them to repentance, telling them they were liars, cheats, stealers, and belonged to the church of the devil and were all going to hell if they didn't get baptized. This naturally turned the audience off, and we didn't make much progress. For this reason I basically called on them to clarify a single point or to bear their testimony, then I took the meeting back.

I remember one particular evening when I felt we were making progress with the audience. You could tell from their eyes that some of the people were quite interested. I was just to the point of bearing my final testimony, but my throat was so raw I couldn't go on. I felt like I had to finish this particular point and testify of its truthfulness. I prayed with all my heart and asked the Lord to help me. I remember feeling something like a voice saying, "Okay, if you have a desire to bear testimony, I'll give you the strength to do it." I was able to finish. There were many spiritual experiences at these meetings, including holding back the rain, seeing would-be interrupters silenced, bearing testimony using exactly the right words, and sensing testimonies received by honest people.

At the conclusion of these meetings, I would announce that we were going to have a closing song and prayer, after which they could ask questions or return home. I asked them to study the tracts more and pray about what they had heard that evening. If they felt it was right and had the witness of the Spirit (and I testified that they could have it), we would be down by our boat early the next morning before we left for the next island, to baptize any who truly believed. Hardly ever did anyone show up, but once in a while someone would be by the boat and say, "I want to be baptized."

After we baptized them, they would ask, "What do we do now?" For those who had a branch on their island, we referred them to the branch president. For those who didn't, we left them a Book of Mormon and some tracts and said, "Study these and we'll be back in a month or two and tell you what else to do." Generally, they were faithful, and we didn't have to worry about them falling away.

There was a lot of persecution against the Church then, and the words *less active* and *prospective elder* didn't even exist. There were a few people who weren't active, but not many. The pressure of society was so strong against joining that when they made the commitment and joined, they were generally good members and stayed faithful.

In a month or six weeks we came back, and if they had other family members or friends who were interested, which they usually did, we would teach and baptize them. When we got a few families as members, we would call a couple on a mission to go to that island and be the branch president and help the new families. If the original convert family had done well, which most of them did, we often called them on a mission to be a branch president on some other island. In this way, they rapidly learned the doctrine and how to lead in the Church. Most of them became powerful members of the Church. Gradually we built up branches in this manner.

When branches got enough members, we asked members from a nearby island to come and help them build a chapel. If we baptized someone on a very small or distant island, we asked members who had dealings on that island to check up on them, strengthen them, and help them, similar to being home teachers, I suppose.

On these preaching circuits, we nearly always slept on the floor of someone's home or on the ground under a tree. Someone usually loaned us a wooden pillow and some *tapa* cloth as a blanket. *Tapa* cloth can be very warm. I got used to sleeping on the floor or ground and using a wooden pillow, with *tapa* cloth for bedding.

We never brought bedding or food with us, but relied on the goodness of the people. I told the people that all we carried with us was the Spirit of the Lord and our testimony. They were nearly always good to us. The only physical things we carried with us were our scriptures, a change of clothing, and some tracts. Usually someone would volunteer to wash for us, and we always found people who were willing to let us use a tub for a shower and help us in other ways. Most of the time we were given food to eat and something to drink.

*Pangai Harbor.*
*Our mission sailboat is on the far right.*

The next morning, after baptizing anyone waiting, we would sail to the next island, arriving about midafternoon, and start the cycle all over again. We repeated this process day after day, week after week, and month after month. Some of the strongest Latter-day Saints in Tonga came into the Church from these preaching circuits.

# 38

## "Ko E Maama E"

As we traveled by sailboat week after week, month after month, from island to island, we learned to rely on the winds and the currents of the usually friendly seas and especially on the love of our Father in Heaven. It was a glorious time, full of the normal challenges of seasickness, becalming, strange situations, different foods, and unusual customs. But mostly it was a time of spiritual closeness to our Father in Heaven, whose love and goodness so far overshadowed any temporary pain or problems as to make the latter shrink into obscurity.

On one occasion, we received word that a missionary was very ill on a somewhat distant island. The weather was threatening, but we felt responsible for the missionary's well-being. After prayer, we left to investigate the situation. Extra heavy seas slowed our progress, and it was late afternoon before we arrived. The missionary was indeed very ill. Fervent prayer was followed by a priesthood blessing, during which the impression came very strongly to get him back to the hospital on the main island, and to do it now!

The weather had deteriorated to the point of a small gale. The seas were raging, the clouds were thick, the wind was fierce, the hour was late, and the sun was sinking rapidly, betokening a long, black night ahead. But the impression was strong—"Get back now"—and we had learned to obey the all-important promptings of the Spirit.

Many on the island expressed concern, and we talked much about the darkness, the storm, and the formidable reef with its narrow opening to the harbor we would be attempting to gain. Some found reasons to stay behind. But soon eight persons—including an ill missionary, a very experienced captain, and a somewhat concerned district president, boarded the boat. The spiritually prompted voyage began.

No sooner had we committed ourselves to the open seas than the intensity of the storm seemed to increase sevenfold. The small gale became a major storm. As the sun sank below the horizon, bringing with it darkness and gloom, my spirit seemed to sink into the darkness of doubt and apprehension. The thick clouds and driving rain increased the blackness of our already dark universe. No stars. No moon. No rest. Only turmoil of sea, body, mind, and spirit. As we toiled on through that fearsome night, I found my spirit communing with the spirit of the father of an afflicted child in the New Testament, as he exclaimed, "Lord, I believe; help thou mine unbelief" (Mark 9:24). And the Lord did, and He does, and He will. That I know.

As we rolled and tossed closer and closer to the reef, all eyes searched for the light that marked the opening—the only entry to our home. Where was it? The blackness of the night seemed to increase; the fierceness of the raging elements seemed to know no bounds. The rain slashed at our faces and tore at our eyes—eyes vainly searching for that life-giving light.

Then I heard the chilling sound of waves crashing and chewing against the reef! It was close—too close. Where was the light? Unless we entered the opening exactly, we would be smashed against the reef, ripped and torn by that thousand-toothed monster. It seemed that all the elements were savagely bent on our destruction. Our eyes strained against the blackness, but we could not see the light.

Some began to whimper, others to moan and cry, and one or two even to scream in hysteria. At the height of this panic, when others were pleading to turn to the left or to the right, when the tumultuous elements all but forced us to abandon life and hope, I looked at the captain—and there I saw the face of calmness, the ageless face of wisdom and experience, as his eyes penetrated the darkness ahead. Quietly, his weather-roughened lips parted, and without moving his fixed gaze and just perceptibly shifting the wheel, he breathed those life-giving words, "Ko e Maama e" ("There is the light!").

I could not see the light, but the captain could see it, and I knew he could see it. Those eyes long experienced in ocean travel were not fooled by the madness of the storm, nor were they influenced by the pleadings of those of lesser experience to turn to the left or to the right. He calmly guided us forward. On one great swell, we were hurled through the opening and into calmer waters.

The roaring of the reef was now behind us. Its plan of destruction had been foiled. We were in the protected harbor. We were home. Then, and only then, did we see through the darkness that one small light—exactly where the captain had said it was. Had we waited until we ourselves could see the light, we would have been dashed to pieces, shredded on the reef of unbelief. But trusting in those experienced eyes, we lived.

That night I learned this great lesson: there are those who, through years of experience and training and by virtue of special divine callings, can see further, better, and more clearly than we can. They can and will save us in those situations where serious injury or death—both spiritual and physical—would be upon us before we ourselves could see clearly.

I sense in the world today an almost exact duplication of that voyage of many years ago. We are in the midst of a major storm over moral values that will get worse before we arrive home.

Just one example: We hear much of the so-called problem of overpopulation and the possible future horrors it could bring. We hear claim and counterclaim, fancied fact and interpolated figures. We hear the call for planned families, for delayed families, for free abortions, for personal aggrandizement in many ways.

It is true that we have a sick world on our hands and that it needs help. But in delivering that patient to help, we must not listen to the calculated plan of this or that professor, or to the pleading of some group, or to the hysterical screaming of some faction, or to any combination of man-made philosophies, but only to the calm voice of the prophet as he says, "Have your families in a normal way; accept all the spirits the Lord sees fit to send you; do not delay your families; always be considerate of one another; have nothing to do with the sin of abortion." Therein is safety. He will guide us through this or any storm.

As I think back, I thank the Lord for that wonderful Polynesian captain who saved my life and the life of the sick missionary. I am eternally grateful for his experience, much of which, I am sure, was not pleasant. I am grateful for his wisdom, for his eyes, for his not yielding to the fury of the moment, but steadfastly holding the true course to safety.

I felt at the time that he was more than himself, more than the sum total of all of his experience. In some marvelous way at the moment of desperate need, he drew upon a power and a strength from generations of faithful, seagoing people that only those who know Polynesians well can begin to understand. My admiration and love for him and all other faithful descendants of father Lehi knows no bounds.

In like manner, and with even deeper meaning, I thank the Lord for our great prophet-leader of today. In our moment of great need, the Lord has provided one tested, molded, trained, instructed, and clothed with divine authority, who in addition to the total of all his experience, which is great, draws upon the strength and power of not only generations of faithful leaders but also of angels and of Gods.

As we moved into that calm harbor and glided through the darkness to the anchorage, I thanked God over and over again for His goodness to us. I thanked Him for that wonderful captain who saw the light in time. I thanked Him for our modern-day prophets whose eyes can see the light that will save us and the world. I thanked Him for the assurance that when all about us are sinking in darkness and fear and despair, when destruction seems close and the raging fury of men and demons ensnares us in seemingly insoluble problems, we can listen as the prophet calmly says, "There is the light. This is the way."

# 39

## Mud, Horses, and Familiar Voices

When it was time for one of our regular preaching circuits to the nearby island of Foa, our boat was under repair, so five of us sailed to Foa on another boat. When we finished our circuit a few days later, we couldn't find a boat going back to Pangai, so we decided to return by foot. I had promised to attend a meeting in Pangai the evening of the next day, but we felt we could easily make it back by then.

The islands of Foa and Lifuka are close together. At that time, when the tide was out, you could walk from one to the other across a narrow isthmus. But you had to be careful, as the isthmus was full of jagged rocks and deep pools. At one time the government tried to join the two islands with a continuous seam of cement with no breaks. Anyone who knows the ocean knows that can't be done. The sea gets angry and the tide picks up whatever is blocking it and throws it away, which it had done with the cement, making the isthmus even more treacherous. Today there is a causeway that connects the two islands, with arches that allow lots of breathing room for the ocean tides, but back then it was a dangerous crossing.

Normally it would have taken us most of a day to walk to Pangai, but it had been raining heavily and walking was very hard as we were often up to our knees in gooey mud.

After several hours of walking (slogging), we arrived at the village of Fotua near the end of the island closest to Pangai. We were very tired and muddy. Some of the members in Fotua had compassion on us; they gave us food and drink and agreed to let us use their horses for the balance of the journey. We were very happy with this arrangement, but soon found that even horses couldn't handle the deep mud very well.

The tide was still mostly out, so we thought there was enough time to take the horses to the seashore and get to the end of the island along the beach, as the sand was much firmer than the muddy trail through the center of the island. We turned toward the ocean, found one of the few openings in the high wall of coral that protected the fertile island, and descended twenty or thirty feet to the narrow, sandy beach below.

We made good progress along the beach for an hour or so, but then the tide started coming in very strongly. With only a narrow, sandy margin between the ocean and the high coral cliffs and very few places to get up through the coral to the land above, we were in a precarious position. Some of our group said we should find an opening and get back on top because it was too dangerous to stay below, as a large wave could easily dash us against the sharp coral and hurt or kill us.

By now, however, we could see the end of the island and thought that since we didn't have much farther to go, we could probably make it. We knew that if we climbed back on top and tried to go through the mud, it would take us forever to get to the end of the island. We were prayerful about the decision but didn't receive any strong impression, so on a three-to-two vote we decided to make a dash for the end of the island.

The tide came in much faster than we expected, and we came close to losing our lives, or at least suffering serious harm, as huge waves started rolling in and smashing us against the coral, bruising and cutting us and the horses. It was scary.

Our biggest concern was the horses, because if they got mangled, we were out of luck. Horses are pretty strong, but even they can only take so much. Waves are powerful and coral is sharp and not to be fooled with. We had some close calls, but eventually made it to the end of the island. The tide was almost fully in now. How grateful we were to be at the end of the island and away from the relentless pounding of the waves against the treacherous coral cliffs! We offered a deep and sincere prayer of thanks for our safety. It was evening.

Now we had another decision to make: Should we try to cross the isthmus at full tide or wait till morning and then cross? Everyone gave their opinion. Some said to wait; others said, "We have the horses and we need to get to Pangai. Let's go now." We made it a matter of prayer, and by the same three-to-two vote, we decided to move on.

We felt fairly confident, as horses are pretty sure-footed animals, even in water. We got about two-thirds across the isthmus without too much trouble, but the last third was the worst, as that was where the tides and currents were the strongest.

As we looked at the deep section ahead and saw the heavy currents running there, some of us started to have second thoughts about proceeding. We were wet and tired and felt like we were stuck between two bad options. We didn't want to go back, but the section ahead looked dangerous and our horses were exhausted. We counseled together; by the same three-to-two vote, we decided to keep going.

Partway across the last section, my horse suddenly stepped into a *loloto* (deep spot) and lost its footing. As the horse fell, struggling into the deep hole, I was sent sprawling into the turbulent ocean. All of my books, papers, scriptures, and change of clothes were washed away with the heavy tide, and I found myself flailing away to keep my head above water. The heavy tide pushed me and the horse off the trail into deep water. We were both fighting for our lives now. By some miracle, I was able to grab hold of the horse's mane. It took every ounce of energy the horse had to swim back onto the trail and keep from getting washed out to sea. I felt hanging onto the horse's mane saved my life.

Eventually our whole party made it to the other side. The five of us and our horses were completely exhausted, but the first thing we did was kneel down and thank the Lord for sparing our lives. We knew He had. We also thanked Him for the powerful and faithful horses. We could not have made it without them.

We were now on the far end of Lifuka. We needed to be back to Pangai, in the middle of the island, by that evening to meet my commitment, but we were so tired, we decided to rest for a while right where we were before going on. We moved high enough up the beach to be out of the reach of the tide, lay down in the sand, and slept.

Toward morning while we were still sleeping, someone very distinctly called my name in Tongan. I awoke immediately. I recognized the voice even though it was the voice of someone who had been dead for a long time. I knew it was the father of someone who had helped me a great deal in Ha'apai. I had never met him, but I had heard about him and knew he had been a faithful member of the Church in Ha'apai. There was no question as to who it was. I listened intently and heard him say just once, *"Kolipoki, kuo pau ke ke alu ki Uiha 'i he vavetaha* (Elder Groberg, you've got to go to Uiha right now)."

The message was very definite and very clear. I got up and looked around to see who had called. Even though I knew this man had died some time ago, I still looked, as the voice was so real. I couldn't see anyone and I didn't hear anything more. Everyone else was still asleep, so I said, "C'mon, let's get up. We've got to go to Uiha."

They sleepily said, "What do you mean, Uiha! We're going back to Pangai! Why Uiha?"

I replied, "I don't know why, but that's what we have to do."

What good men my companions were! They did not complain, they simply got up and asked how we were to get to Uiha. I said I wasn't sure, but I knew we had to get there and I knew the Lord would provide. We all knelt in prayer and asked for help. When we finished, we still weren't sure what to do, but shortly after the sun came up, we saw a boat heading south. We hailed the boat and asked where they were going. They said they were going to Pangai and from there to Uiha.

I asked, "Could you change that and take us directly to Uiha first and then back to Pangai?"

They said they would rather not. I said, "Look, I need to get to Uiha right now!"

"What for?" they asked, and I said, "Because there are troubles over there."

"What kind of troubles?" they asked, and I said, "I don't know. But there's trouble and I need to get there right now." Logically that didn't make much sense, but there's something about the power of the Spirit that carries a lot of persuasiveness. Someway, through the influence of the Spirit, along with some strong determination, they responded, "Well, we can only take two of you. But we'll go to Uiha first if that's what you need." So, we sent the other three to Pangai with the horses, and two of us swam out to the boat.

The wind was strong and we made good time to Uiha. As we got close to the harbor, I saw several people along the seashore. I recognized a couple of them as members. Some of the ladies were weeping and wailing. I called to them, "What's wrong?"

They responded, "They're killing the missionary!" As soon as I heard that, I dove into the water and swam to shore as fast I could. Once on shore, I ran directly to the chapel. As I got there, I heard lots of confusion and yelling. I saw a group of men with hammers and crowbars smashing away at an outhouse made of wood and tin siding. It was about ready to come to pieces under the blows of those six angry men.

I ran up and yelled, *Tuku ia!* ("Stop it!"). I guess the shock of someone from outside coming up and yelling at them knocked some sense back into them. It was, of course, really the power of the Spirit. With that same power and authority, I said, "What are you doing? What is going on here? Whatever it is, stop it!"

They all turned and looked at me and started whispering, "Oh, it's *Kolipoki.*" It was like a moment frozen in time. Their eyes got wide and the crazy anger that was there just a second before began to dissipate. They dropped their heads, hands, and hammers, and all of them sheepishly left. I heard some almost animallike whimpering from inside the outhouse. When I opened the door, I saw a young missionary curled up with his hands over his head, making strange sounds. I stood there not knowing exactly what to do.

I reached for his hand, but he jerked away and curled up even tighter. With some help, we eventually got him to a nearby home and had him lie down. I began to investigate to find out what the trouble was. The mission president had previously asked me to work with this young man because of serious problems he'd had elsewhere. Apparently he had been harassing the local workers. They told him to lay off and mind his own business. But he kept needling them, and that morning when some of them reached the breaking point, they took after him. He had run into this outhouse, and they were beating it down to get to him.

How someone's departed father, who talked to me the night before, knew this was going to happen, I have no idea. I guess he could see it brewing and helped get me there as fast as he could. Even at that, there was no time to spare before real tragedy would have struck.

Why did the Lord send someone to warn me to be there? I suppose part of it was that he did not want harm to come to the missionary, but I'm sure that can't be all because some missionaries do die or are killed on their missions. I thought maybe another part was that these were members of the Church, whose anger was out of control, attacking a missionary. It would have been a terrible thing for them, and for the work, had harm been inflicted upon him. I don't have all the answers, but I was very grateful the problem had gone no farther.

We got the offending and offended parties together, and amidst tears, sobs, and apologies, got things worked out. We told the branch members that all was under control, and soon everyone was sitting together having lunch and laughing about the whole thing. I was pretty sobered at knowing how close we had been to real disaster. I knew that this was my responsibility, and I wondered about this sort of thing happening again. We got some pretty strong commitments and worked out specific understandings and agreements, which I felt would be kept.

This whole process took a couple of hours. Just as we finished, somebody came to me and said, "There are people on a boat in the harbor saying you promised to be here only a little while and they are anxious to leave for Pangai." I felt things were okay, so I returned to the boat and we left for Pangai. We had a good wind back, and that evening I was in Pangai in time to keep the commitment I had made.

I recorded in my journal that evening: "Had some problems getting back to Pangai from Foa. Had to go to Uiha, but with the Lord's help, I made it home in time for my meeting."

As I reflected on what had happened, I became more appreciative of the Lord's help. I watched the situation with the missionary in Uiha carefully. Fortunately, the agreements worked, and we never had that type of problem again. We continued to work with this missionary, and he was able to finish his mission.

Something happens when you put everything on the line and go through a harrowing experience in the Lord's cause, not for just a few minutes, but for hours and hours. I suppose slogging through the mud, getting smashed around by the waves, being thrown from the horse, and struggling for your very life softens you. You sincerely feel to thank God for preserving your life. I know my companions felt the same way.

I have wondered if one could hear that voice, receive those instructions, or have that type of guidance under other circumstances. It may require this type of softening up to put one in a position to be sufficiently receptive to actually hear. Even though much of the action was physical, it was the Spirit that gave control and power.

As I look back, the whole thing was a miracle. I know for sure that the physical circumstances of getting the boat to Uiha that soon, having the strength to swim ashore, then to run and stop those angry men at the right time, could have only come from God. Only the power of the Spirit could have enabled me to command those men to cease what they were doing and have them obey. Only the power of the Spirit could have caused the people with the boat, who weren't members of the Church, to agree to take me to Uiha, wait there, and then take me back to Pangai in time to meet my commitment. I still marvel at all the other things that had to go just right, but which did.

At the time, it all seemed fairly natural and logical, and my main

*Missionary conference in Ha'apai.*
*Most of the missionaries were couples with families.*
*Elder Groberg is standing second from the left.*

concern was getting back to Pangai in time to keep a promised commitment. I still don't know why it happened the way it did, but for some reason it seems this faithful, departed brother had been given some responsibility to handle that particular situation. I guess the Tongans beyond the veil have as much faith as their counterparts here. How grateful I was it turned out as it did. Not much was said by the others about the events. They take things like that in stride, not questioning, just doing.

We asked some members going to Foa to take the horses back to Fotua the next day. A while later I was in Foa and again thanked the members in Fotua for the use of the horses. I told them I hoped the horses weren't too beat up. They told me they were fine and said that anytime I wanted to use them, just let them know.

As I was leaving, one of the members said, "I heard you had a hard time getting back to Pangai. I'm glad it worked out for you. But I shouldn't wonder. Things work out for missionaries." I hoped that statement would always be true.

# 40

## *Forms and Substance*

While I seldom saw my mission president, I had great respect and admiration for him. We all tried to do what we felt he wanted us to do. We worked hard in the school, in the district, in missionary work, and with the branches. We were constantly on the move, teaching, preaching, baptizing, building, interviewing, and the like. I remember thinking, "If I'm this busy, imagine how busy my mission president is!" I never questioned not being able to talk to him much.

After several months, I received a telegram saying the mission president was going to Vava'u, and on the way the boat would stop overnight in Ha'apai. He wanted to meet with me and hear a report. I was happy and excited to report on the things we were doing.

When the boat arrived, we met him at the wharf and took him to the guest house where he was staying. He asked me to sit down. After a few pleasantries, he asked, "Well, what are you doing?"

I enthusiastically replied, "I believe we're doing what you asked us to. We are working with the school, teaching as much as possible, traveling a lot to the outer islands, preaching the gospel, baptizing people, strengthening the Church, building up branches, and constructing chapels . . ." I was rather general, but soon could see that he wanted specifics.

"Who have you baptized? What chapels have you constructed? What branches have you formed? Who have you put in as branch presidents?"

"Well, we baptized Sione, Mele, and Vika . . ." I responded.

"I have no records of them, nor any reports on your work."

"What records? What reports?" I asked.

"When you baptize someone, you are supposed to fill out a baptismal slip. And you're supposed to send in weekly reports telling me what you've done." I could tell he was a little irritated.

I was quite taken aback, because no one had told me about any reports or forms to send in. I reminded him that his instructions to me were to "clean up the mess in Haʻapai, start a school, get the missionaries going, and generally build up and strengthen the Church." I told him I thought we were doing these things.

He acknowledged that those were his instructions and said he appreciated what we were doing, but he repeated that he needed forms and reports with names and dates. I told him I had kept a journal and I could create that information for him if he wanted. He said he needed the names and dates of all those we had baptized, ordained to the priesthood, and set apart to various positions, and a list of all the missionaries we had called—and he needed the lists now!

I said, "Fine. I'll get started and have them for you in the morning, before you leave."

I had mentioned a good branch we had in Felemea, and before I left he looked through some papers and said, "Another thing. We don't have a branch or a chapel in Felemea."

I said, "Oh, yes, we have a good, strong branch of thirty-two members and a nice chapel there."

"Who authorized you to organize a branch in Felemea? Who authorized you to build a chapel? Where did you get the money, and whose property is it built on?"

I detected some further irritation, but responded: "I'm sorry, but I thought when you asked me to build up the Church in Haʻapai, that was my authorization. We baptized a lot of people in Felemea, and they needed a chapel, so together with some other members we built a chapel. It didn't cost us any money. We all worked together and built it. I am not sure whose land it is on, but everyone in Felemea knows it is our chapel. We've been holding meetings for several months and have had no problems."

He gave me a lecture and said it was against Church policy to form new branches or build chapels without prior approval. He seemed upset and kept talking about money and authorization. I repeated that there was no money involved, and I guessed we didn't have any authorization. I apologized and asked what we *should* do.

He said, "Well, you've got to list all these things down on paper—

all the branches you've organized, all the chapels you've built, and all the branch presidents you've set apart—and I'll see if I can get approval for them. And another thing, don't do any more of this without prior authorization from me!"

I assured him I wouldn't. I was worried and thought, "What if he can't get approval for what we've done, what will we do then?" I wanted to ask but didn't feel it was appropriate.

I don't want to give the wrong impression—he was a nice man whom I greatly respected. He might have had a bad ride up, or maybe he had been reprimanded by someone in Salt Lake City, or perhaps he felt the pressure of other major problems. But at this time he was quite stressed and seemed very concerned about authorization. I wondered if I had gotten him in trouble by baptizing a lot of people, forming several branches, and building a few chapels. I hoped he wouldn't be too unhappy when he saw the fairly long list I would bring in the morning.

I stayed up all night with some of the nearby branch clerks and others, using their records and my journal and gleaning the information on whom we had ordained, whom we had baptized, whom we had called as missionaries, what branches we had formed, who the branch presidents were, and what chapels we had built. After an all-night vigil, we had quite a list of information on several sheets of paper.

The guest house and our quarters were both close to the wharf, but on opposite sides of it. The boat was to leave at 8:00 A.M. and we finished our lists at about 7:30 A.M. I ran as fast as I could to the wharf so I could explain the sheets to the mission president. I got there and waited and waited and waited. No one came from the guest house.

The captain, whom I knew, was pacing back and forth. He said, "Look, we are leaving at eight o'clock. I don't care whether your man is here or not!" About then, we saw the mission president coming down the path with some other people. He got to the wharf a few minutes before eight, just as they were starting to pull up the gangplank, but they waited for him.

I said, "President, here's the information you asked for. I'm really sorry that I've apparently done things out of order and caused you some problems. I hope this is all right. In the future, do you want me to put this information on a sheet of paper and send it to you, or are there specific forms to use? What do I do from now on so that I don't get you or me or the Church into trouble? I won't move ahead without authorization from you. Just let me know and I'll do whatever you say."

There then followed one of those never-to-be-forgotten experiences. With a saintly smile, he took the papers and without even looking at them put his hand on my shoulder and said, "Elder Groberg, I've spent a sleepless night. Forget about everything I said yesterday. Just keep doing what you are presently doing. God bless you." He turned and got on the boat and was gone. That was all there was to it. I never asked for any more explanation, and he never offered any.

You can leave it to your own interpretation whether he had a sleepless night because he had eaten something wrong, was tired from the trip, or had been disturbed for some other reason. Whatever it was, I will always be grateful for the kindly look in his eye and the love in his voice as he responded to my concerns by saying, "Just keep doing what you are doing; forget about what I said yesterday."

We kept working hard, but we also filled out forms, made lists, and sent them to mission headquarters. There was no more discussion of this issue.

I learned that it is important to keep your superiors informed, and it is important to fill out the proper forms and get the necessary authorizations, but I also learned that substance is more important than form. I was glad to know Heavenly Father was aware of what we were doing and that He was pleased (at least He continued to bless us with success) even if we had not filled out the right forms.

I was also glad to have a feeling that forms, as we know them now, probably apply only to this world. I suppose when we have a better way of communicating, such as sensing substantive personal changes rather than just reading reports (as we hopefully will beyond this world, and maybe even here during the Millennium), we can focus more on things that really make a difference. Using paper and keeping records was not a part of Tongan culture then. The heat, humidity, and lack of storage, as well as the cost of pens and paper, made it basically impossible. More than that, however, I wonder if they didn't understand better than we do that substance is much more important than form, and the Spirit always measures substance and justifies action.

Of course, forms and records *are* important, at least in this life and probably beyond. The Lord has placed great emphasis on records— witness the brass plates, the gold plates from which the Book of Mormon was taken, the Bible, other sacred records, patriarchal blessings, records of ordinances, and all sorts of historical and family history records that are kept with such great care.

But sometimes I wonder if the other Book of Life isn't the actual substance of what we are, our character as formed by our thoughts and deeds, permanently encoded into us. I have a feeling that in the eternities outward signs of power from any source—a document from a university, stripes from an army, or wealth from gold or silver—will be meaningless. The only power that will have any validity will be the power we possess within ourselves. That's why the Savior's prayer for us—that we may be one with Him as He is one with the Father—is so important. Heavenly Father and Jesus Christ do have all power and are willing to share it with the humble, the meek, and the obedient.

That may seem a deep doctrine, but it appears fairly simple to me. I am confident that many of the good Tongan people understood it better and lived it better than many of us *palangis* do. I learned that just because something is "legally" possible doesn't necessarily make it right in God's eyes, nor does it imbue it with any eternal power or authority. Only obedience to God's will does that.

In the meantime, I learned that while forms and records are important because they provide valuable information, substance is still the essence of all true progress.

# 41

## *The Lord's Wind*

Finding someone willing to listen to the discussions was like finding a piece of gold, especially if a member had referred them. One day we received such a referral. We were told that if we would be at a certain harbor on a particular island when the sun set the next day, a family would meet us there and listen to the discussions.

What joy such news gives to missionaries! I quickly found four members who were experienced sailors to take me to the island.

Early the next morning, after prayer, the five of us started out in our sailboat. There was a nice breeze, and we moved swiftly along the coast, through the opening in the reef, and out into the wide expanse of the open ocean. We made good progress for a few hours. Then as the sun climbed higher in the sky and the boat got farther from land, the wind played out and soon quit completely, leaving us bobbing aimlessly on a smooth sea.

Those familiar with sailing know that to get anywhere, you must have wind. Sometimes there are good breezes without storms and heavy seas, but often they go together. An experienced sailor does not fear storms or heavy seas, for they contain the lifeblood of sailing—wind. What experienced sailors fear is no wind, or being becalmed!

Time passed and the sun got higher, the sea calmer. Nothing moved. We soon realized that unless something changed, we would not arrive at our appointment by sundown. I suggested that we pray and plead again with the Lord to send some wind so we could get to the harbor. What more righteous desire could a group of men have? We wanted to get to a family to teach the gospel. I offered a prayer.

When I finished, things seemed calmer than ever. When it was obvious nothing was happening, I said, "Okay, which one of you is like Jonah? Who lacks faith? We'll throw you overboard so the Lord can send the wind and we can get on with our journey." No one would admit to being like Jonah, so we just drifted.

Then one of the older men suggested that everyone kneel and all unite their faith and prayers, each one offering a silent prayer at the same time, which we did. There was great struggling of spirit, but when the last person opened his eyes, nothing! No movement at all. The sails hung limp and listless. Even the slight ripple of the ocean against the side of the boat had ceased. The ocean seemed like a sea of glass.

Time was moving, and we were getting desperate. Then this same older man suggested that everyone kneel again in prayer, and each person in turn offer a vocal prayer for the whole group. Many beautiful, pleading, faithful prayers ascended to heaven. But when the last one finished and everyone opened their eyes, the sun was still burning down with greater intensity than before. The ocean was like a giant mirror. It was almost as though Satan was laughing, saying, "See, you can't go anywhere. There is no wind. You are in my power."

I thought, "There is a family at the harbor that wants to hear the gospel. We are here and we want to teach them. The Lord controls the elements. All that stands between getting the family and us together is a little wind. Why won't the Lord send it? It's a righteous desire."

As I was thinking, I noticed this faithful older man move to the rear of the boat. I watched as he unlashed the tiny lifeboat, placed two oars with pins into their places, and carefully lowered the lifeboat over the side.

Then the old man looked at me and softly said, "Get in."

I answered, "What are you doing? There is hardly room for two people in that tiny thing!"

The old man responded, "Don't waste any time or effort. Just get in. I am going to row you to shore, and we need to leave right now to make it by sundown."

I looked at him incredulously, "Row me *where?*"

"To the family that wants to hear the gospel. We have an assignment from the Lord. Get in."

I was dumbfounded. It was miles and miles to shore. The sun was hot and this man was old. But as I looked into the face of that faithful brother, I sensed an intensity in his gaze, an iron will in his very being, and a fixed determination in his voice as he said, "Before the sun sets this day, you will be teaching the gospel and bearing testimony to a family who wants to listen."

I objected, "Look, you're over three times my age. If we're going to do it this way, fine, but let me row."

With that same look of determination and faith-induced will, the old man replied, "No. Leave it to me. Get in the boat. Don't waste time talking or moving unnecessarily. Let's go!" We got into the boat with me in the front and the old man in the middle with his feet stretching to the rear of the boat, his back to me.

The glazed surface of the ocean was disturbed at the intrusion of this small boat and seemed to complain, "This is my territory. Stay out." Not a wisp of air stirred, not a sound was heard except the creaking of oars and the rattling of pins as the small craft began to move away from the side of the sailboat.

The old man bent his back and began to row—dip, pull, lift, dip, pull, lift. Each dip of the oar seemed to break the resolve of the mirrorlike ocean. Each pull of the oar moved the tiny skiff forward, separating the glassy seas to make way for the Lord's messenger.

Dip. Pull. Lift. The old man did not look up, rest, or talk. But hour after hour he rowed and rowed and rowed. The muscles of his back and arms, strengthened by faith and moved by unalterable determination, flexed in a marvelous cadence like a fine-tuned watch. We moved quietly, relentlessly toward an inevitable destiny. The old man concentrated his efforts and energy on fulfilling the calling he had from the Lord—to get the missionary to the family that wanted to hear the gospel. He was the Lord's wind that day.

Just as the sun dipped into the ocean, the skiff touched the shore of the harbor. A family *was* waiting. The old man spoke for the first time in hours and said, "Go. Teach them the truth. I'll wait here."

I waded ashore, met the family, went to their home, and taught them the gospel. As I bore testimony of the power of God in this Church, my mind seemed to see an old man rowing to a distant harbor and patiently waiting there. I testified with a fervor as great as any I have ever felt that God does give power to men to do His will if they have faith in Him. I said, "When we exercise faith in the Lord Jesus Christ, we can do things we could not otherwise do. When our hearts are determined to do right, the Lord gives us the power to do so."

The family believed and eventually was baptized.

In the annals of Church history, few will be aware of this small incident. Hardly anyone will know about this insignificant island, the family who waited, or the obscure, old man who never once complained of fatigue, aching arms, a painful back, or a hurting body. He never talked about thirst, the scorching sun, or the heat of the day as he relentlessly rowed uncomplainingly hour upon hour and only referred to the privilege of being God's agent in bringing a missionary to teach the truth to those who desired to hear. But God knows! He gave him the strength to be His wind that day, and He will give us the strength to be His wind when necessary.

How often do we not do more because we pray for wind and none comes? We pray for good things and they don't seem to happen, so we sit and wait and do no more. We should always pray for help, but we should always listen for inspiration and impressions to proceed in different ways from those we may have thought of. God does hear our prayers. God knows more than we do. He has had infinitely greater experience than we have. We should never stop moving because we think our way is barred or the only door we can go through is seemingly closed.

No matter what our trials, we should never say, "It is enough." Only God is entitled to say that. Our responsibility, if we are faithful, is to ask, "What more can I do?" then listen for the answer and do it!

I'll never forget the example of that old man.

# 42

## Totally Exhausted

The mission president basically let us operate on our own in Ha'apai. Once in a while he came up or I went down, but not often. My counselors, the members, and the locally called missionaries were wonderful! Because we were more united now, in one sense we were indeed left alone, but in a bigger sense we were not alone but were directed by the Spirit of God. What a wonderful director the Spirit is!

We were constantly going on preaching circuits. They were arduous, both by land and by sea. We traveled long distances over trails of mud and ocean. There is a scripture that says that we should "waste and wear out our lives" in the service of God (see D&C 123:13). Great joy comes as we try. I remember many times being so tired that I could hardly move. It is exhausting to teach families, particularly when you go so far to reach them, put forth so much effort to bear testimony, and try to help them all you can. There were no cars or bikes, so we walked or rode horses. To me it was hard work riding horses, especially for long distances. We always rode bareback or with a burlap sack because no one could afford saddles. Horses are pretty bouncy, so most of the time I walked.

It was always good to return home from preaching circuits, whether by land or by sea. I remember returning from long sea voyages and entering the calm harbor at Pangai, called Fanga Ko Paluki, with deep feelings of gratitude and appreciation. It is rough out in the open sea, but once you are inside the reef, it is calm and you know you are nearly home. What a wonderful feeling to be home, to be in the calm of a protected harbor after a rough voyage, and to feel the calmness of soul that comes from knowing you have done what the Lord wanted you to do. The same principle of gratitude held when we returned by land from preaching in distant villages.

I remember one particular time when we had some families to teach on the north end of our home island. Three of us were ready to go when a good member family brought us some salted whale meat to eat before we left. We were hungry, so we ate quite a bit and then started on our journey. Within just a few hours we knew we were in trouble. The meat hadn't been properly cured, and we paid the price: diarrhea, throwing up, and all that goes with eating bad meat. We continued anyway, as there was no way to get word to the families that we were sick. We taught all the lessons and then started back.

It was very late and we had "had it." I think I know what being totally exhausted is. Perhaps I haven't fully experienced it yet, but being ill and having miles and miles to walk in mud, sand, water, and the heat of a hot night must come close.

Generally, I was in good health on my mission, but this was one of the few times when I had no strength. I began to realize that a few steps from a sick person may require as much internal effort as a one-hundred-yard dash from a skilled, young runner. I learned that everyone at every age and under every condition can have his or her determination tested fully!

I wanted to get home that night because I had school to teach the next day, but it was hard just to put one foot in front of the other. I wondered if we would ever make it. We rested often and finally got to within a mile of our home when our strength seemed to leave us completely. We all fell down in a heap in the middle of the road and slept for ten or fifteen minutes. We got up, went a few yards, and fell down again.

Although I was absolutely exhausted, I was still determined to get home that night, so we continued on, alternately moving a few yards and then resting in the middle of the road. We never worried about sleeping in the middle of the road, because the only things that came down the roads were people, horses, or carts drawn by horses, and horses can smell pretty well. We must have stopped and rested twenty times to cover those last several yards.

We finally dragged ourselves up to our house, which was built on cement blocks a few feet above the ground. There were three steps to the floor of the house. How many times had I skipped up these steps effortlessly, but that evening crawling up those three small steps was a formidable task.

*A few young Tongans were called on proselyting missions.*
*They carried everything with them in mat rolls and baskets.*
*Painting by Clark Kelley Price.*

When we finally got to our mats, we wanted to sink down and sleep, and sleep, and sleep. Before we did, however, we looked at each other and in near unison said, "Let's say a prayer of thanksgiving. We're home." We always did that when we returned. I gave our prayer of thanks. I don't know when I felt more sincere in expressing gratitude and letting God know how good it felt to be home.

After the prayer, I collapsed on that familiar mat and seemed to sink into oblivion. Yet as I sank, I seemed to enter another element—a buoyancy, a calmness, a beauty that is beyond description. I didn't see anyone or hear anything, but I felt a peace and calmness such as I have seldom felt before. It was as though I was totally enveloped in peace and beauty, love and calmness, certainty and softness, and every other good and beautiful thing. How well I rested!

That buoyant feeling stayed with me for a few days and then gradually faded. Even now, at times, I can remember how it felt and sometimes longingly wish to feel it fully again. I know there is a correlation between how much honest effort we put forth, particularly in building God's kingdom, and the good feelings we experience. When life is through, I am sure those who have worn out their lives in the service of others, which is serving God, will have a feeling that is impossible to describe but will include a feeling of total love. Those who have not sacrificed for others simply cannot experience it, not because someone is angry with them but rather because they haven't done what is necessary to experience it.

The Lord said something about our needing to experience the bitter to know the sweet (see Moses 6:55; 2 Nephi 2:15). I know we must work hard in the Lord's cause to feel good, and I know God can and does give us deep feelings of love, peace, and comfort. Being totally exhausted in the Lord's cause isn't all that bad.

# 43

## *Who Will Help?*

As a district presidency, we called many couples on missions. They were very good to accept and then go wherever and whenever we asked them. On one occasion I got word that a missionary couple was very ill on an outlying island. We left immediately to investigate and indeed found them extremely ill. We brought them back to Pangai where the hospital was.

When the doctor saw them, he was alarmed. They had typhoid fever and had deteriorated to a point of being basically helpless. He didn't want them around any of the other patients. At that time the only way they handled typhoid fever was to put the afflicted people in a barbed wire enclosure, away from everyone else, and hope they got well. They weren't treated badly, but they were isolated.

At that time in Tonga, the hospitals furnished medicine and other medical treatment, but each family was responsible for feeding their own patients, providing a bed for them, and caring for them in every other way. Since we were the "family" of this missionary couple, it was our responsibility to care for them. We gave them a priesthood blessing, during which I felt the assurance that they would be all right but that it would take time. We made arrangements for someone to watch their two small children. Then I helped nurse the couple and had some of the missionaries trade with me in providing for their needs.

The law then was that the couple could not leave the compound until they were well. We couldn't hire anyone to help them, because people generally were pretty scared that they might catch the same fever. I assigned a couple of missionaries to the job; they were pretty obedient, but scared also. Caring for this missionary couple became a major challenge.

I knew we needed someone more permanent, so I walked to the nearby branches, then took the mission boat and went to the various outlying branches, everywhere asking members, "Who will help? Is there anyone who will stay with these missionaries to nurse them back to health?" I knew the Lord wanted them to live. After visiting many branches, I found that no one was willing. I didn't put pressure on them, I just asked. They all had excuses.

Finally, on the island of Uiha, there was a young girl of about sixteen who, after we had explained our need, looked at her father and said, "I'd like to go." Her father, on the spot, said, "If you want to, you can." So she came back with us.

What an act of love! Here was a young girl in the prime of her life, willing to come and, in effect, give her life (because she might catch the disease) to help a missionary family in need.

She asked how long she would be there. I told her I did not know and neither did the doctor. She went straight to the hospital compound. When I closed that barbed wire fence behind her I thought, "What have I done?" In effect, she was a prisoner with them. Yet someway I knew things would be all right because she had such a beautiful attitude.

It took several months for the couple to fully recover. The girl stayed with them day and night and nursed them back to health. She did her duty even though it took a long time. By the time the missionaries were well, I had a deep feeling of love and admiration for her.

She came from a poor family. The only thing I could figure out to do to help repay her kindness was to enroll her at the Liahona College on Tongatapu. However, she didn't qualify, because she hadn't done well in school. I pulled rank a little and explained to the mission president the sacrifice she had made. We got her into school, and she did well. She ended up marrying a returned missionary, and they then went on a mission together. They had a large family, nearly all of whom served missions and married in the temple. Her husband has been faithful and held almost every responsible calling in the Church, and she has not been one whit behind.

Every time I see her, I realize again the blessings that come after we have proven our love for others. I have asked her how she felt when we came looking for volunteers. She says, "I was as scared as anyone, but I had a feeling that someone needed help and it was my duty to give that help."

She learned to love that family just as she loved the Church, her husband, and her family, because she served them. I was impressed by this young girl and by many others who willingly served unselfishly. I wrote home:

"Pangai, Ha'apai, 29 September 1956

"After conference, one of the older ladies invited me over to her house for a meal and to bless her mother. I found that her mother was about ninety-five years old and had been blind and lying on her back for over five years, with this woman caring for her. This woman was also taking care of a little girl of her sister's after her sister had separated from her husband. There she was, just assigned to that little house. For over five years she had gone no further than to the church house and to the store; she just watched her aged mother and the little girl. There is no such thing as government care for the aged in Tonga. The family does it all, and they do it willingly. I think that this woman is doing the Lord's will a lot more than some of us who run around in circles trying to accomplish some good along so many lines that have been assigned us. I guess the main thing is to do that which is given us to do and do it well and not worry about the job that has been given to another to do. I am sure it is not so much the work we are assigned to do or where we work that is the saving factor, but rather the kind of heart we do our assigned work with. I have seen some great examples of willingness to forget self for the good of others. I think the basis of all spirituality and the means of exaltation is to just forget about oneself and help others. I wish that I knew how to serve better. I guess all of these things will come with time and experience.

"When we come into closer contact with the Lord, the importance of true love and service comes to the front. I'm sure when my work in Tonga is over, all that will be remembered is how much love I had in my heart for the people. Maybe all that will be left when we leave this earth is how much we have loved others."

I learned that feelings follow actions. I learned how important it is to do good and unselfish things so we can have good, godlike feelings.

# 44

## *The Trumpet*

My trumpet played a fairly significant role on my mission. I had played the trumpet in high school and had been asked to bring it to Tonga. I wondered why, but soon found that it was a real hit with these musically gifted people. I didn't play it a lot, but when I did, there was always a crowd. I was asked to play at rugby games, flag-raising ceremonies, and a few other events. I learned several British bugle calls.

Everyone wanted to play the trumpet, and I let them try. I guess it is a miracle that no one caught diseases, because I only had one mouthpiece. I tried to wash it out before I played. My trumpet became so popular that everywhere I went I was branded as the *palangi* with the trumpet. I used it mostly in our school and on public holidays.

I remember one day teaching my students the Idaho state song, "And Here We Have Idaho." I put the words on the board and played it once for them on the trumpet. Then something came up, and I was called away on an emergency. When I came back an hour later, the students were all smiles. These were children from six to sixteen years old. I wondered what kind of mischief they had been in. "Listen," they said. Then in absolutely perfect four-part harmony they sang the whole song—all from hearing it one time! They have an unbelievable musical ability. Music is a big part of their lives.

On the seventeenth of March I led a parade of Saints from our branch in Vaipoa, on Niuatoputapu, to a big rugby match in the next village. The game was the big event of the day, but Church members came with banners celebrating the anniversary of the founding of the

Relief Society. No one would have paid much attention to us if it hadn't been for the trumpet. Leading that small group with a trumpet got everyone's attention, and from then on the whole island knew that the Relief Society of The Church of Jesus Christ of Latter-day Saints was organized on March the seventeenth.

More than once people told me that they might forget me and my sermons, but they probably wouldn't forget my trumpet! I hoped they would remember my testimony as well.

Queen Salote was the queen of Tonga while I was a missionary. What a regal lady she was! She visited Ha'apai a few times. She was a very nice woman and very strong in the Methodist Church. She was not against our Church, but as the titular head of the Methodist Church in Tonga she felt she had some major responsibilities to her church. Over the years there had been some anti-LDS decisions made, but they were more in the context of not wanting competition than in anger.

When Queen Salote visited Ha'apai, we were always told we weren't invited to the big feasts or to any personal visits with her, despite the fact that we had a fairly large school. That all changed when, on one of the queen's visits, the government leaders in Ha'apai wanted to have a flag-raising ceremony with all the schoolchildren in their uniforms. It was arranged that the queen would stand at attention as the flag was raised and then walk by all the schoolchildren, who would line her route.

I told the local government officials, "We have a school. We ought to be part of this."

They replied, "We just can't include you." I reminded them that we had official permission for our school from the Commissioner of Education in Tonga, so they shouldn't exclude us. They still refused.

Then I said, "I'll play my trumpet for the flag raising. Their eyes lit up and they said, "Maybe we could arrange it." And they did.

They put us at the head of all the schools so we would be closest to the flagpole. That was a big thing because up to then our school had not been included in anything official. I'm sure the trumpet made the difference.

We practiced and practiced. There were hundreds, even thousands, of schoolchildren, all in uniforms.

Finally, the big day arrived. It was beautiful and clear and we all lined up according to the plan: the Mormons in green, the Catholics in red, the Methodists in blue, and so on. Everyone was excited. The queen came by, smiled at us, and shook hands with some of the children as they stood at attention. You should have seen their smiles! I played the trumpet while they raised the flag. It was the British equivalent of "To the Colors."

When we got through, the queen turned and said, "I understand you are the headmaster of the Mormon school." I said, "Yes." She said, "I would like to have you come to tea," which is a meal, not a drink. So I had the opportunity to sit next to her and visit for a long time. She was wonderful and gracious and made sure her servants brought me orange punch. She was very complimentary, asked many questions, and thanked us for what we were doing.

She made it very clear that she was interested in our school and what we were doing for her people, but not in talking about religion. The event was probably more symbolic than anything, but it was an important turning point. From then on, there was a great increase in the stature of our school and our Church among the people generally, as well as an increase in righteous pride among the members. They told their friends and neighbors, "Did you know our missionary was sitting next to the queen, and our school raised the colors?" The Mormon school was well established now, and many subtle problems we had been experiencing seemed to melt away. We still had our detractors, but things were moving in the right direction. I wrote home:

"I just received four new missionary couples and families, so I have lots of work getting them acquainted with missionary work. The missionaries who had typhoid are better now so they will be more help, too. Keeping the branches working is a real job, and this school-work is an enjoyable job, over 100 students now. I'm still trying to convert some people to these schools, but it's fun because I'm pretty sure of the ground I stand on. My trumpet has been helpful in the school."

I recalled all the times I had balked at lessons and practicing. Now I was glad Mom had pushed me. I've heard it said that behind every boy who plays any musical instrument, there is a pushy mom. I don't know if that is universally true, but it probably was in my case.

I enjoy good music. I remember as a child sometimes waking in the morning and hearing Mom playing Grieg's "To the Spring" or "Morning" on the piano and thinking to myself, "How could anything be prettier?"

I was glad I had my trumpet, as I am sure there were several occasions when it was a decisive factor in favor of the Church.

# 45

## My Aching Back

We had many opportunities to preach the gospel, and we consistently had baptisms. All of the baptisms in Ha'apai were performed in the ocean. As we baptized people and built up branches, the Saints often outgrew the homes they were meeting in. When this happened, we proposed to the members that they build a separate chapel of their own. In every case, they were supportive and excited. We asked them to furnish all the material, all the labor, and a piece of land to build on. No Church funds were used. As a district presidency, we checked attendance, evaluated the future, decided on the size of chapel to be built, called for a vote of the branch, and then gave our official permission. We usually worked along with the members as they began the buildings, which were generally small, thatched *fales*.

It normally took several weeks to complete a nice chapel of about fifteen by thirty feet. They were nearly always built on some member's land and never cost any money because everything was donated. Building chapels was a positive experience for the branch members. Those who worked hardest on the chapels were invariably the best attenders and the most active members. Many who had not been very active participated in the building process, and many became active again. Lots of nonmembers helped too, and a few of them joined the Church, but not many.

On one occasion, I went to a small branch to help them start building their chapel. We had previously agreed on a certain size for the chapel. When I got there, they had already put the four corner poles in and were starting to build the roof structure. I saw that one of the corner poles was too small for the size of building we had approved.

I got a little upset and said, "Look, we agreed to build this chapel so big and that post will not support that size, so it must be removed and a larger one put in." They were not happy with that suggestion because the poles had all been set and filled. They said the other three poles were larger and would be strong enough to support the roof. "Absolutely not!" I replied. "That pole must come out and be replaced by a larger one."

They refused to help and sat down. I was really perturbed now, so I grabbed a shovel and started digging the undersized pole out. One or two started to help me, but most of them refused, saying, "If you want it out, take it out yourself." They were not exactly angry, but strongly disagreed.

I was determined to get that pole out. It was hard work as the wet dirt seemed to cling desperately to the pole. We would dig for a while, then twist and pull to loosen it, but it was difficult to get any movement at all. In the process of straining at this obstinate pole, I felt something pop in my back and fell to the ground writhing in pain. I knew I was in trouble. The others came over to see what had happened. They carried me to some mats and apologized. They said they were sorry and asked what they could do to help.

"If you want to help, get the pole out," I said. They quickly rallied and in no time had it out. I could tell they were scared, and so was I. I was experiencing intense physical pain and they felt their disobedience had caused it. They hoped by getting the pole out, the pain would stop, but it didn't.

They gave me a blessing. In the blessing, they said they felt I should go to Tongatapu. I was afraid I might pass out as I was starting to lose my grip on exactly what was going on. I could tell they were very concerned and wanted to help. I was aware of faces looking at me and heard someone say there was a small sailboat just leaving for Tongatapu. They hailed the boat, and as it came closer to shore they explained to the captain what had happened and asked if he could take me to Tongatapu. He agreed, so they carried me out in the ocean and put me on the boat. They told me to lie still, remember the blessing I had been given, and all would be well. I was in no position to argue.

There were about ten people already crowded onto the small sailboat, but they quickly shifted around and made room for me. They even got some nice mats and *tapa* cloth and made as comfortable a place for me as they could. None of them were members of the Church, but all of them were kind and helpful. One of the older men had a bottle of special Tongan oil and asked if he could rub my back where it hurt. He said he was sure he could make it feel better. I didn't think I had anything to lose, so I told him to go ahead. His skillful hands began to work their miracle—and before long, the intense pain began to subside, and I started to feel that at least I wouldn't faint.

I was still in a lot of pain, but part of it was apprehension and wondering what had happened to my back. I knew something was wrong but didn't know what, or how serious it was, and I seemed helpless to do anything about it. I had experienced broken bones in high school and knew they were broken, but this was different. I didn't know what was wrong.

It was midafternoon and the seas were fairly heavy, but there was a strong wind and I could tell we were making good time. The undulating motion of the boat, along with the warm afternoon sun and the warmth of concern I felt from everyone, eventually lulled me to sleep. I slept for a few hours.

Suddenly I was awakened by a dash of cold ocean spray as a wave crashed across our bow. I started to jump up, but firm hands held me and kind voices assured me all was well. They said they were sorry the sea was getting a little rougher, but I should not worry. "Just try to rest," they said. I tried, but found I was fully awake now. My back still hurt, but not as much as before.

It was nearly sundown and I was able to think more clearly. I began to realize I was somewhat alone in a small boat, among strangers, in the midst of God's great ocean with no land in sight. I trusted the experience of the captain but realized we were all relying on the goodness of God and on the winds and the currents He controls. I thought of something I had read in the Book of Mormon about "being wanderers in a strange land" (Alma 13:23).

I was quite melancholy and not very comfortable with the boat going up and down, and turning and twisting as I tried to hold on. The people were helpful, but they could do only so much. I was still feeling pain and wondering what was happening.

This was probably the first time I had thought much about good health. Like many young people, I took good health for granted. I felt I could do anything. I thought my body was strong and agile and always would be. I suppose I felt my body was impervious to physical problems. Now I hurt badly and couldn't do what I wanted to do. It was a rude awakening and I was forced to think about the gift of good health, the gift of strong bodies, and our responsibility to treat this gift from God with more respect and care.

The sun was almost down now. I raised myself a little and looked into the friendly, concerned faces of faithful people as they prepared to spend the night on the open ocean, trusting their lives to the skilled hands of the captain and to God. I could tell they had deep faith in God—faith that they would not overturn or be washed away during the night, and faith that they would eventually arrive at their desired destination.

The captain told me that on their previous voyage, three people had been washed overboard during the night, and they had only been able to recover two of them. The third, a young girl, was now in the "Lord's hands," as they put it.

They seemed happy as they sensed I was feeling somewhat better. They knew I was a missionary and asked if I would be willing to give the evening prayer and commend our souls into the hands of the Lord for the long, dark night ahead. I agreed.

They sang several beautiful hymns of praise and pleading, such as "Jesus, Savior, Pilot Me" and "Brightly Beams Our Father's Mercy." I thought of all the hymns that have water travel as a theme: "Master the Tempest Is Raging" came to mind, especially the phrase, "they all shall sweetly obey thy will: Peace, peace, be still" (Hymns, no. 105).

I wondered if anyone could fully appreciate the words and the pleading of these songs until they had been on "a tempestuous sea." I sensed that it is probably beyond the grasp of most who have not been in a small boat on a dark night to understand fully the great value of a beacon light on perilous waters. For some reason I felt sorry, not for myself but for those who have never been in a small boat on a stormy sea, where they can feel the truth and beauty of the pleading verse. "Wondrous sovereign of the sea, Jesus, Savior, pilot me" (Hymns, no. 104).

After the songs, I offered the prayer. It was a moving, spiritual experience. Words of gratitude came easily and many scriptures came to mind, such as "Humble yourselves therefore under the mighty hand of God, that he may exalt you in due time" (1 Peter 5:6). Words of praise and words of pleading seemed to flow into my heart and fill that darkening evening with the fluid Tongan tongue, so rich in phrases of praise and metaphors of gratitude. For a while it was almost as though I was lifted above that small boat and could see God's hand covering us for the night, His face smiling in appreciation for our heartfelt hymns of praise and prayers of gratitude. It was a strong, spiritual confirmation of His goodness to all people, as well as the goodness of honest people everywhere who try to help others and who humbly submit themselves to God. I know He hears sincere prayers.

As we finished that subdued devotional, there were many tears— tears of gratitude, tears of pleading, tears of love, and tears of simple emotion as a small group of believers felt deeply their need for the Lord's help. God was very close to us that evening.

During the long night, the wind howled, the spray flew, the boat creaked, and the sails and ropes moaned as we alternately rode the crests of waves and plunged into valleys of darkness. There was no intense fear, however, for we all knew we were in God's hands. Many times during the night I heard people whispering, "Yea, though I walk through the valley of the shadow of death, I will fear no evil: for thou art with me" (Psalm 23:4). Faith and love were our covering that night, and what a warm, wonderful covering they were!

I was awake most of the night, partly from physical pain but mostly from awe, wonder, and a desire to help others as they had helped me. I talked to the captain and a few others and tried to express my love and gratitude to them and to God. We had some good gospel conversations. I can truly say I was filled with the Spirit.

I had been on many boats but none quite like this, because I didn't feel whole physically. Something happens when you know you don't have much physical strength and you must rely totally on others and on God for your life and your future. The circumstances are not necessarily pleasant, but the feelings of love and appreciation surely are.

Sometime during the night, it dawned on me that I had nothing with me. Usually when I traveled from island to island, I carried my scriptures, a few tracts, a change of clothing, perhaps a little food, and had at least one companion. Now I had nothing: no change of clothing, no scriptures, no watch, no food, no wallet, no money, no passport, not even good health. I had nothing but the clothes on my back.

At first I shuddered and wondered what I would do. Then I realized it didn't matter. Money, clothes, tickets, passports—all these things of the world were not important. Even physical health was not critical. I had what was important. I had a testimony. I knew God was my Father. I knew I was a missionary, a witness for His Son, Jesus Christ. I knew He knew who I was, where I was, what my needs were, and where I needed to go. I knew with certainty that He was the "Master of ocean and earth and skies" and that through Him, everything would "sweetly obey His will" until the fulfillment came: "peace, peace, be still."

I thought of Moses in the wilderness as he left Egypt. He likely had no passport, money, or maybe not even a change of clothes. I thought of Abraham and others as they traveled through the deserts and waste places, and of the pioneers among sagebrush and sand. It may actually be easier to find God in places and circumstances like these—at least there are not so many worldly distractions. I was grateful for that night. I was also grateful when it ended.

As the eastern sky began to grow light, everyone gathered again and sang songs of praise and thanksgiving. They asked me to offer another prayer of gratitude for the protection during the night, for being on course, and for not losing anyone. In the prayer I praised God and thanked Him for His help and asked for His continued protection through the coming day. Words from the Psalms came easily and seemed natural in meaning and setting. They were felt by every heart, including many above. I thought of the sweet little girl from the last voyage now in the "Lord's hands."

The seas were heavy, but we were making good progress. I noticed how large one of the women close to me was. I remember thinking, "She is huge." I suppose I was thinking a little negatively. Not long afterwards, I tried to get up and was hit by a sudden pain in my back. I started to fall just as the boat hit a large wave. I went flying off balance and could easily have gone over the side. I felt something strong encircle me and found myself securely held by very stout arms. I realized I was in the lap of this heavy woman, and all the seas in the world could not rip me loose from her grip or shake her from the deck of that boat. When the danger was over, she let me go and cautioned me not to stand again but rather to sit, crawl, or just lie down. I was sorry I had felt even slightly negative towards her.

During the day the old man massaged my back for hours, using special ointments. I felt much better. Others shared some boiled bananas and coconuts with me. They tasted good. How solicitous they were of my needs! What wonderful people!

Late in the afternoon we sighted land; just before evening, we pulled into the harbor at Nuku'alofa. I felt so much better, I was almost ashamed I had come. As I stepped ashore, my spirit literally soared with gratitude and deepened understanding. We had arrived safely, and the pain in my back was almost gone.

I thanked everyone for their help. They refused any payment, for which I was grateful as I had no money. I assured them they would be richly rewarded for their goodness. They thanked me for my prayers and said they had felt the Lord's protection with a missionary on board. The old man with the "magic fingers" assured me I would be okay. I embraced him in a heartfelt hug of gratitude. We parted with tears of joy and appreciation for one another. It had been a good experience. I am aware of two in that group who later joined the Church.

I was able to walk now without too much pain, so I headed towards town. I was hungry, tired, and thirsty, but I felt great. I still didn't know what had happened or what would happen, but I remembered I had been given a blessing and a promise. I reflected on the blessing and on the assurance from the old man on the boat that I would be okay. I felt I would, but I still had some concerns.

Eventually I found the mission president and explained what had happened. He took me to the hospital. It wasn't much, but it was more than anything we had in Ha'apai.

A TMP (Tongan Medical Practitioner) checked me and did a few tests. He knew I had come on a boat from Ha'apai in fairly stormy seas and asked if I had been hit by the side of the boat or been struck by anything during the trip. I told him I didn't think so, but I couldn't remember for sure.

He said my back was all black and blue and had gone through some major trauma. I also had some badly torn muscles, but there were no broken bones or damaged discs. "Whatever it was it's okay now," he said. "You're free to go back; just take it easy and don't lift anything heavy or do any hard work for two weeks."

The mission president wanted me to stay for a few days and make sure things were all right. I assured him that I felt fine and that I wanted to return to Ha'apai as soon as possible. He sighed, but then agreed. I stayed overnight at the mission home and left the next morning. I have had no trouble with my back since then.

# 46

## Lost and Unknown

The morning I left for Ha'apai the president said, "We have one hundred membership cards of lost and unknown people from Ha'apai that have been in the office for a long time, so we are going to send them to Salt Lake City."

I asked, "What do you mean lost and unknown? There isn't anyone lost and unknown in Ha'apai."

He replied, "Well, here are one hundred membership cards that no one seems to know about. Do you know any of them?"

I looked and could identify no one. I asked if, before sending them to Salt Lake City, he could give me a couple of months to see if I could find them. He agreed.

I returned to Ha'apai. Even though my back was still hurting some, I was feeling much better, especially knowing there wasn't anything seriously wrong.

Over the next few months we asked everyone we could about the people whose names were on the "lost and unknown" cards. One of the problems at that time with records in Tonga was that people often changed their names. I used to get after them for changing their names, and they would always come back to me and say, "Do you *palangis* die with the same name you are born with?"

"Yes," I said. Then I explained how for the records of the Church that is the best thing. They looked at me in disbelief and said, "Then you don't progress at all through life?"

At first I did not understand, but they explained that in their culture, when they changed their attitude or position or proved themselves in life, they changed their name as a sign of their new situation. They would quote from the Old Testament and show how Abram's name was changed to Abraham, Sariah to Sarah, and Jacob to Israel. They used many examples in the Old Testament and explained that when you do something, proving yourself in a certain way, then you change your name accordingly. They seemed to feel that was the pattern God followed.

They pointed out that our wives take on them the family name of their husbands and that all the faithful will take on them the name of Christ. I couldn't answer much. They continued explaining that according to their custom, if you die with the same name you were given at birth, it is a sign of failure in life. Their arguments reinforced my feeling that to understand Tonga, you must understand the Old Testament.

Most of their examples came from the Old Testament, but they also used examples from the New Testament and the Book of Mormon, such as Saul becoming Paul, the Lamanites becoming Anti-Nephi-Lehis, and King Benjamin giving his people a new name when they changed their hearts.

They used other more obscure references that I had never heard of before, but that to them were significant. This may be one of the reasons Tongans take to temple work so naturally. Their kings are given new names when they become king (as is often done with English and other kings). There is so much similarity between the Old Testament, the temple, and the Tongan culture that I am convinced they are of the blood of Israel, their forefathers had the truth and had temples, and at one time they understood correct gospel principles. An outsider may not think so, but I have no question.

We continued searching and asking questions about the "lost and unknown people" everywhere we went. Even though there were more than fifteen thousand people in Ha'apai, everyone knew everyone or at least could make a connection very quickly. When there are not a lot of material things to take your time and attention, you tend to concentrate more on what you do have, such as families, friends, and relationships. All we had to do was talk to enough people and before long we found, or accounted for, ninety-nine out of those one hundred. Most of them were still in Ha'apai. Several had died or had moved, and many had changed names, but they were all real people and they were there. It was one of the most fascinating detective adventures I had ever had.

We found many people to teach as we contacted them asking about these cards. We finally got down to the last membership card, which seemed to be the biggest puzzle of all. We thought ninety-nine out of one hundred was pretty good, but still felt like trying to make it a perfect job and find all one hundred.

One day we were on a boat that we seldom used to go to another island. Most of the time we used our own sailboat, but often it was in such bad shape that we could not use it and had to take passage on other boats. As we traveled, we talked about the person on that last card. The membership cards at that time gave a lot of information, such as who baptized them, who their father and mother were, and the like. When I mentioned the name of the Elder who had baptized this "missing" person, I noticed out of the corner of my eye the captain sort of ducking his head. I went back by the rudder and talked to him—sure enough, he was the man. He had been baptized long ago, which was the last he had to do with the Church. But when the Elder's name who baptized him was mentioned, it brought back a distant memory of that baptism and he responded. The captain had changed his name since then, and no one had any idea he was a member.

Things are gradually changing in Tonga now, as they realize the need to consistently use the same name in issuing birth certificates and passports for international travel, among other reasons. I'm sure this is more convenient, but I'm not sure that it indicates progress.

Most of the people we located came back into activity, but some did not. I was convinced then, and still am now, that there is no such thing as a lost and unknown person in the Church, especially in Tonga. There are only "unidentified people," and with effort they can all be found.

# 47

## Conversations

We continued to have new challenges with the members, the missionaries, and the school, but they were mostly minor compared to what we had already been through. Every day there was something exciting and challenging to accomplish, and we tried to go about our work with enthusiasm. There was little time to rest. I remember feeling that there is no greater blessing than to have challenging and important work to do, with the authority to do it and good people to help you. These were glorious times.

The days evolved into weeks, and the weeks into months. There was a little progress here and a little better feeling there. The new missionaries at the school made a huge difference. The branch president missionaries and the proselyting missionaries were more in tune with one another and with the members, and more people were attending meetings. The feeling of unity was starting to become a reality. Occasionally an argument or a nasty problem came up, but by and large, progress towards achieving the goal the mission president had set for us "to get rid of the bickering and quarrelling and achieve more unity among the people" was gradually happening.

Nowhere was this more evident than in the school. The spirit of helpfulness, love, and unity among the teachers was nothing short of marvelous. I don't know how it would be possible to have better feelings. No one complained. Everyone went out of their way to help one another. Everyone worked hard, and there was lots of hard work to do.

The teachers constantly told me they would take on more of the load if I needed them to. They wanted me to feel free to perform my duties as district president. They knew of my responsibilities to the other missionaries and members on the far-flung islands. "When you need to leave, just let us know; when you return, you'll have no regrets. We'll work twenty-four hours a day if necessary," they said. Gradually I turned more and more responsibility over to the missionary teachers. I felt the school improved as I did.

This same feeling of unity seeped over to the district presidency, the district council, and the other missionaries and members. Each person took their own responsibility more seriously, and as they consciously tried to help others, a feeling of unity and oneness started to pervade the whole district in a manner that brought great joy to me and to everyone.

About this time I went on a preaching circuit to Lulunga (a southern group of islands) for ten days. When I left, the feelings among the members and teachers were very positive. As we visited the outer islands, the feelings among the members and missionaries there were also very positive. It seemed that everyone *wanted* to help. They all wanted to do their part, and more. What a wonderful change!

As we finished that preaching circuit and started home, the winds were somewhat against us, so we had to make long tacks with the sailboat to make any forward progress. That is, to move a mile forward, you had to go several miles sideways at a small angle and several miles back at a small angle, just to get a little closer to your forward destination.

The seas were not overly rough, but because of the head winds, what could have been a half-day's journey took over two days. I was past the immaturity of complaining about the wind, so as we sailed back and forth I had lots of time to think and contemplate.

As I did so, a spirit of wonder came over me. I felt so good about what I had left at home, what I had found in the outer islands, and what I felt among my companions. I felt sure I would find good feelings when I returned home and could sense that unity and its blessings were starting to become a reality.

As I sat there in this contemplative mood, I reflected on the great contrast between how good things seemed now and how bad things had seemed just a few months ago. There were only five of us in the boat, and with the brisk wind coming straight at us and the ocean being fairly strong, there was lots of work to do to keep us moving forward. I offered to help, but they were sensitive and could see I was studying and thinking. They said they could handle it and just left me alone with my thoughts. Never once did they complain about my not helping. With their skillful hands and cooperative attitude as a backdrop, I leaned back and fell into a state of deep pondering.

Without realizing it or even thinking about it, I started a type of conversation with God. It was not a real conversation in the sense that I might now have with my wife or children, but nevertheless a conversation. To me it was very real. It was basically a one-sided conversation as I asked the questions and also gave the answers. I had been reading the scriptures a lot and had been thinking about the changes that had come to pass in Ha'apai. Even though I gave the answers to my own questions, I felt good about them and felt they were at least somewhat prompted by a divine source.

I hope it is not sacrilegious to give just a few thoughts from that conversation. I started out saying: "It's marvelous to see and feel the change that has come over the Ha'apai District. How did it come about?"

*Through faith in My Beloved Son. All good things come to pass through faith in Him.*

"But there was so much chaos, so much quarrelling, so much dissension. Things seemed to be in such disarray. And now they seem so peaceful and orderly, and there seems to be so much unity of purpose. How does that change actually happen? It's like a miracle."

*I've had a lot of experience bringing order out of chaos. I've done it lots of times. I can bring love from quarrelling and order from chaos in individuals or families, branches or districts, even worlds or universes. It's just a matter of obedience to eternal law.*

*I work with people and all my creations until they obey, and then peace and order replace anger and chaos. Chaos comes from disobedience; peace comes from obedience. Some elements and some people take longer, but they eventually learn.*

"It seems so wonderful, so desirable to have peace and unity and oneness. Why is there disharmony or lack of unity, and why would anyone do anything to bring that result?"

*There is a principle of moral agency that must be kept intact. Some learn faster or better than others, but all learn. Eventually the realities of eternity become apparent. Truth eventually prevails. Light always overcomes darkness.*

"But what about those who seem bent on doing evil and deceiving and lying? How is that handled?"

*I've had plenty of experience with that also. You teach correct principles and bear fervent testimonies, but you also learn to love with all your heart and develop patience as deep as eternity.*

"How do you develop that love and patience?"

*You develop love by loving, and you develop patience by being patient. But remember what was said first: All progress comes through faith on My Beloved Son. Follow Him. Study His life and teachings. Learn of Him. All things in the Church and even in the earth and in the heavens testify of Him. Sense Him and see Him and His life and teachings in all things. Rely on Him. Be patient and accept His tutoring, and you will learn.*

"I still don't understand how to work with those who seem to be unwilling to change, who in effect seem to want to disobey. How do you do it?"

*Follow what I've said before.*

Sometimes I would ask questions and feel no answer. Yet sometimes my questions were answered with, "Not now," "Not yet," "It's not time," or "You can't understand yet." Mostly it was a wonderfully fulfilling experience of reading scriptures and sensing answers that, while not necessarily hidden, I had at least not understood before.

These conversations went on for hours and hours. Maybe I have said more than I should, but I don't think I have said anything that can't be found in the scriptures. It was a wonderful time for me. I felt like a child looking into a lake and marveling at its beauty, depth, and width, and wondering at all that was going on in it, yet sensing there was a whole ocean, even an eternity of oceans, beyond the next mountain range. I was happy for the conversations but knew I had hardly started.

Two days later as we finally pulled inside the reef and made our way to home port, I was still contemplating and reflecting, marveling and thanking. I wondered how people understand these things if they don't have a few days to sit and contemplate in a sailboat in the South Pacific with a faithful crew who never complain. I assumed that people find their own days and places of reflection, but I was glad we had a head wind and it had taken us two extra days to get home.

As I returned to the school, the branches, and the missionaries, I was not disappointed. In fact, my most optimistic expectations were surpassed. The school was running smoothly, even beautifully. The members and missionaries were united and were very close to being one in heart and purpose. What a blessing!

What marvelous things the Lord gives to those who obey him and help others, who are humble and united, and who do not seek their own good but constantly seek the good of others.

I learned that language, culture, physical surroundings, technology, time, place—none of these things make any real difference. Only unity, obedience, love, helpfulness, hard work, patience, humility, and willingness to allow agency its full play, and then developing deep faith in the Lord Jesus Christ, make any real difference. These are the important things to learn in this life. Only these things bring blessings.

I learned that God is intimately involved in our lives, that the more faith we have in Him the more we can comprehend that involvement and the less faith we have in Him the less we can comprehend that involvement. I learned that no matter how things may seem, God is always there. We must obey, endure faithfully in Christ, and always remember that for us the last chapter has not yet been written.

# 48

## *Auhangamea*

Unlike Niuatoputapu, there were lots of boats to and from Haʻapai. I doubt a week went by without some type of boat arriving. Some carried mail, but most of the little ones didn't. After boats from Tongatapu arrived, I always checked the mission post office box 6 for mail. Like all missionaries, I was very happy when I received mail. Letters now came and went much more regularly, and I was sure my family felt a little more at ease.

One day a letter came from the mission president saying that he had received permission to build several brick chapels in Tonga, including two in the Haʻapai District—one in Pangai, and one in Uiha. We were excited! The word spread fast. After years of rather shabby chapels, the Mormons were finally doing something first class!

Stories circulated everywhere, among members and nonmembers alike: "I hear the Mormons bought a motor launch and it's coming here." "I hear the Mormons are going to build with cement, which is hard like coral." "I hear builders are coming from America." On and on went the rumors and questions. I couldn't say much because I didn't know much.

In his letter, the mission president said we must get long-term leases in Pangai and Uiha before we could build. He also said we should raise a considerable sum of money (£500 or about $2,500 U.S.) and furnish several able-bodied men as building missionaries. He asked me to let him know when we had accomplished these things, and then one of the builders from America would come up, make a survey, and tell us what to do next.

I was a little concerned about someone who didn't know the language or understand local ways coming to Ha'apai and telling us what to do, but I had faith in my mission president and tried to do everything he asked.

We did our part, and before long the first builder arrived. He was a kind and understanding man. While he was required to do certain things, he was also willing to listen and make changes to better accomplish what needed to be done. Thus, the Church building program began to unfold in Ha'apai, and before long we started construction of two block chapels. For good or bad, things would never be the same again.

It is hard to imagine how far-reaching the new ways were. The biggest impact was the introduction of a new way of thinking. Motor launches were used instead of sailboats. Lumber, cement, tin roofing, and nails were all introduced as building materials. Electricity (through generators) provided power to do jobs formerly done by hand. Using schedules, paying people to work, following a written plan, keeping records, expecting people to work so many hours or get so much done in a day or a week—all were concepts basically foreign to the normal way of doing things in Ha'apai. These concepts took on great importance and reached into almost every facet of our activities.

It was interesting to watch two cultures clash. The Tongan culture was largely oriented towards moving with nature. The Western culture was largely oriented towards moving despite nature. The Tongan culture seemed to bend to the will of nature. The other seemed to bend nature to its will. It was often sad and sometimes painful to see many aspects of a centuries-old culture swallowed up by a more powerful one led by advanced technology, new ideas, and different ways of doing things, a culture that seemed to run roughshod over seas, storms, rain, darkness, and sometimes even people's feelings.

For a while there was a lot of confusion, even in my mind. However, I quickly learned that the basic principles of the gospel were not changed at all. Even though we now often traveled by motor launches rather than sailboats, there was still need for faith. Even though people were paid wages, there was still need for honesty. Even though people were given specific assignments, the opportunity to go out of their way and help others was still there. And even though a schedule was now required, this did not need to keep anyone from performing those basic acts of kindness of which Christianity is made. No matter what the new technology brought, the need for faith and kindness would never be outmoded.

The builders brought a motor launch to Ha'apai. They cautioned that it was to be used for "building purposes only," as the Building Department (whoever that was) was paying for it. They made it clear that the launch was not to be used for branch or proselyting work, but they wanted *me* to be responsible for it.

I *was* confused now. I thought branch work, proselyting work, and building work were all the same. I could see no way of separating them, but I told them I would do my best.

When the builder left, he promised to send a mechanic to keep the launch in good repair as I knew nothing about diesel engines. He also said that since the only wharf in Ha'apai was in Pangai, they would send a double load of cement there and asked if I could get half of it over to Uiha. I said I would. I didn't know what I was getting myself into!

When the shipment of cement drums arrived in Pangai, it was so heavy no one knew what to do. It may well have been the heaviest load ever delivered to Pangai. We could tell it would take us forever to get the dozens of heavy, waterproof barrels of cement to Uiha using our small sailboat or even the motor launch.

The copra board had a big *lafa lafa* (barge) they used to haul loads of copra (dried coconut meat) out to large British ships that were too big to come into the harbor. With some negotiation, we soon had an agreement to use the barge to haul the cement to Uiha.

On the appointed day, the members came down to the wharf and loaded those heavy drums of cement onto the wooden barge. By the time the barrels were in the barge, it was so low in the water that I thought it was going to sink. But it stayed afloat.

We bought a lot of strong rope. (It seemed a miracle that the Building Department could always come up with money to buy those things. We could never buy enough good rope for our old sailboat.) We hooked the barge to the motor launch with a long length of heavy, new rope. We started the launch moving forward and as the rope tightened and came out of the water, the launch tried to move forward, but couldn't. The heavy old barge just sat there laughing, as though to say, "Try and get me to move."

This was terribly frustrating. Many of the members were jumping back and forth from the wharf to the barge, yelling and laughing and having a great time. I enjoyed seeing them have fun, even at our expense, but I couldn't help feeling that maybe we were getting into something beyond our ability. There were five of us on the launch, and the situation wasn't very funny to me.

After lots of effort, the barge began grudgingly to move, at first only a few feet, but eventually with a more steady rhythm. When I realized we were really under way, I signaled that everyone, except the ten men we were taking to help us unload in Uiha, had to jump from the barge and swim ashore. There was lots of laughing and running about—and a great game of cat and mouse as the young boys ran from the older ones, who were trying to throw them off. Eventually only ten men were left. By now we were close to the opening in the reef that separated us from the protected harbor and the open sea.

Once we got into the deep ocean, the swells started lifting us and the barge up and down—often at different times. Even though we had made the venture a matter of prayer, that latent sense of foreboding I had felt earlier returned. Occasionally the barge was pushed back by a large wave, which would pull the launch backwards, no matter how fast our motor was running. It was scary. The barge must have weighed 100 times as much as the launch. I was grateful we had as long a rope as we did. With time we learned when to move forward, when to slow down, and how to play the ropes and the waves to achieve the maximum forward movement.

We had started early in the morning under broken clouds. The seas were fairly strong with whitecaps all around. The launch had been to Uiha once before on its own and made it in four hours, but with this heavy load, we anticipated it would take us most of the day to get there.

The place we were most concerned about was the *auhangamea* (the destroyer of things). This was an area where parts of separate islands come relatively close together. The currents and tides got deflected and channeled by the islands into a fierce multidirectional force so powerful and unpredictable that the *auhangamea* is a major danger zone.

On a previous voyage I had thrown a long stick like a spear into the *auhangamea* with all my force. Down, down it went and then surfaced one hundred feet away. A little later I threw another one, and it surfaced seventy-five feet away in an entirely different direction. I could only imagine the giant battle going on between opposing currents down there.

It had taken us till early afternoon to get to the *auhangamea*, which was about three-fourths of the way to Uiha, but we all knew the last part was going to be the hardest. We had been relaxing and singing but as we neared the *auhangamea*, all of that stopped and a tenseness gripped everyone. Would it be smooth? Would we find riptides? How would it affect the launch, the ropes, and the heavy barge? We all knew it was unpredictable, but what would it be like today? Many heartfelt prayers ascended to heaven.

When we entered the destroyer, we could feel an eerie tug and pull from the powerful currents. The launch would careen to one side and then would shoot back as though being whipped by a sinister force.

We moved slowly forward, but when the heavy barge got into the *auhangamea*, we knew we were in trouble. The heavy currents seemed to grab it and move it at an angle away from the launch. The rope tightened, and we could actually feel the launch being pulled backward. Then another current took over, and the barge moved rapidly to the other side, dropping the rope deep into the water. Then just as the launch moved forward to take up the slack, the barge would move in a different direction, and we would be pulled backwards or sideways. It was crazy and scary.

The engineer revved the motor but said it couldn't take this much strain for long. Working with his lookout man, he tried to coordinate the various movements of the launch and the barge. For a while, things would seem to go better, then unexpectedly a shift would come, and the launch would be jerked to one side or the other. The waves seemed to grow bigger, and we were all soaked from the constant breaking of the ocean over us. But the worst part was the unpredictability of everything.

The strong currents were forcing us in a course we did not want to follow, and the barge was bobbing up and down with ever greater force. Sometimes the barge would almost sink out of sight, then ride high above us. We seemed to have no control over it! The launch was at the mercy of the heavy, aimless barge, which at times nearly pulled us underwater.

Tongans are generally calm in tight situations. It takes a lot to frighten them, but before long I sensed some real terror in the eyes and voices of those around me. It was obvious we were in deep trouble, and none of us knew what to do.

The swells deepened and the winds blew harder. Often we could not see the barge, but we could certainly feel it! Without warning, we would be partially submerged or whipped to one side or the other. The engineer kept the motor at full throttle but reminded me that at that rate it would soon burn out. Yet when we slowed the motor, we were jerked around even more, so there seemed to be no alternative but to keep it racing at top power.

I couldn't see the ten men on the barge very clearly, but I could sense the deep concern among them. Breaking waves were filling the flat bottom of the barge with water; because the barge was so loaded, it was almost impossible for them to bail it out. The added weight of the seawater was sinking the barge ever lower. The men were bailing as fast as they could, but ten men with small buckets were no match for the large waves. It seemed this sea of terror was trying to rip us to pieces. We knew something had to change, but what could we do?

There are times in our lives when nothing seems to go right, when nothing seems to make sense, when we feel there is nothing we can do. Perhaps we feel our prayers are not bringing any inspiration or direction, or the turmoil about us is ready to engulf us and we want to scream in agony. Yet while we often don't know what to do, we generally know what *not* to do. God sees to that. This was such a time.

I could see the panic in those about me, feel the fear in my own heart, and sense the same was going on in the hearts of those in the barge. The engine began to cough and sputter a little. We were taking on too much water ourselves and could hardly keep it bailed out fast enough. All of us were working as hard as we could. Finally, the captain shrugged his shoulders and said, "We can't get any more power, and soon we will have none. Something must change." He looked at me as though he was sure I knew what to do.

I had no answer. I had been praying as hard as I knew how, but had no impressions at all, only mounting fear. Suddenly one of the most terror-struck young men screamed, "The next time the rope loosens up, release it. At least that way we'll be able to escape."

"What about the people on the barge?" I asked. "Without the rope pulling them, the barge won't last a minute."

"Maybe they can swim when it sinks. Then we can swing around and pick them up."

"But what about the cement?"

"Forget it! Release the barge now!"

I didn't feel good about that. Just then the rope tightened and we were jerked into a wave that totally engulfed us. As the water subsided, this same man yelled, "If they go down, they'll drag us with them! Release the rope now!" I looked. The rope was taut. We couldn't release it. The young man brought out his machete and said, "I'll cut the rope. Just say so. We have to save ourselves so we can try to save them!"

I was immobilized. I couldn't talk. I couldn't even think. I just stood there staring back and forth at the rope, the barge, and the launch. Everyone was waiting.

I continued staring. *Why aren't my prayers being answered? Why is there no direction?* Another wave smothered us. I looked back. The barge seemed to be listing heavily, and the men were gathering on the side highest out of the water. I could feel their fear. It seemed to resonate with mine.

The young man with the machete yelled again, "Cut the rope! Cut the rope!" In my mind's eye, I could almost see the barge sinking and pulling us down with it. I sensed that if I didn't act, we could well lose the barge, the cement, the launch, and our lives. I knew I must say something, but for some reason I couldn't. Another man frantically yelled at me, "You're a missionary. You can't be a good missionary or do missionary work if you're dead! Cut the rope now!"

Their arguments made sense. No one knows how badly I wanted to tell them to cut the rope. Time was moving, but I just stood there. *Why can't I answer?*

Finally an impression: no voice, no manifestation, no calming of the seas, just a feeling to speak—and even I was surprised at the words that came from my lips as I said, "I can't be a good missionary or do missionary work if I value my life more than others. Don't cut the rope. Keep the engine at full speed."

There was dead silence. Everyone was shocked, including me. They looked at me in disbelief. I stood transfixed. It took a few moments for me to realize what had happened, to realize I had received an answer to my prayers. I was not particularly calm, but I was certain what was right. I knew it didn't matter whether we lived or died, it only mattered that we were loyal to God and to others for whom we were responsible.

Slowly the young man lowered his machete. The lookout man climbed back to his post. The captain started tinkering with the motor. The rope man made sure all was secure. I stood and stared at the barge. It was over. I had no idea how it would end, but the decision was made. It was out of my hands and into much better ones.

Almost imperceptibly we began to move forward. The fear, the wind, the jerking, and the crashing sea were all still there, but now the entire scene seemed to take on a slightly different hue. I knew whether we made it to Uiha was not really important. We had already made the important decision, and all were obedient.

We tend to fuss so much for our lives, maybe because it's natural, or because we haven't fully repented, or because our lives are not yet full of love and compassion and charity, or maybe because we haven't unselfishly helped others sufficiently. It may be that our faith in God is not as full as it should be, so we don't yet realize that when our lives are filled with these and other Christlike qualities, it doesn't really matter whether life continues here or there.

In the middle of that raging sea, I pondered these things. The tenseness in my eyes and heart began to soften. I signaled as best I could to those in the barge that we were making progress. I saw several clasped hands moving back and forth in a sign of encouragement and gratitude. I even thought I detected smiles on some of those weary faces. We all redoubled our efforts at bailing water. It kept us busy.

Before long it became clear we were moving forward. The motor was running smoothly, the currents seemed more subdued. The barge was not twisting and bouncing quite so much. Soon we were beyond the *auhangamea*.

One could explain this physical turn of events in many ways. Maybe enough time had passed so the tides were starting to equalize each other, or maybe some vagrant current had tipped the balance of power. The simple fact was, regardless of how He did it, God allowed us to move forward. He caused the powers of destruction to loosen their grip. He is all-powerful, kind, and loving. I know that!

Slowly, foot by foot, we moved toward Uiha. We pulled into the relative calm of the harbor just as the sun sank into the sea. After we secured the launch and the barge, we swam to shore. The Saints had a great feast prepared for us. How good it felt to be on firm ground and see the smiles and feel the happiness of those who had committed their all to getting the Lord's cement to Uiha. Not much was said about the trip. When people asked, the response was simply, "God protected us. He helped us bring His cement safely here." It was almost like, "What else is there to say?"

I tried to be as calm as the others, but somehow my *palangi* nerves were jangled. The men from the barge were all laughing, eating, and asking for help to unload the cement in the morning. None of them talked much about the ordeal. However, in a quiet moment just before we retired, one of the older men from the barge came over and whispered, "Thanks for not cutting the rope. We knew God would help us. Thanks for listening to Him."

I knew it was the power of such faith that had allowed God to bring us safely through. I sensed that God had as much concern for their faith as for their lives. I rested well that evening knowing both had come through unscathed.

# 49

# *The Granddaughter*

It is warm in Tonga at Christmastime, the weather is hot and humid, but the spirit of the season is beautiful. People tend to think more about others and less about themselves, and what a blessed thing that is! I reflected on my first Christmas in Liahona waiting for a boat to Niuatoputapu, the second on Niuatoputapu, and now the third in Pangai, Ha'apai.

There was not a lot of physical gift-giving in Tonga because there were simply not a lot of things to give. People were poor in terms of worldly possessions, but they gave marvelous gifts of love, service, and kindness. During the warm evenings around Christmas, many singing groups and assorted bands went around serenading. Even with the oppressive heat, the feeling of peace and good cheer seemed to permeate everything.

A few months earlier we had been asked to raise £500 so we could start our new brick chapel in Pangai. We made an assessment of £50 each to ten separate families, and everyone was to have the money in by 1 January. Most of the families had completed their allotment, but one older couple, who lived close to our home, was still struggling. They were a faithful grandparent couple, all of whose children were married and gone. Most of their children were active in the Church, but some were not.

The grandfather originally thought he could get his money from other sources, but one by one those sources failed. At last he realized he must go to his plantation on another island and make copra to sell. Making copra was done by gathering coconuts, cutting them open, extracting the meat, drying it in the sun, and selling it to the *mataka* (copra board) to get the needed money. (Copra is used commercially for soap, oils, etc.) He was determined to meet the deadline, so two weeks before Christmas he left for his plantation. He planned on being back by Christmas, but he wasn't.

Shortly after he left, a nine-year-old granddaughter came from Tongatapu to spend the holidays. Her arrival was unannounced, but welcomed by her grandmother as the girl's mother was one of their more wayward children.

The grandmother and her granddaughter had a good time together, but a few days before Christmas the granddaughter became very ill with a high fever. Even though her grandma put her to bed and cared well for her, the fever seemed to get worse. The grandmother asked us if we would administer to her granddaughter, which we did. I felt she would be all right, and we continued about our other activities.

The day before Christmas, one of the missionary schoolteachers and I visited families and wished everyone the season's best. As we concluded our visits, I asked my companion where else he thought we should go that Christmas Eve. He replied, "I've heard the granddaughter is still doing poorly and that the grandfather has not yet returned. I'm sure the grandmother is very tired from the constant care she has been giving her granddaughter. Why don't we go to her house and volunteer to watch her granddaughter tonight and let her get some rest?"

"What a great idea!" I thought. "Why don't I think of things like that?"

It was early evening when we arrived at her house and explained what we proposed to do. Seldom have I seen more grateful eyes or felt more sincere appreciation. The grandmother looked at us a long time, I suppose studying our seriousness, and then said, "She is very ill. I have been up day and night with her for the last three days. I am very tired, and I'm not sure I can make it another night. Thank you. Thank you! I have been using this cloth and bowl of water to cool her brow and this woven fan to give her some air movement. She has not talked at all the last few days, but only moaned. I'm not sure if she will get well or not. Maybe I should try to stay up and help."

My companion said, "No, you go and rest. *Kolipoki* and I will fan her and cool her forehead, and she will be all right. Now run along and sleep." She looked at us again for a long time, then left. I imagine she was asleep the second she got to her room.

We were on the front veranda of the house, where it was a little cooler. We immediately started fanning the granddaughter and cooling her forehead with the wet cloth. She seemed in a bad way. Her breathing was strange, her fever was high, her eyes were closed, and her moans were pathetic. We devised a system where one would hold the wet cloth and the other fan air through it to get some cool air moving around her mouth and head.

It doesn't sound like much work, but the anxiety of the situation, the sultry evening, the exertion to get water, rinse the cloth, and constantly wave the fan, caused us both to tire quickly. I appreciated the grandmother and her constant care for the last several days more than ever.

There was an old wind-up clock on the porch, and at around 11:00 P.M. we realized we must do something different to make it through the night, as we were both very tired. My companion again came up with an idea, "Why don't we take turns?" he said. "You sleep for an hour while I care for her, then I'll wake you and you care for her an hour while I sleep, then you wake me and so on. At least we'll get through the night that way."

"Fine," I said. "Who should start?"

"I'll start," he replied. "You rest first." So I lay down, and he started caring for her alone. At midnight he woke me and I fanned with one hand and sponged her forehead with the other until 1:00 A.M., then I woke him. He woke me at 2:00 A.M. and I again woke him at 3:00 A.M. I knew he would wake me for my next turn at 4:00 A.M. Even though I was very tired, I knew this was fair.

The next thing I remember is sunlight streaming into my eyes. I awakened, jumped up, and said, "What time is it?"

"It's six o'clock," my companion replied.

"Six o'clock! You were supposed to get me up at four o'clock! Why didn't you wake me?" I asked.

He had a broad smile on his face, which was intensified by the bright rays of the early morning sun. That smile seemed to come from deep within his soul and encompassed his whole being as he replied, "Oh, you looked so tired. I decided to let you sleep. It's my present to you. Merry Christmas!"

I couldn't say *anything.* I just looked at him in admiration and wondered, "Why don't I think of things like that or do things like that? My companion is a great man. God loves him. He stayed up for me. Why am I so weak?" I thought of the Savior coming to His sleeping disciples and asking, "Could ye not watch with me one hour?" (Matthew 26:40.) The Savior stayed up most of the night performing the greatest work of love in the world, while those close to Him slept. Yet, as He returned again and saw them sleeping, He merely looked at them and quietly said, "Sleep on."

I felt ashamed, yet I also felt happy as I could see the joy in my companion's face. He had such a radiant smile—it was almost angelic!

Sometime during those early morning hours, the girl's semi-delirious moaning ceased, her fever broke, and before long we could tell the crisis had passed. She stirred and opened her eyes. While she was still very weak, we knew she would be all right. We waited till midmorning, then knocked on the door to wake the grandmother. She answered the knock quickly, possibly expecting the worst. As she came out on the porch, her granddaughter was sitting up. We were all smiles as we said in unison, "Merry Christmas!" It was good to have her and her granddaughter both feeling so much better. We had many other things to do, so we left and went about our regular missionary activities. It was a wonderful way to start Christmas Day.

Over time I largely forgot about this experience. Many years later, however, I was asked to speak at the funeral for this faithful Tongan brother. He had lived a good life and had died of cancer. While speaking in Tongan, I suddenly received a flash of understanding which, while totally unsolicited, made a deep and clear impression on me. I emphasize that this was not a vision, revelation, or dream, but rather a feeling and an understanding wherein I sensed the following:

I saw a beautiful place with throngs of people anxiously waiting to get to a certain area. There was no pushing or shoving but rather a respectful and excited pressing forward to this particular place.

I saw a young man in the throng smiling and patiently moving along with the others. Suddenly his name was called, and someone in authority came, took him by the arm, and led him past the waiting crowds directly to the desired area. His guide said a few words to someone who seemed to control the entrance, and this person smiled and ushered the young man through the entrance.

Even though there were huge numbers of people waiting, everyone seemed to be aware of what had happened. People turned to one another and began to comment, not in anger or jealousy but rather in wonder and happiness for the young man who had gotten to that desirable place so quickly.

The guide came back and began waiting patiently with the

throngs of people. Someone leaned over and asked him about the young man. The guide whispered something to him and immediately the questioner's face lit up with a deep smile. He nodded his head approvingly and turned and told his neighbor. Almost instantly everyone seemed to know the answer. I strained to understand and finally heard someone say, "Oh, he let his companion sleep when he was very tired."

I offer no more explanation than what I have related. I learned that deeds of sacrifice, deeds of selflessness and honesty, deeds of effort in sincerely trying to help others, especially at the expense of one's own comfort, never go unnoticed by the powers of heaven.

# 50

## A Different Way of Thinking

In Ha'apai everyone worked hard. There was no welfare as we know it today from either church or state. Everyone helped whoever needed help, but this was done almost exclusively through the family. The term *kainga* (family) means a much broader, extended family than we usually think of. Everyone seemed to be related to everyone else and often claimed the privileges of that relationship. Of course, to claim the privileges on one side meant you were obligated to perform the duties on the other side, so there was a wonderful balance to the system. The thought of having someone just give you something was foreign to everyone. You worked for what you got, and you worked for what you gave to others as well.

Life was hard in one sense, yet fairly easy in another. I remember going to another island one time in our small sailboat with several men. Just before we got to the opening in the reef, we noticed a movement under some canvas at the front of the boat. It turned out to be the ten-year-old son of one of the men on the boat who had stowed away, hoping to come with us. I recalled trying to do the same (only in a car) as a young child and now felt some admiration for this young fellow for being so quiet for so long. There was certainly no turning back now as we were a long way from shore. I wasn't sure what his father would do.

Imagine my concern when the father picked the boy up, scolded him, and told him he couldn't miss school. He told him it was wrong to stow away, spanked him once, and then threw him into the ocean and yelled, "Now swim home and hurry up about it."

I tried to protest that it was a long way to shore, and he was a very small boy, but the father would hear nothing of it. "How will they learn if you give in?" he said. I mentioned that there could be cramps or dangerous fish and that we could go back if he wished. He steadfastly held course and didn't even look back as he said, "He'll be just fine, don't worry."

I did worry, but when we returned a few days later, the first person to greet us was this young boy. He was all smiles, especially for his dad, as I'm sure he was proud to show him he had made it. The father only briefly winked to me but said nothing. I should have learned more from this, I suppose, but it is hard for some of us *palangis* to not give in more.

On our sailboat I forbade ever carrying a harpoon. I explained that we were fishing or hunting for men, not whales. We often saw whales and sometimes went right among them and got very close to them, but we never chased or hurt them. In return, we were never chased, hurt, or even threatened by a whale. Whales are beautiful mammals. My respect for God's handiwork in the seas increased greatly.

Many of the island men did hunt whales—not for the blubber, but for the meat. When they harpooned one, it started a wild ride until the whale eventually tired and came to the surface. They would then finish it with a killer stick, a harpoon with a long, spearlike end. When the whale quit struggling, they would quickly dive in and try to sew up its mouth so it wouldn't swallow too much water and sink. They would then raise a flag as a signal, and someone with a motorboat would come out and haul the whale in. It hurt me when I saw a whale being hauled in to the reef closest to shore. They are such magnificent creatures!

On the other hand, it was always a wild and happy time when someone caught a whale, which didn't happen often. They pulled it to the reef and started butchering it. They cut the blubber away to get to the meat, which was sold by the pound to the anxious islanders. After a few hours, when most of the meat was cut out, the owners complied with the government requirement to haul the remains beyond the reef for the sharks to finish the disposal process.

Whales are so large that most of the meat was either salted, dried, or both. Of course, a lot was cooked and eaten right then, but salting seemed to be the main means of preservation (although I learned from experience that that form of preservation was not always very good).

To me, whale meat had a rather bland taste, more like beef than fish, but not much like either. I didn't like it and ate very little, except when there was no other option, such as when eating with a family.

I didn't learn any good whale recipes. In fact, I didn't learn any recipes at all, because the Saints wouldn't hear of me cooking my own meals. Food was always brought in, or I was asked to eat with other families. The same was true of washing and mending clothes, so I'm afraid I didn't become very self-reliant in those areas.

We wore short-sleeved white shirts, ties, and heavy-duty slacks. The native missionaries wore a *tupenu* and a *ta'ovola* (skirt with a woven sash) and went barefoot, but my first mission president told me I should always wear socks and at least sandals, so I did. Washing was done with strong lye soap and stones or corrugated washboards, so clothes wore out rapidly. The knees of my trousers always seemed worn. I had three or four patches on patches before I got out a new pair.

I remember when one of the sisters put a fourth patch over one knee, she told me she felt the trousers were so worn that I should get a new pair. They still looked fine to me, but when she said, "If you can't afford it, I and a few others will buy some cloth and sew you a new pair." I quickly got a new pair on my own.

Clothes were an interesting phenomena at that time. I remember talking to one of the wealthier men on the island who, though not a member, had donated a nice shirt to me. I thanked him for the shirt and commented that it was a nice, new shirt, but I seldom, if ever, saw him in new clothes. He asked me to sit down and talk for a bit. He told me he had plenty of means to buy new clothes, but explained, "If I wear new clothes, how do you think that would make the rest of the people feel? They would either try to get more new clothes, which they can't afford, or they would dislike me. I think both options are bad."

He then explained that even though he had the means, he felt that part of his duty to his people was to dress like they did so they would not be offended or jealous or try to do what wasn't really necessary. The people, though poor, were neat and clean, and he thought he should help with the tried-and-true theory: use it up, wear it out, make it do, or do without. I thought, "He is a good man."

This conversation had deep impact on me, and I tried to follow his theory and literally wore almost everything completely out. Ever since then it has been difficult for me to buy new shoes or clothes.

Even when people suggest my suit is quite shiny or my shoes are pretty worn, I hesitate to replace them because I feel there is still wear in them. I guess I remember too well how happy people were in Ha'apai with old but clean clothes.

Sometimes we hear the phrase, "Clothes make the man (or woman)," In our society there may be some truth to it. But at that time in Ha'apai, the Tongans realized that clothes did not make the man or woman—character did. They were not fooled by the ways of the world and realized that no amount of finery—clothes, makeup, rings, or jewelry—could compensate for something that wasn't actually there.

It made me think of the account in 3 Nephi 11:8 where the Savior, the greatest of all, appeared to the Nephites wearing a simple white robe. I suspect we ought to get used to simple clothing, as it appears to be the way of life after this one.

There were many other impressions made on my mind in those days. I remember coming back from a preaching tour and arriving in Pangai just at sunset. There were some people at the wharf and others on shore waiting. We got the boat tied up, and I went to our house. I put my things away and heard a quiet tapping. One of the neighbor ladies whispered that there was hot food and drink waiting for me at her home. I was hungry and thirsty, so I went to eat.

As we ate, I asked, "We have been gone a long time. Your husband was in the boat with us. Why weren't you at the wharf to meet us?"

She said, "Elder Groberg, listen carefully. You have much to learn. There are good reasons for some people to be at the wharf to meet you, but remember that people generally fall in three classes.

"There are those who will be at the wharf with broad smiles to meet you. If you do not know them well, beware of them, for they may take advantage of you. Then there are those who wait on the shore. They may help you if you ask, but often they are just looking for a chance to make money. Then there are those who stay home and cook a good meal for you to eat. They are your true friends. Many will appear to want to help, but few will actually be found helping. Trust them the most."

It may not be too profound, but it made a deep impression on me. I have found it to be largely true. Friendship or loyalty can only be measured by what we do for others, or what they do for us, not by what is offered only. Jesus not only offered his life as a ransom for all but also gave it.

I remember being very hungry at one time and being given a banana to eat. I peeled it and started to eat while standing. Someone quickly asked me to sit down. I did, and later asked why. They explained that in Tongan culture one of the worst breaches of etiquette was *kaitu'u* (to eat while standing). The idea is that food is from God and is often fixed by others after much effort. The Tongans feel that to show respect to God and to the preparers, we should take the time to sit down and enjoy the food. If we are in such a hurry that we feel we must eat standing—or as we say, "eat on the run"—then according to their customs, we shouldn't eat. In other words, if we haven't time to show respect and enjoy the food, we aren't worthy of it. I suspect there are some health overtones here as well. That Tongan custom is at the other extreme of our "fast food" concept, which seems such a part of Western culture. I grew up in a large family, and I learned to eat fast, more out of self-preservation than anything, so I have appreciated the ameliorating influence of this Tongan custom about food and eating.

In Western cultures we give offense if we burp during or following a nice meal. In Tonga, at least back then, you showed respect or appreciation for the meal by burping. That was the sign that it was good and you enjoyed it. Some say the louder and longer the burp, the greater the show of appreciation, although I never found that to be the case. A simple heartfelt (stomachfelt?) burp did the job nicely.

Some of the things Tongans valued most were grace and loyalty, usually expressed in singing, dancing, and speaking. They were great orators, dancers, and singers. Many have said that Tongans are born with perfect pitch, graceful movements, and silver tongues. I doubt that, but they were born into a society where they grew up learning those things. Both men and women danced, sang, and even preached with the same vigor.

I often watched *laka laka* (line dancing) practice, performed by residents of a particular village where literally the whole population participated. I saw small children and teenagers imitating the graceful movements of their parents. Behind the line of active dancers was a group of singers made up of older people, nursing mothers, or others who for whatever reason were not dancing, at least at that time.

I looked at those small children and even the nursing infants and realized that from their earliest days they were hearing music, harmony, and rhythm, and watching and participating in graceful dance movements—it just became part of them. Under those circumstances, you could say it did come naturally or at least was second nature.

*Group dancing and singing like this* laka laka *was an all-community event. Stories were told and praise given through this medium.*

I remember late one evening seeing a mother dancing gracefully, and singing beautifully with a village group. Her whole body was swaying in perfect coordination. One arm was following exactly the outlined routine, fingers curling, then extending in a symphony of beauty that would be hard to duplicate. Her other arm was cradling a newborn infant, who was nursing with closed eyes and bearing a look of perfect contentment.

As I watched for a few moments, I realized where those Tongans got their natural instinct for music and graceful movements, and how loyalty to family and community were part and parcel of living. There is much to learn from this island people.

# 51

## *The Governor*

I had not been in Ha'apai very long when people started asking if I had met the governor. I had not met him and actually was a little afraid to do so. I had been told he was a fine man but, along with others, was quite anti-Mormon. I had seen him from a distance a few times and noticed that one of his legs was somewhat withered, so he walked with a limp.

Before long it became evident that I would have to eventually meet and talk to him, so I made an appointment and decided to get it over with. I arrived in the best clothes I had. As I met him, I realized how much he outshined me in his brilliant white outfit with brass buttons, and elaborate *ta'ovola,* and his many well-dressed aides who moved quickly at his slightest request.

I was duly impressed and somewhat intimidated by the finery of the setting and the formality of all that went on. Fortunately, over and above all of that, I had a feeling that he was basically a good man and that I liked him. I knew that feeling came from God, and I was grateful for it.

He asked me to be seated and soon had his servants bringing biscuits and drinks. He said, "I am having tea, but you'd better not as I am sure someone would report you." Though he said it rather matter-of-factly, I sensed a slight smile. He asked the servants to bring me orange juice. Now I knew I was going to like him. The initial "ice" of formality was broken.

We visited quite easily for a long time. That first meeting turned into a continuous series of conversations, during which I felt I had been given a good friend. Even though he disagreed with the Church and could even in some ways be considered anti-Mormon, he was kind and helpful to me.

He often called me over "just to visit." He was very pro-Methodist and quite open about being opposed to the proselyting program of the Mormon Church. His opposition was not based on doctrine but on history. He explained to me that the first Wesleyan (Methodist) missionaries to arrive in Tonga were killed by the natives, then the next missionaries were run out, and others suffered a great deal before they finally got a foothold. He felt that "his" church had paid the price, and they ought to get the rewards. He felt we were sort of interlopers; as he said, "You come in and take away our sheep, and what price have you paid?"

I explained that several of our missionaries had died in Tonga, not from being killed but from illness. I mainly tried to explain that with religion, it isn't a question of finder's rights but rather a question of truth.

Almost every time I would approach an issue from a doctrinal or scriptural point of view, he would counter with a historical fact, and since he was so much smarter in history than I was, I didn't get very far. I often bore my testimony, but it didn't seem to affect him much.

He was a good teacher, and I almost felt like I was taking an advanced Tongan history class. During one of our conversations, he brought up a historical situation that I was not familiar with. When he saw I didn't know much about it, he said, "If you don't know history, you don't know much." For some reason that triggered a thought, and I responded, "I know more about the history of your forefathers than you will ever know!"

That got his attention. He asked what I meant and how I knew anything about his forefathers. Up to that point I hadn't said much because I didn't know much about the history of the first kings in Tonga or the first missionaries, or the interesting interaction between them that he had so carefully explained to me.

I told him about the Book of Mormon and explained some of the history of the real "first kings" of the Tongans. It turned out that someone had given him a copy of the Book of Mormon years before, but he had never read it and had no idea what it was about as it was a deluxe gift-type book, and he didn't want to get it dirty, so I gave him another "working copy" and we started studying it together.

We spent many evenings, sometimes long into the night, reading and discussing the Book of Mormon. His advisors sometimes got a little perturbed and came in and said, "We must go over this case or this bill or this proposal with you now. We have a court date tomorrow." I tried to leave, but nearly always he would tell them, "Can't you see I am talking with the Mormon missionary? Leave me alone. I'll get to those things when I am through here."

He gave me no quarter and argued about some of the things we read. I tried not to argue back but bear my testimony and explain that the book speaks for itself. He was a good student of culture and history, and every once in a while he would acknowledge, "Yes that makes sense. That's probably right."

While he was friendly to me, I felt he was quite hard on the Church. He defined this opposition as being "correct" and didn't allow us any extra privileges. For instance, he had an official government boat, but he wouldn't allow us, as missionaries, to ride on it, since it was only for official government use. When I told him I noticed some of the preachers from *his* church riding on it, he just changed the subject.

The captain of his launch also felt it was unfair not to allow us to ride, so when he knew the government boat was going someplace we wanted to go, this captain would leave the wharf and send word to tell us to be down the island a ways. He would pull in close to the shore there, and we would paddle out in a canoe, get on board, and go with him. Before long people told the governor what was happening, and the captain got reprimanded and warned severely. The governor never said anything to me about this, so we continued to ride on the boat occasionally. Our schedule seldom coincided with the government boat schedule, but when they went to distant islands, we often tried to go with them.

As unofficial passengers on these trips, we had many hours, even days, to talk to the captain. He asked us, "Why do they hate you so much?" I told him I didn't know, but maybe if I explained to him what we believed, he could see for himself what they didn't like. He agreed so we gave him all the discussions and used those hours of travel to answer his questions. Eventually he began to believe and asked us to visit him and his family in his home. The word got around that he was pretty friendly with the Mormons, and he was warned again to stop visiting with us, but he continued.

We baptized the captain and his family one Saturday and confirmed them members on Sunday. Monday when he went to work, there was a package containing his personal belongings and a note saying he was fired and not to come to work anymore. He told me about this and said he felt it was coming, but it did not matter as he now had the truth, and with God on his side, he would be okay.

I told the governor how unfair I thought his firing of the captain was, and he basically told me to mind my own business, so we dropped it. In some ways I thought the governor was a hard man, but I still felt he was basically a good man. We maintained our friendship. The captain struggled for a while, but remained faithful, eventually got another job, and things worked out well for him.

At that time, nearly everyone we baptized remained faithful—mainly because there was so much pressure against the Church that there was no turning back once you made the commitment. Some think it is great today to not have so much persecution against the Church, and I suppose it is. But I can see the other side, such as having so many "less-active" now, whereas back then, there were virtually none. I have a feeling that everyone must endure testing or "persecution" sometime, someway, in their life, either before baptism or after or both. Only the faithful will make it, and I guess it does not matter a lot when that persecution or test comes. What does matter is that we remain faithful.

In those days when the government passed laws, they would disseminate them by sending them to each governor, who in turn would take his boat and go around to the different islands and read the laws to the people. It was like the old town-crier system. Each district and each little village had a *pule fakavahe* (district officer) and *pule fakakolo* (town officer) who called the people together for the governor and who was expected to enforce the laws.

Not long after firing the captain, the governor's boat broke down. It was bad timing for him as he had just received a set of new laws from the palace and needed to read them right away on the various islands under his governorship. He called me over and asked if he could use our Church launch to go around and read these laws. I reminded him how he hadn't let us ride his boat, how he chastised the captain when we rode with him, and how he had fired the captain when he joined the Church. "Yes, I know, I'm sorry," he said. "That wasn't my doing; those were directions from above me."

I assumed he was telling the truth, and I still had a good feeling towards him but nevertheless said, "No, the boat is strictly for Church work, I am sorry, but those are my instructions," which was true. I left his office and returned home feeling a little sorry for the governor, but also a little like justice had been served.

I felt uncomfortable that evening. As I said my prayers, I wondered what kind of bread I was casting on the water. I seemed to hear the Savior talking about returning good for evil, but I thought, "Who am I to change the policy?" I couldn't figure out why I continued to feel uncomfortable. The whole situation smacked so perfectly of poetic justice. Still, I didn't sleep well that night.

Fortunately, the next day he sent for me again and said, "Look, I'm desperate. I've got to get these laws out. I'll lose my job, and if they assign someone else up here, that will be worse for you than anything. At least we're friends. Can't you please make an exception? I'll pay whatever you ask."

I didn't think I should make an exception, but I felt I had better do some explaining. As I started to explain the policy, a flood of light came to my mind, and I knew exactly what to say, "Look, your Honor, I'll make you a deal. The boat has to be used for Church work. I can't rent it out. But just now I have decided to make a preaching tour to the very islands you want to go to, and you can come along. You can't pay rent in money, so here's what the rent will be: when we get to the islands, you call all the people together and tell them that there is a lot of business and they have to stay for two hours, instead of the normal one hour. Tell them the first hour will be the *faifono* (reading of the new laws), but then they must stay another hour and listen to the Mormon missionary, because it is his boat and you must comply with his regulations. Tell them if they don't stay and listen, I won't take you to the next island and you will be in trouble." He swallowed hard, but I suppose because he had no other choice and was desperate to read the laws, he agreed.

We left the next morning for the first island. Through the town officer, the governor called all the people together and told them exactly what we had agreed. When he finished his hour, he repeated, "Now it's the Mormon missionary's hour. None of you leave, and I'm not leaving either." I got up and explained what I felt were the most important principles of the gospel. I bore testimony of the Savior, of Joseph Smith, of the Book of Mormon, and of living prophets and priesthood authority.

I sensed that some people were angry and not willing to listen, but they stayed. Others, however, listened intently. While we didn't baptize anyone on that trip, many members have since told me that they probably never would have listened to the missionaries had it not been for that introduction. The Lord does move in mysterious ways.

We continued our rounds, and on island after island the governor, as well as the people, sat through the preaching. He set a good example and kept his word. We concluded with a big feast on each island. We basically ate the same type of food over and over and never tired of it as we were hungry each time. I realized that we, including the governor, were also having a spiritual feast and hearing the same principles and testimonies over and over and not tiring of them either, because we hungered spiritually each time.

Sometimes we forget that the basic spiritual food we need is composed of the first principles and ordinances of the gospel—faith in the Lord, Jesus Christ; repentance through Him; baptism by His authority; the gift of the Holy Ghost to testify of Him; and enduring faithfully in Him to the end of our lives. These are the most important things, just as taro, rice, potatoes, or bread sustain life and also allow us to enjoy some of the desserts, which may be pleasant but which without the nutrition of the basics have no power to sustain life on their own, physically or spiritually.

We had only visited a few islands when the government sent up another boat from Nuku'alofa for the governor to use. I don't know if they found out what was happening or just had an extra boat. The governor didn't say anything and I never asked him. We had, however, been to several of the most difficult islands, and I felt we had been able to do things we could not have done any other way.

After this trip with the governor, I noticed our conversations became a little less frequent, but also a little deeper. He had heard truth enough times that he was wondering. Soon after this, he told me he had diabetes quite badly and knew he was dying.

He came close a time or two to acknowledging his understanding but could never quite make it all the way. He did tell me he felt the Book of Mormon was the correct history of his forebearers. One time he told me that he would be fired immediately if he ever joined the Mormons or even showed too much sympathy for them. He felt for his health's sake and for his family's sake, and even for tradition's sake, he must stay where he was.

It was interesting how the roles changed during the year and a half that I knew him. I first came to his office scared and overwhelmed with his dignity and power. He was an official who could grant or withhold favors, and I was the outsider wondering what to do. But as

I prepared to leave Ha'apai, I had a good friend. We talked openly and with a degree of friendliness that belied the big difference in age.

At times he in effect asked for help to understand his feelings and to have the strength to do what he ought to do. I pleaded with him to act on what I felt he knew was true, but he was always the governor and had the pride of generations of fierce warriors and rulers in his veins. He never took additional steps, but when I left Ha'apai, I had a good, loving feeling toward him. I believe that feeling was mutual.

He died shortly after I left Ha'apai. I feel sure he at least had a testimony of the Book of Mormon. He never would admit it publicly but told me on more than one occasion that Tongans were descendants of Israel and this was the record of their forefathers. It was hard for him to acknowledge things publicly, but he was still a good man and a good friend. I wish I could have helped him more. Maybe I still can. I hope someone is. I sometimes wonder how they get around in the hereafter. I'd love to go on another law-reading–preaching circuit with him sometime.

# 52

## "The Best £10 I Ever Spent"

We continued working hard each day and always felt there was more to do than hours to do it in. It is a good feeling to be busily engaged in important work. One evening I received a telegram from the mission president stating that he would be staying overnight in Ha'apai on his way to Vava'u and he needed to hold a Church disciplinary council for one of our prominent members. He asked me to contact this man, tell him of the charges, and ask him to be present with any witnesses he wanted on the designated evening.

A few days later, we met the mission president and one of his counselors at the wharf and helped them get settled in the guest house. After supper we all went to the chapel where he was to hold the disciplinary council. He did not ask me or his counselor to take part, but decided to handle it by himself. I asked no questions as I knew he was in charge.

There was a fair amount of excitement about this case as the person involved was well known and basically everyone knew what was going on. It was next to impossible to keep any event like this from both the members and nonmembers. In these small islands, it seems that everyone knows everything about everyone else.

We all waited outside and visited with the many people who were milling around the chapel that evening. Occasionally the mission president would ask someone to come in and tell what they knew about the situation. Speculation was abundant. The man in question was in the chapel for a long time with the mission president. Finally the woman involved went in, and we felt it would soon be over. We were all aware of the charges and what had actually taken place.

After what seemed like forever, the door opened and the mission president, the man, the woman, and a couple of others came out. I asked what had happened because I needed to know what to do with this man.

I was shocked, as was everyone else, when the mission president said I could use him any way I wished as he had been found "not guilty." I asked the president why, and he replied, "There was insufficient evidence. You probably should leave him and this girl and the whole situation alone. I have handled it and, so as far as I'm concerned, it's over."

I couldn't figure out what had happened, because the evidence seemed so clear. I was afraid this would be a setback to the forward momentum in terms of proper living that was occurring in Ha'apai. However, since he was the mission president and his instructions were very clear, I decided not to worry about it and go on about my duties. I was confident the Lord would continue to help us.

The mission president left for Vava'u the next morning. Almost immediately after he left, several people came and told me what had happened. It seems this man knew he was guilty, as did everyone else, so he went around and pleaded with people to not testify against him. The girl involved came from a poor family, and he gave her £10 (about $50, which was a large sum then) if she would reverse her testimony and say he was innocent. She did and he was not disciplined, at least not by that council.

The man made the somewhat boastful comment, "That was the best ten pounds I ever spent." He knew he was guilty and knew that everyone else knew he was guilty, and he felt he had really "put one over" on the mission president.

Several people came to me and said, "He can fool a *palangi*, but he can't fool us. Why don't you talk to the president and tell him what happened?" I told them the mission president had asked me to leave it alone, so that was what I was going to do.

"But he can't just get away with it," they cried.

"Of course he can't," I responded. "God is the ultimate judge. He knows the truth. This man knows the truth. He is trying to deceive the Lord. He will not be successful. You can fool other people, but you can't fool God. Watch him and learn a great lesson. You cannot lie and be successful, at least not in God's ways, and those are the only ways that count." So everyone dropped it because I asked them to, as I had been instructed. It did not seem to affect our forward progress, in fact, it probably helped because the deception was so blatant.

I watched that man, not only for the balance of my time in Ha'apai but also later as I served as mission president, then Regional Representative, then as a General Authority. He eventually moved from Ha'apai and then left Tonga altogether.

He stayed active in the sense of coming to meetings but never was able to do much in the Church or in a profession. He seemed so capable, but each time he was about to accomplish something, a strange twist would occur, things would fall apart, and he'd be right back where he started. It was as though there was a lid above him that he kept hitting against and above which he could not rise.

We talked occasionally, but he refused to acknowledge his problems as having any other cause than "bad luck" or "someone else interfering." I tried from time to time to explain that it was not "bad luck" but his own bad performance that was at the root of his problems.

"You can't try to cheat God and still think straight," I told him. I tried to help him understand that his bad performance was not only what he did first but possibly even more his refusal to properly repent from it. I told him, "We all make mistakes, but we should not compound those mistakes by trying to hide them. The greatest mistake any of us make is to not repent and acknowledge our errors to God, to ourselves, and to others when necessary."

Some people look upon repentance as a negative thing or something used only when we do wrong things. I remember a story I heard of a Mia Maid teacher who asked her students what the first step of repentance was. One of the girls on the front row quickly responded, "The first thing you do is commit sin, so you have something to repent of." I suspect a lot of people have that feeling, and hence they look upon their leaders' constant call to repent as a negative, judgmental call. The fact is, we all do wrong things and need to repent from our negative actions. But if the celestial kingdom is our goal, and all we do is cancel out our negative behavior through repentance, how will we ever make our goal?

I tried to explain to him that repentance is improvement. It is positive change. It is coming closer to God. I drew the following chart.

Life →

+ Celestial Kingdom

+ Good Actions

Point Zero

- Bad Actions

I told him that if we only use repentance to go from negative be-havior back to point zero, we're still a long way from our goal. He once asked me, "Are you telling me we can repent from good things?" I responded, "Yes, if we can do them better. If we are doing anything either good or bad, and can improve, we need to do so. That is repen-tance. The gift of repentance comes from God, and He is just as anx-ious to help us improve on the positive side of the equation as He is to get us out of Satan's side."

He still refused to accept my counsel and said I was "judging." I tried to explain that this was not true and that by asking people to re-pent we are just inviting people to improve their lives, no matter where they are. It is easy to tell we still have improvement to make, for we are still here in mortality. Those who feel they don't need to repent, just don't understand. To say we don't need to repent is to say we are perfect, and that isn't true and won't be true until we have repented fully. We can never cover sin, only repent of it. There is no other way of getting rid of it.

He listened and thought for a while, but finally repeated again that he had been cleared by the mission president so I should "leave him alone."

He was never successful in anything. Right to the end of his life, he felt he had fooled someone, not realizing he had only fooled him-self. There were times when he seemed almost ready to open up and acknowledge the truth, but he never quite got around to it and even-tually he passed away. I imagine he is in the process of "getting around to it" now and realizes that you can't fool God. I was not available to attend his funeral, but as I heard about it, I thought what a sad under-utilization of talent this man's life had become. That old devil called pride seemed to have carried off another victim.

All meaningful progress is based on honest repentance. The more sincere the repentance, the greater the progress made. As I thought of his vastly underutilized life, I thought of the scriptures that tell us we are to preach nothing but repentance to this generation (for example, see D&C 6:9; 11:9).

I guess I wasn't too effective, for as far as I know, he left this life never acknowledging the real problem. I hope he has by now. I have often felt that his statement, "That was the best ten pounds I ever spent," should be, and maybe now is, "That was the worst ten pounds I ever spent."

# 53

## Baby-sitting and Other Activities

The Queen of Tonga had two sons. The oldest, Tungi, was the crown prince. He and his wife, Mata'aho, occasionally came to Ha'apai and stayed in the royal summer home by the harbor. Normally they were on vacation retreat and stayed about a fortnight (two weeks).

When they heard there was a *palangi* missionary in Ha'apai, they invited me over to visit. They were very kind, helpful, and supportive, and I enjoyed visiting with them. We eventually became good friends and had many meals and discussions together.

Sometimes they asked me to help with their children. I didn't really baby-sit in the sense of feeding them or getting them ready for bed, because they had servants who did that. But I played games, read stories, and generally entertained them several times when their parents went out for various functions.

Princess Mata'aho jokingly told me that there is no "free lunch," so reading stories to her children was how I paid for the meals they gave me. I became quite attached to their lovely children, particularly the two oldest, Tupouto'a (now the crown prince) and Pilolevu (the king's oldest daughter).

Nine years later, on the death of his mother, Tungi became King Taufa'ahau Tupou IV and, of course, Mata'aho became the queen. Tupouto'a and Pilolevu have grown, and Pilolevu now has four children of her own. We have maintained a good friendship throughout the years.

I remember once telling them the story of "Goldilocks and the Three Bears." I had told it many times before, but this particular time Pilolevu stopped me at a certain place and said, "That isn't right."

"What do you mean it isn't right? I'm the one telling the story."

She surprised me by saying, "I know that isn't right because that's not the way you told it yesterday! Here's how it should go . . ." She then repeated almost word for word what I had said the day before.

I thought, "She's a sharp girl! These are smart children! I'd better write things down so I tell them the same way each time." It was a fun association and has been helpful to all of us on many occasions over the years. Their kindness to me, as all kindnesses shown to anyone, will never go unnoticed or unrewarded by the powers of heaven.

Once the mission president sent me a local missionary who had been dubbed as lazy. He requested that I try to use him in the school or someplace where he didn't have to do much, and see if I could salvage his mission. I came to like this young man, who seemed to want to try but tired easily and was short of energy. He worked as well as he could and helped some in the school.

After a few months, I received a note that he should be transferred to another district. He cried and said he didn't want to go, but was faithful and obedient and left for his new assignment. I'll never forget the look in his yellowish eyes as he bid me farewell and clearly said, "I'll see you in heaven." He died of yellow jaundice two months after leaving Ha'apai. Regular health care was not very advanced at that time. How glad I was in this particular case that the Lord never allowed the term *lazy* to cross my mind!

We had very little in Ha'apai. There were stores, but their shelves were mostly bare. Whenever we got a package from home or from mission headquarters, we untied the string, undid the various knots, and wound it into a ball for future use. We never considered cutting the string or tearing the wrapping. The brown paper was always carefully taken off, folded, and saved for future use. There were no magazines or newspapers, and every scrap of anything that looked like it might be useful was saved.

I remember watching young children having great fun with a stick and some rocks or a coconut shell, which they pushed through the dirt and sand. If they ever got a can or a bottle to push around, they squealed with delight as though they had received the latest toy craze. They laughed and ran and pushed and smiled in such heartfelt glee that I wondered if we, with our doll houses and computer games, can even come close to their joy.

In Ha'apai much of the tithing and fast offerings was paid "in kind," i.e., coconuts or chickens or pigs or *ufi*. Some was paid in coin also, and we tried to sell what produce we received for coin. It took

considerable time to account for everything paid as tithing, fast offerings, budget, and building funds. We had very little problem with
stealing, but still we generally took the money to the post office the
Monday after we received it.

One evening we returned quietly and unexpectedly and found
one of the older students rifling the tithing and fast offerings funds. It
was a shock to me. He put it all back and I assigned one of the good
schoolteachers to work with him. He became a model student and, as
far as I know, overcame that terrible problem of taking things that
weren't his. How grateful I was for the teacher who willingly took the
challenge and saved a boy.

I had many opportunities to be involved in a variety of activities,
from legal work to real estate negotiations to building supervisor. At
various times I wrote home:

"The mission president can't come and has asked me to be his official representative for the ground-breaking ceremony next Tuesday. It
will be a big occasion as the whole island will be there. The mission
president has also given me the money and the authority to make a
deal on some other land so I am going to get some practical real estate
business experience. I like that kind of work. Land is very valuable,
even on these remote islands, especially if more than one person
wants it. There are many factors to be taken into consideration, but
the main one is fairness.

"I think that I have been blessed with much valuable experience
here and I feel that the times that weren't so pleasant have been some
of the most valuable.

"As the work gets harder and more prolonged, more and more of
the people I trusted fall out until there are very few whom I can really
rely on. But they are the very best. The business of leading in the
Church is really hard at times."

Later I wrote:

"One of the Tongan missionaries jumped on an old Ford tractor
without permission and started to bring things from the wharf to the
Church for the building project. It has a hydraulic lift with a scoop in
the front, which someone jumped in and was hoisted up to pick some
coconuts to drink. We were eating when all of a sudden we heard a
cry from about a block away. I jumped up and ran down there as fast
as I could, and sure enough there had been an accident. The scoop
had come loose and dropped the fellow that was riding in it and he
had been run over by the tractor. The driver, who had tried to get out

*The Royal Family.*
*Queen Salote in the center, Prince Tungi*
*and Princess Mata'aho on the left, and*
*Prince Tu'ipelehake and Princess Melenaite*
*on the right.*

of his way, had run into a store and torn off part of the veranda that had fallen on him and knocked him out. The driver was just stunned and shocked, but the other fellow looked in pretty bad shape. Accidents are sure unpleasant things. I thought that the fellow who had been run over was dead, as he looked pretty broken up and bloody, but we rushed him to the hospital where he first gained consciousness and asked for administration and was quite miraculously found to be free from any serious breaks or fractures, only bad bruises. It turned out that the driver had no license, so he will have to go to court. I, being the official Church representative in Ha'apai, will have to handle the Church's case. I have also had to make the adjustments for the damages done to the store and have really had a good experience out of it all. These two new missionaries that just arrived bring the total up to 40 missionaries in the district, and it is a full-time job looking after them."

# 54

## *Emotions at Sea*

There is a tremendous amount of emotion involved whenever you deal with the sea or with ocean travel. I remember one day assigning a group of seven priesthood brethren to go to a small island and get some special sand for some building we were doing. I stayed home as I had to teach school. The day started out fine, but by afternoon it became very stormy. About the time the boat was due back, a huge storm hit. The winds shrieked, the clouds thickened, and darkness hid the sun. Six of the seven men were married, and their wives and families were very concerned.

I went to the shore with the wives and mothers and other family members to see if we could see the men, but we could see nothing. The weather seemed to be getting worse, and the boat was long overdue. We looked and listened so hard our eyes and ears actually hurt, but despite all our efforts and prayers, nothing happened. The emotions I felt from those women and children were indescribable. I tried to comfort and encourage them.

Another hour or two went by, and still no boat. Some were resigned to the worst; others maintained hope; all prayed fervently. Seldom did boats come in after dark, and it was now pitch black and hard to see anything. Some suggested that we return home, but most said they would stay through the night. I felt I should stay. I was the one who had asked them to go.

I can't fully describe the sinking feeling of helplessness I had. It was as though I was hollow inside. Even though nothing was said, I sensed the feeling among some of those women: "You're God's servant. If there was danger, why did you ask them to go?" I didn't know what would happen but tried to calm and assure them that all would be well. I prayed fervently and felt a heavy responsibility. *Had I acted rashly?* I hoped not. I pleaded with God not to hurt those families for my mistakes. I wished I had gone with them. I was very torn emotionally, but eventually, after deep wrestling of the spirit, I began to feel a peace that things would be okay.

For that whole night, we jumped at every unusual sound as a possibility of hope, only to have it fade away to nothing. Finally towards morning a distant shout was heard. It was a long way off, but every ear strained and every person perked up. Several minutes passed . . . nothing. Then again a distant cry, *"Oku 'ife'ae uafu?"* (Where is the wharf?)

Everyone was up now—eyes peered into the darkness, hearts pounded in anticipation and love. A chorus of voices went up—some crying, others yelling, some almost hysterical, others calmly calling, "The wharf is over here!" Kerosene lanterns flickered brighter as wicks were raised and chimneys cleaned. Again a voice, somewhat closer now, *"Oku 'ife'ae uafu?"* Then came back and forth communication and identification. It was them—they were back! In the understatement of the year, their leader said, "We had a bit of a hard time getting back, but we have the sand for the Lord's chapel."

As the sailboat was tied to the wharf, the men came ashore and were greeted by their wives and other family members. I'm not sure I have ever felt a stronger feeling of love, faith fulfilled, and gratitude to God for His help. Needless to say, everyone was relieved at the close of that nearly all-night vigil.

I can relate to the all-night vigil in the final scene of the opera *Madame Butterfly.* Fortunately, this vigil in Ha'apai had a happier ending, but the emotions felt have something in common. I guess we need to experience those types of feelings to even glimpse what God might feel as so many of His loved ones seem so lost in the darkness of evil. I can understand a little the feeling in the scripture that says, "How great is his joy in the soul that repenteth" (comes out of darkness and returns back home) (D&C 18:13). I felt this great joy in Pangai when husbands and sons came out of the dark into the arms of their loved ones and returned home safely.

Emotions are powerful things, and deep feelings are not soon forgotten. I learned that emotions need to be directed in the right way, but anyone who says he needs to go outside of religion to express his emotions has never felt the full power of true faith and pure love for God that is completely within religion. It is all-encompassing.

# 55

## "*Tahi Kula*"

One day I woke to the cry, "*Tahi kula, tahi kula*" ("Red tide, red tide"). I had never heard this before and wondered what it meant. One of the islands in Ha'apai is a fairly active volcano, and earth tremors were a common occurrence. Some of the tremors were quite strong, but most were mild. The people explained to me that once in a while a seismic movement sucks the tide way out (red tide), and everyone runs to the shore. For the islanders, a red tide is a food hunter's paradise as the tide goes out so fast and so far that it leaves pools of water full of fish and other sea life ready for the grabbing.

I noticed, however, that no one went out very far. I was told that if they went out too far, they might get caught, because when the tide comes in, it does so very rapidly. I was amazed at the discipline I observed: they simply did not go beyond a certain point no matter how tempting the next pool was. I was also amazed at how quickly the tide came roaring in and realized that had they not stayed close to shore, some would surely have been lost. The young people stayed close to their mothers and other family members, and I realized again what a different way of thinking was being inculcated into them because of the circumstances of their upbringing.

Many times I was reminded of the advantages and disadvantages of these rather small, close-knit societies where everyone knows everything about everyone else. One of the advantages was the almost total absence of crime, for if someone did something wrong everyone knew about it. Another plus was the feeling of loyalty to, and identity with, family and community. Another positive was the clear understanding of what was expected of you and exactly how you fit in. Everyone fit into the picture someway or another. Some liked it, some did not. I suppose all people have these same feelings to some degree.

One negative was the frustration felt by those whose personalities didn't seem to fit the mold they were placed in. Some felt very oppressed by everyone knowing everything about them. This group often desired to get away and be on their own.

Occasionally a Tongan would return to Ha'apai with tales of the outside world, of cars and big cities, of working and getting lots of money, and of living in places where people don't know you and even ignore you and leave you alone. To some that seemed terrifying, to others it seemed like paradise.

I suppose one of the reasons some Tongans have problems when they go to big cities is the lack of the close societal structure that is so effective in the islands and so lacking in big cities. To be nameless and unknown is foreign to their background, so gangs and other forms of false closeness loom large for some.

As I read the scriptures, the eventual society we are striving for appears to be much closer to the Tongan society I knew in the mid-50s than our aloof, secretive, everyone-do-their-own-thing society of big-city life in the 1990s. If God knows our thoughts, actions, and even the intents of our hearts (see Alma 18:32), which He does, then we ought to get used to being open in our dealings and not try to appear to be something we are not.

I can understand why Jesus spoke harshly against hypocrites, not only in His day but in all days. When any of us try to cover our sins, mask our vain ambitions, or exercise control, dominion, or compulsion on anyone in any degree of unrighteousness, including deceit in any way (see D&C 121:39–42), we have no chance of getting any real power, for true power comes only from God and is given based on faith and obedience, not on appearances or smooth talking. He wants us to have this power, but it is only available as we position our lives in perfect harmony with His commandments.

This positioning comes a little at a time. This "line upon line" process may appear to be frustrating and slow—at least Satan tries to convince us it is—but if we have faith (recognizing God's hand in our lives) and humility (willingness to acknowledge our errors and our need for help) and constantly repent (improve), we can adjust to that celestial society here and hereafter. Again, I feel that when this ideal is achieved, it will be closer to the Tongan model I knew than the models we seem to espouse today.

I felt so good as I heard the Tongans sing in such beauty and watched them dance with such joy and unity. I had the feeling that what we are striving for will contain more singing, dancing, grace, and loyalty than many of us are used to. Maybe they will feel more at home and these things will seem more natural to the Tongans—and to all Polynesians and others who have been raised under the circumstances I have mentioned.

The Tongan outlook on the human body was also interesting to me. Those born with deformities or mental problems were considered part of the overall society and accepted for what they were. They were generally treated with respect and loving care.

People's weaknesses (especially of the body) were accepted quite openly. There were plenty of sins committed, just as there are in any society, but I noted much less hypocrisy or attempted covering up of these sins among the Tongans. Some say the Polynesians generally are more lax morally than people in our western culture. I don't believe it. I feel that when all the truth comes out, which it will eventually, in these things the Tongans will compare very favorably to other cultures. My experience was that living God's moral laws had much more to do with the individual than with the culture.

The Tongans look upon the body not only as the housing of our spirits but also as a means of expressing gratitude to God for all he gives us. Thus, their skillful and beautiful dancing and singing, done with such grace and finesse, can at times become another testimony and means of praising God. They are also great orators and wonderful poets, and no Tongan is worth his salt who cannot quote several poems. Of course, some are much better than others.

Being heavy was considered a plus rather than a minus. I remember some friends asking me to go to a movie so I could interpret for them. The mission president had not said anything about not going, and the movies were high class then, so I went along with nearly everyone on the island. In those days going to a movie was a big event that seldom occurred. There was never a movie on Niuatoputapu, and I remember only this one in Ha'apai, which was shown outside with a generator for power and a sheet for a screen.

My friends were interested in this movie as they had heard it featured a lovely American movie star, who was supposed to be very beautiful. As the movie proceeded, they kept asking me where the beautiful lady was. I kept pointing her out, but they thought I had made a mistake. When the movie was about half over they finally accepted that she was the "beautiful" lady, but they felt deceived. They turned to me and said, "She's not beautiful. She's skinny!"

I tried to explain that in our society, this lady was the ideal model of desirability for American men. They were aghast. A rough translation of what they said is: "Surely American men are smarter than that. Surely they want a *wife* and not a *doll!* Surely they are smart enough to know that dolls are a 'dime a dozen,' but a good wife and mother is worth her weight in gold." I couldn't say much, so I just listened.

As a missionary I had little to do with romance and marriage, except for performing a lot of marriages and giving some counsel when asked. Often young men would ask me what I thought of So-and-So as a possible wife. Those who were members of the Church looked for strength of testimony first, but a close second was the perceived ability to bear children and remain healthy. Being thin was a definite drawback to them.

I remember listening with sadness several times as a young man would say, "Oh, I couldn't marry her, she's too thin," or "She appears unhealthy." I tried to persuade them that other qualities were more important and that thin girls could have babies too, but the mind set was pretty strong and my reasoning didn't make much of an impression. I suppose they were reflecting some of their Israelite background. I recalled a passage from the Old Testament—Proverbs 31:30: "Favour is deceitful, and beauty is vain: but a woman that feareth the Lord, she shall be praised."

Having children and families was very important to the Tongans. Most families were large and united. It was common to have six, eight, ten, or a dozen children. I know several families with more than twenty children from one mother. There were no unwanted or uncared-for children. Even those born out of wedlock were taken in by the extended family and cared for as any other.

Often children were "given away," but in a different way than it sounds. Many Westerners look on this practice with horror, but when you consider the circumstances it is easier to understand. For instance, if a couple could not have children, some of their relatives who had lots of children would "give" them one or two to raise as a *pusiaki* (sort of like adoption). Being a *pusiaki* was no different than being any other type of child.

Once I mentioned something a little negative about giving a child to be raised by someone else, and the couple giving the child said, "But you don't understand! We're all together. We trust our sister, who can't have children naturally. Our son will be raised right." Then they put me to silence by saying, "Would your culture actually be so cruel as to allow a couple to go through life without children when it's so simple to fulfill that need for them? God wants us to help one another and take care of our own, and that includes *all* our family!"

I could not answer, or at least didn't feel like I should. I tried to do as the Prophet taught—teach correct principles and let the people govern themselves. Eventually, they will have to face their Maker and give an accounting, as will we. If desire to help and lack of selfishness are major criteria towards perfection, I have a feeling some of them may be much further along that path than others might think.

Another interesting custom was having grandparents do a major part of child rearing. Often a young couple would live with the grandparents, or the grandparents with them, and the division of responsibilities was such that the mother and father would work in the garden while the grandparents raised, taught, trained, played with, and disciplined the children. When I questioned such a situation one time, the grandmother involved told me she felt that when her daughter (the mother) was older and more experienced, she could do a better job of raising the children. She then caused me to think a lot when she asked, "What is my experience and life for if I can't help raise my grandchildren?"

There was deep respect for grandparents by grandchildren and deep love by grandparents for grandchildren. I suppose this came largely from the great amount of interaction they had; this interaction didn't seem to reduce the love and respect between parents and children either. There were lots of advantages to this extended family type of living.

The Church teaches the correct concepts that families are important and that families are forever. We need to do more than understand the concept—we need to practice the principles that allow the concept to become reality. We have heard the phrase: "the future belongs to those who are prepared." I have rephrased that to say, "the future belongs to those who are there." You don't have to look far to see which cultures are not keeping their families intact and thus not reproducing themselves to know what people are going "to be there" in future generations.

There were very few tourists in Ha'apai. But one day a tourist yacht came in for a few days. Several of the members asked me about a "poor lady" on the yacht who didn't have much protection from the sun and was obviously sick as she was lying on the deck of her boat when the sun was high with hardly any clothes on. They wondered what they could do to help her. I could not convince them that there actually were people in the world who *wanted* to lie out in the sun. It was inconceivable to them that anyone in their right mind would do so.

I guess to white people, getting darker or more tan seems more important than the risks. Despite my explanation, the Tongans still thought the lady must be crazy, or sick, or both. The Tongans try to protect themselves from the sun as much as possible. To them being lighter rather than darker is the preferred skin color. I have heard of Tongan parents having their children play in caves and under roofs all day so they would grow up with as little sun exposure as possible. I suppose most of us value that which we don't have and undervalue that which is common to us.

The Tongans were very class conscious, and everyone tried to make some connection to the king, the nobles, or others of high birth. While I was there, the feeling of loyalty to royalty was very deep and heartfelt. The queen was loved by all, and everyone had a reverence and an awe for the royal family that permeated nearly every aspect of life. The only negative I was aware of was when people believed in the true Church but couldn't quite pull themselves away from "the queen's church" out of loyalty to her. As hard as I tried, many people could not see the difference between loyalty to an earthly monarch and loyalty to a heavenly monarch. There was, and still is, religious freedom in Tonga and many people joined the Church when they obtained a testimony, regardless of peer pressure.

In the Tongan village, everyone seemed to know their role. If people were unhappy with their role, they seldom showed it. Everyone's role was respected, and each person had their "day in the sun." In our society, we respect those with wealth, training, or position, such as company presidents, doctors, or mayors, but in the Tongan village hierarchy, the *punaki* (most respected and talented poet, singer, choir director, dancer, or choreographer) was on top. They love a person with these talents, and if someone is good, he has no need to worry about food, clothes, or other necessities of life.

I remember once calling a man to be a branch president. He asked if the job of choir director was already filled. When I told him it was, he sighed and accepted the "lesser" calling as branch president. The Saints loved to sing in choirs, and it was not uncommon to have more people in attendance at choir practice after church than at sacrament meeting.

Choir competitions and festivals drew large crowds and were somewhat akin to sporting events in our society in terms of interest, participation, and so forth. The members sang the hymns almost exclusively from memory and with great force and feeling. There were no pianos or organs, and the perfect harmony of the congregation and choirs (which were virtually the same) helped me feel that I was listening to the most majestic sound on earth—that of a human pipe organ.

As an outsider and a missionary, I am not sure how the Tongans perceived me, but I felt I had their love and respect. All missionaries were looked up to. It put extra responsibility on us to be circumspect in all we did. One role I played in Ha'apai that I neither sought nor particularly liked was to calm down one of the perennial drunks. Most people couldn't afford liquor and were afraid of the side effects of bush beer and other cheaper forms of intoxicants, which occasionally caused blindness and other physical disabilities, including death. But there was one nonmember who seemed to have enough money and who drank to excess fairly often. For some reason, when he got "soused" he started wandering the streets and yelling loudly. This disturbed the people, and they asked me if I'd talk to him. When he was sober, I did talk to him, but made little headway, as he kept on drinking.

For some reason, the next time he got drunk, he started wandering the streets yelling *"Kolipoki, Kolipoki!"* I tried to ignore him as I felt I couldn't talk to a drunk and do much good, but eventually he got so loud that I went out and said, "I'm here, come on in!"

He came in, calmed down, and started to cry. We had a nice visit. I am not sure how much he understood, but he was quiet and soon went to sleep. The people were so happy (including his wife) that I automatically had a new role. When my being in town coincided with his drinking too much, maybe once every month or two, I had the responsibility of talking to my friend until he started crying and went to sleep. I am not sure what I learned or what good I did because things didn't seem to change much, but I felt okay about at least trying to help. The other villagers were grateful also.

# 56

## *My Ocean*

By now, I felt so at home with the people and the islands that I wrote to my family: "There are times as we ride the rolling seas that I feel I own this part of the ocean—own it in the sense that I can come and go at will and usually find the ocean cooperative. It is like a second home."

I had deep respect for the ocean and its various moods. Along with many others through the ages, I compared the ocean to a lady. I wrote home: "The sea is like a lovely lady—beautiful, mysterious, powerful, deep, moody, unpredictable, loving, helpful, and life-giving. I realize that at times both can be fierce and angry, and at other times soft and caressing. I love the ocean. I hope I will love my wife as much. I'm sure I will."

In Tongan the word *hala* means road or path, but it is incomplete by itself and needs to have a modifier, such as *hala uta* (path on land) or *hala tahi* (path on sea). I became convinced that many of those old captains were as sure where they were on their sea paths as we are on our land paths. The ocean is home to them and they develop a feel that is hard for us to comprehend. Let me give an example: I remember returning home from a long voyage in very contrary weather with heavy seas, strong winds, and a cloudy, rainy sky. We were out of sight of land all afternoon, all night, and into the next morning. I became a little concerned and asked the captain if he knew for sure where we were.

He looked at me rather quizzically and then gazed at the shape of the sun through the heavy clouds for some time, felt the wind as he moved his head slowly back and forth, then put one hand in the water while holding the rudder with the other hand. After several minutes, he withdrew his hand from the water, pointed partway across the sky and announced, "When the sun is there, the island of Lofanga will appear there."

His statement was strictly factual and nonemotional, and when he saw I accepted his word, he went back to concentrating on moving the sail and the rudder just so, feeling the currents, and intently watching the sky.

Several hours passed, but when the outline of the sun was right where he had pointed, the mists and shrouds seemed to lift and, almost like magic, the island of Lofanga *"na'e kite mai"* (appeared). It was as though it materialized out of nowhere to fulfill his words.

I looked at the island and then looked at the old captain. He just smiled and nodded and continued concentrating on the sky, wind, and current.

I marveled and thought, "We spend years going to school, getting an education in astronomy, weather forecasting, navigational engineering, or electronic maneuvering of various kinds, and then we say we *know* something. Yet encapsuled in this old man is more knowledge of celestial navigation than all the degrees the world can give." I realized that his eyes, his hands, his face to the wind, his sense of sight, sound, smell, and temperature were so refined that he knew exactly where we were and exactly how to set the sail, use the wind, and move the rudder to get us safely to our destination.

We arrived home that evening and I thanked the captain for the safe journey. I asked how he knew where we were. He talked of the warmth and strength of the currents, of sun and moon and stars, of the feel of wind and waves, but basically said, "I just knew." He couldn't really explain it to me, or maybe he knew I couldn't understand. I was glad I had "my captain" to take me over the sea paths of "my ocean."

I thought of how we honor our great scientists and engineers and mathematicians for their intelligence and understanding, yet that old man who had no degrees was more knowledgeable about currents and directions at sea than anyone I have ever known.

It was a sad day for me when he died just before I left Ha'apai. I have watched rather wistfully as his compatriots one-by-one have left this existence. I am unaware of any of that old group who are left. I imagine they are charting beautiful courses through the endless realms of space and eternity. I have the assurance that true knowledge gained here, especially that used to help others, is never lost and is ever useful.

I remember another time returning to Pangai when the winds completely quit on us and we just bobbed around for a couple of days. There were ten of us on the boat, it was hot, and we soon became very thirsty and hungry. One man had a fishline that he patiently dangled in the placid ocean hour after hour. In the afternoon of the second day, his line suddenly pulled tight and everyone jumped up with excitement, yelling encouragement. The fish ran with the line and it took a long time to bring him in as there was a lot of fight in this good-sized tuna. After a long time, the tired fish was brought alongside and several sets of strong hands quickly flipped it into the boat.

The men were so hungry and thirsty that rather than taking the time to properly kill and clean the fish, they gave him one hard knock on the head, which stunned him sufficiently to quiet his frantic flipping some, then they just started eating him raw. As the fish was passed from one man to another, someone mentioned that they should save some for me as I was probably hungry and thirsty too. I told them, "Just cut me off a piece and go ahead and finish him off." They gave me a nice piece, which I ate and enjoyed greatly. They continued eating the fish until there was nothing but bones left. I was not shocked or amazed, just interested. As I watched this process and saw the smiles on their faces, I remember thinking how nice it was that they could catch the fish and get some nourishment, and how wonderfully well man, nature, and the ocean could work together. That evening a good wind came up and we were in Pangai by early the next morning.

I remember that one of my counselors always brought a rectangular sealed can with him on our journeys. It was about nine inches square and twelve inches deep. I asked what it was and he told me to never mind. After a while I forgot about it until on a particular voyage I noticed him hiding the tin can, and I insisted on knowing what it was. He finally showed me a letter in English that was ingeniously sealed to the side of the can. I read the letter and found that the can was a hermetically sealed tin containing a temple burial outfit in which to dress any American Elder who died of disease or other causes and had to be buried in Ha'apai.

I was aware of some Elders who had died in Ha'apai, as our branch kept up their grave sites. I asked if he knew what to do if anything happened to me. He replied that he could not read English, but

*Typical sailboat coming into the calm harbor of Pangai from the outer islands.*

he knew he would know what to do if the occasion arose. I asked if he had ever dressed anyone before, and he said, "No." I asked again how he would know what to do and he gave me that look of "Why do you always wonder about such things? The Lord will tell me through an angel or some other means. Why do you *palangis* always worry about such silly details?"

It was a constant learning experience to see the degree of faith these wonderful people had. I was comforted when he smiled at me and said, "Don't worry. You won't die here. I know that. You have much work yet to perform." I wasn't sure whether he was speaking qualitatively and meant I had much more to learn now and he needed to teach me better, or whether he was speaking quantitatively. I hoped he meant both.

After the temple was dedicated in New Zealand, many Tongans went there and temple clothing became more available, so the need for these hermetically sealed tins became less and less and I doubt they even exist there now.

There were times when I didn't want to go on the boat, especially when the winds and the seas were boisterous, but except in the worst situations, we went anyway. There were other times when I rode those beautiful silver seas, felt the breeze filling the sails and powering us forward, sensed the rising and falling of the solid, curved wood beneath me, listened to the whistling of the wind, marveled at the many beautiful shades of blue and green and white all about me, and realized I was falling in love with the sea. To me, at that time, it really was "my ocean."

# 57

## *Letters Home*

Even though I was busy, I felt impelled to write regular letters to my family and loved ones.

How grateful I am to my mother, who retyped and saved all these letters. I include a few selected samples, written mostly toward the end of my mission.

"Pangai, Lifuka, Tonga.

"I think that being able to have your plans thwarted and not letting it upset you is a mark of maturity. I think that this mission has matured me in a lot of ways, although I don't say that I have learned to take disappointments as I know I must learn to take them.

"I often wonder if I'll let delay frustrate me anymore, but I suppose as soon as I get back into the fast swing of things at home, I'll probably be upset by delays.

"Already most of the mission seems like just a dream, especially that year up on Niuatoputapu. There is more meaning to that year than any of us will ever realize, I am sure."

"Pangai, Ha'apai.

"One of the reasons a mission is such a happy time is because by its very nature it requires one to seek out only the good in others and this makes one happy all of the time. Seeing good in others and trying to develop those qualities of goodness, and trying to take the bad things from one's own life so that one can become a good example to the people—these are the elements of happiness. Anyone can be happy under any set of conditions, if only he makes up his mind to be. Before I learned the Tongan language, I felt that was the key to happiness in the Tongan mission. When I learned the language, I found the degree of happiness that went along with that particular accomplishment, but that was not the key to happiness. The key to happiness is to serve others.

"We all seek happiness in this world, and I am sure that there are many thousands of volumes written upon it and many years of totaled lectures on it. But still, above all, the real elements are: to 'love the Lord with all your heart and to love your neighbor as yourself.' Nothing else can be said, no more elaboration given. That is the summation of it all. If we want to be happy, we must make up our minds to be happy, and we will if we have lots of love in our hearts."

"Pangai, Ha'apai, Tonga.

"Many of the missionaries have been sick. I myself have been touched a time or two—nothing serious, but enough to make me realize the value of good health. I hope that you don't worry about me. All is well. I appreciate Dad's blessing before I left for this mission. If we could all keep our spiritual health and our physical health up to top peak by constant exercise, we would indeed be much happier. I hope we make enough time to be friendly and kind and considerate of those who do not have good health, either physical or spiritual. We do need to visit and help the sick and the afflicted in spirit or body. I am grateful for the good example of Mom and Dad."

"Pangai, Tonga.

"I hope I can always remember the great lessons I have learned from these wonderful people. Their humility and faith are wonderful. I have learned to love them and have had to humble myself among them to do so. The Lord has been with me in these adjustments, and He will help me adjust to home. The Tongan language is a part of me. I appreciate more and more the various languages and their place in the world. The language of love is the most important language of all. If one learns that language, he can speak to every heart. Love is the only lasting thing in the world. When everything else is done, our value might be summed up by 'how much did he love?' Love is deeper than we know. I think that by being kind and considerate and never being angry or cross, we can keep love more of the time. I'm sure anger drives love from our hearts. Cross words and bad tempers check and starve the seeds of love within us. Love, trust, and sacrifice for others are the greatest forces in the world. Love is shown by how much we are willing to deny ourselves for the good of others, how much we are willing to go through that others might benefit. We need lots more of it. When all else is done, they will only remember, 'How much did he love us?' When all else is done, we will only remember how much one loved us. The Savior set the example; it's deeper than I know, but I hope it goes to its full depth of meaning as I say 'I love you all.'"

"Pangai, Lifuka, Ha'apai, Tonga.
"To all of my loved ones at home, I just want you to be assured that that great bond of love, which will always tie us, is felt by me here, way off in the uttermost bounds of the earth. Also, there is another love in my very soul now. A love for a people, a love for a culture, a love for a way of life, a love for a language—a beautiful language that is as much a native tongue to me as the tongue I spoke as an infant. It is the tongue which I began to speak as an infant, a spiritual infant, and the tongue with which I have grown up from the infancy state in spiritual things to maybe, possibly, just a little above the infancy state in those great spiritual things of life. A love for songs, a love for nature, a love for the sea—the sea with all of its enchantments, the sea with its overpowering influence on men, the sea with its mysteries urging men on to greater things, inspiring some of the greatest poets to pen words which, though deep in meaning, scarcely begin to fathom the depths of the source of their inspiration. I am among my loved ones here as well as back in America. Here is my second home, my second language, my second love."

"Ha'apai, Tonga.
"I would sum up the Savior's words in Matthew 5:43–48 as follows: 'It is said of old to love those who love you but despise your enemies, but I say unto you, love everyone.' Thus, all limits were taken from this great fountain of love; whether any limits existed or if they were only in the clouded minds of the men of those days is beside the point, but now the new law had been given. That was it, the new commandment, 'Thou shalt love.' Love with all of your hearts. Love God and His children, wherever they might be and however they might treat you. How you are treated is of little consequence; the important thing is to learn to love everyone. Can we really love sinners?

It seems to me that that is one of the requirements for our eternal progression. If we expect to be where the Gods are today, and they have love for all mankind—sinners as well as Saints—then certainly if we aspire to such a height, we must learn to love sinners as well as Saints, dark-skinned people as well as white, foreign tongues as well as our own native tongues."

"Ha'apai, Tonga.

"If God is love (which He is) and if the purpose of life is to become more like Him (which it is), then the greatest blessings in life are the opportunities to develop more godlike love.

"God must dearly love women as He gave them the sacred power to bear and rear children. Doing so develops more love than almost anything I am aware of. In one sense, I suppose God gave men the priesthood as partial compensation, so if they use it properly it can help them become the servants of all and thus have a better chance of developing the love needed for eternal life.

"I suppose both men and women can prostitute their sacred God-given opportunities to develop love and use them for selfish purposes, but they will never have the power of God with them if they do so. Only as they use His powers according to His will can He bless and magnify them.

"I occasionally hear people talking about roles and arguing about authority, and sense anger in some people's hearts over this. I feel that Satan has really put one over on those people by diverting their attention from concentrating on that which brings love (and thus is important) to concentrating on worldly position (which is not important) and thus stirring them up to anger one against another (3 Nephi 11:29), and blinding them from His stated purpose to help us become characters full of love."

"Pangai, Ha'apai, Tonga.

We do not develop love with anger or jealousy or selfishness or unrighteous dominion, or in trying to second guess God and His ways—we only develop it in serving (loving) others with all of our hearts. To love God with all of our hearts, and our fellowman as ourselves, has always been and will always be not only the best way but the only way for achieving the love we need to eventually enter the celestial kingdom.

"The principle seems so simple: when we do selfish things, we become selfish people. When we do unselfish things, we become unselfish people. Satan tempts us to do selfish things; God tries to help us do unselfish things. The Church, the ordinances, the covenants, motherhood, priesthood, and our callings are all calculated to develop deep love as the very essence of our beings. We need God's help to do so.

"We all need the strength and saving grace of the Savior's atoning sacrifice in our life. It is the ultimate in love. We simply can't have sufficient love in our lives without it. It is always available and always needed, but we must recognize that need in our individual lives before we are able to allow Him to be the central part of our lives He needs to be to help us 'change our hearts' to hearts full of love."

"Pangai, Ha'apai, Tonga.

"If there were any eternal value to earthly wealth or position or title or income or physical beauty or prowess, then God would be a partial God, which He specifically says He is not. But there is no value to these things.

"What then is the common denominator that covers all men and all women over all time and all circumstances? The amount of love they choose to develop in their hearts! Everyone is on equal footing to achieve that, to whatever degree they desire. All they need to do is first love God with all their hearts, minds, and souls, and then move on to its earthly expression by loving their neighbor as themselves (see Matthew 22:35–40).

"It is interesting to me that Jesus was talking about how to love as the prelude to His great command or request to be perfect" (see Matthew 5:48).

I thought I had learned a few things since my mission, but in rereading these letters I'm not so sure. Maybe I've forgotten as much of real value as I have learned over the ensuing years.

I do know we need to have more love in our hearts for all people. I am grateful for the Tongan people in helping me understand this great truth better.

# 58

## *Islands upon Islands*

While never a huge number, baptisms in Ha'apai continued to increase each month. I didn't think about going home but I knew it would happen someday. About this time, my mission president wrote and asked how I would feel about staying on my mission a few months longer. I enthusiastically replied that nothing could please me more. He wrote back and said he felt it would be good if I could stay and help take the first group of Tongan Saints to the New Zealand Temple, which was to be dedicated in about a year. He said he would write to the authorities in Salt Lake City and make the request for me to stay. I assumed this extension would be granted, so I adjusted myself psychologically to that end. I even wrote a few letters home explaining what the mission president and I hoped would happen, even though I knew it was not for sure.

You can imagine my shock and amazement when two months later I received a telegram from my mission president saying: *Request for extension denied. Stop. You must report to your draft board within two months. Stop. The SS* Tofua *leaves Nuku'alofa in one week. Stop. Be in Nuku'alofa at least one day before this. Stop. If you agree I propose [Elder X] as the new district president. Stop. Send reply including return costs and details soon. Stop.*

I was stunned, and I left the telegraph office shaking my head. Telegrams were supposed to be private, but whoever thought that didn't know Tonga or Tongans! The word spread like wildfire, and I was inundated with all types of responses—disbelief, love, tears, congratulations, requests for feasts, desire for details, and, I'm sure, relief on the part of some.

I thought, *Elder X as district president? What a joke! I'm glad the president asked my opinion. I'll let him know right away. But maybe I'd better find a boat going to Tonga first and save one telegram. Leaving Ha'apai? How can that be?*

A feeling of melancholy came over me. Part of it was the suddenness of the announcement, especially when I had been so ready and anxious to stay longer, but part of it also was the realization that this was final. It was hard to realize that my mission to Tonga was actually going to end. I shuddered as I thought that I would soon have to *leave* these people, these islands, this language. How could I leave the wind, the seas, the sails, the school, the Saints, the children, the love, the faith, the challenges, and the testimonies—all that seemed important and precious to me?

It took me a day or two to come to grips with the fact that I must not wonder any longer but rather be obedient and move on with the rest of my life. For several days, however, each time I thought I had faced the facts, I seemed to relapse, move back into the protection of the familiar, and try to put off the unknown future.

I started inquiring about boats going to Tongatapu and found there were none readily available. I asked everyone but was told they had all either just left or just returned, and no trips were planned in the near future. There seemed to be no way to get to Tongatapu. *Maybe this is my answer,* I thought. I would never be openly disobedient, but if I didn't show up because there was no boat, that was a different matter! My fleeting hope lasted but a few minutes as I realized if worst came to worst, I could press some of the good Saints into taking me to Tongatapu in our old mission sailboat. It was leaking badly, and the sails and ropes were in terrible shape, but if we had to, I knew the Lord would bless us with a safe trip.

I talked to the best captain I knew and was surprised when he said it would not be wise to even think of taking the mission sailboat. "That boat is in very bad condition, and we should not tempt the Lord when we know things are bad and we have other alternatives," he told me.

"What other alternatives?"

"Have you been to Ha'ano? There is a good boat there."

I was running out of time and we had to get a boat, so he agreed to take me to Ha'ano to check on a better boat to Tongatapu. That last voyage for me in the old mission sailboat was very nostalgic as well as revealing. We had a good wind and made excellent time to Ha'ano. We also had to expend enormous amounts of effort to keep the water bailed out. I was convinced the old sailboat would not reach Tonga-tapu in the shape it was in.

At Ha'ano, I spoke to the captain and owner of the only sailboat available. The word of my pending departure had already reached Ha'ano, and he knew I had to get to Tongatapu in the next few days. He was not a member and was poor, as most everyone in Ha'apai was, so he drove a hard bargain. It is difficult to negotiate when others have the upper hand. We reached some compromises, such as making the voyage a charter and giving me the right to collect and keep any money from passages or freight space sold. Still, when we finally shook hands, I felt I was paying far too high a price. But as I could see no alternative, I decided not to press for more but rather to leave the captain feeling good to help ensure his coming.

He agreed to be in Pangai in two days and get us to Tongatapu before the fourth day was up, which would be the day before the SS *Tofua* sailed. The wind continued fair and brisk, and we made good time back home. Even so, when we arrived in Pangai harbor, we had several rips in our sail, a couple of extra knots in our ropes, and a large amount of bilge in the bottom of the boat. I thought, "It's good we are not testing the Lord by trying to take this boat to Tongatapu."

When we returned to Pangai, there was another telegram from the mission president stating: *Send approval and plans now. Stop. You must be here in four days. Stop. Passage on* Tofua *secured. Stop.* I was embarrassed to tell the president how much it was going to cost us to get to Tongatapu—£40 (nearly $200). I was also concerned about how to tell him my true feelings about Elder X being district president. I decided to pray about it again and send a telegram the next morning.

With all the feasts and farewell parties, and heart-tugging visits from many friends, I realized I would not be able to do all I wanted to do and spend any time sleeping. I thought, "Well, I can sleep on the boat down," so I started that evening packing, praying, thinking, and visiting with people around the clock.

One group would come, then another, then another, then a timid knock, and a schoolchild and her family with some bananas and a pineapple, with a desire to visit for a while. "We're going to be baptized, you know," the parents said. "As soon as our daughter goes to Liahona, we will go to Tongatapu and be baptized. Thanks for teaching our daughter. Thanks for getting her into Liahona. Thanks for teaching us the gospel." On and on went the visits. Before the night was over, I had more food than I could eat in weeks. But no matter, it represented love and appreciation, and that never spoils.

I was now down to two days left in Ha'apai, with the third to get to Tongatapu. Just before sunrise, I dozed for an hour or so. I knew I must send a telegram to the mission president that morning, but was still unsure of what to say. I had prayed sincerely about my feelings, but I felt uncomfortable counseling my mission president.

When I woke that morning, I experienced one of those wonderful, warm feelings that we all have from time to time. I felt words and thoughts coursing through my soul in an unexplainably beautiful symphony: "Listen. This is not your work, it is my work. I will see that it moves forward. Support your leaders. Support your mission president with all your heart. Do not worry about the charter fee. It will be returned. Be obedient. Be supportive. Be loving. Be kind. Be forgiving. Be diligent. Bless these people. It is my work. You can help, but do not worry. It is my work." It was not a voice or a revelation, but a beautiful, peaceful feeling.

I ran to the telegraph office and fired off the following message to the mission president: *Elder X will be great as district president. Stop. Wire £40 for boat charter. Stop. It will be returned. Stop. Will arrive Nuku'alofa Thursday evening ready for* Tofua *passage on Friday. Elder Groberg.*

I immediately made arrangements for Elder X, who was working on another island, to come to Pangai. I went through the school schedule with him and introduced him to my two counselors, whom he would use at least until the mission president came to Ha'apai and made the official change. I would be gone, but that didn't matter. I took him to meet the postmaster, the telegraph man, the governor, and everyone in between. I was happy because I knew things would be all right.

The boat from Ha'ano arrived. It was small but sturdy, and it had strong canvas sails, new ropes, and a solid hull. What a pleasure to ride in such a boat! The sea and the wind were about normal, but even so, we knew we would have to leave before noon the next day to ensure making it to Nuku'alofa by afternoon or evening of the following day in order to catch the *Tofua* the next day.

Since there had been no boats going to Tongatapu for a while, I was able to sell quite a few passages and had contracted to take a fair amount of freight. Sailboats always travel better when they have some weight in them as opposed to being too light on the water, so the captain was happy.

I made arrangements for people to load their things that day, and we agreed with the captain to leave shortly before noon the next day. As people paid for their passages and their freight, I stuffed the money into a small bag I had and didn't bother to count it then.

I now had only twenty-four hours left in Ha'apai. What could I do? What should I do? I had turned as much as I could over to Elder X. I had very little to pack as I gave most everything away, keeping only a bare minimum to get home. I made a few visits, attended several more farewell feasts, and met with and encouraged several investigators and wayward members. By this time I was so tired I could hardly keep my eyes open, so in the early afternoon—after another feast—I crawled into the back of a member's house and slept for a couple of hours.

When I awoke, I went back to my home. Some members had a big *kava* ceremony going in the central room, and I joined them for a few hours. Some of the missionary schoolteachers had written a farewell song for me, which they sang beautifully (a translation is on page 285). It talked of a white bird that flew away but eventually returned. There were lots of tears. People kept coming and going for most of the night. Finally, at what I would judge to be about 2:00 A.M., I excused myself and went for a walk alone on the beach.

The moon was full and the seashore alternated between softly lit and rather dark as the clouds moved by, obscuring the moon for long periods of time and only temporarily allowing it to shine forth in its fullness. A soft, warm breeze was blowing, which gently lifted and lowered the coconut palms, and occasionally whipped them with a quick, strong breath. The sand was warm, and the whole scene was conducive to every emotion basic to man. I reflected, "I am actually leaving Ha'apai. When the moon, the wind, and the clouds play out their nightly act and the sun again takes control and sends the moon away, and disperses the soft mantle of coolness that fills this night, then I will leave Ha'apai. When the sun sends forth its searching rays and causes reality to reign again, I will get in a boat, wave good-bye, and soon drop below the horizon until I can see Ha'apai no more." I accepted these thoughts, but at the same time I fought them.

For a few more hours I could stay in this wonderful world of softness, moonlight, and shadows, and be alone with my thoughts and feelings. I could think, pray, and ponder, and try to understand my swirling emotions.

For some time I had been bothered by the fact that I had only physically gotten to sixteen of Ha'apai's seventeen inhabited islands. The instruction to leave came so quickly and unexpectedly that a trip to that last island had to be cancelled. I felt bad. I felt I had failed in that area. I had not made it to all seventeen islands, even though I had

Translating a Tongan poem or song into English is very difficult if not impossible. Many Tongan symbols have such deep background meaning that it would take a paragraph in English to begin to get the feel of just a few symbolic words in Tongan. Two Tongans who speak English well attempted to translate the song into English. This is their best effort:

*Siu'e Tavake*

As the soft wind from the north begins to blow, we stand, our hearts full with the secret of it all. The fragrance of your spirit lingers in the isles. We feel deep in our hearts your feelings as you take leave, and we try to understand.

You came across the great waters, sending forth the light of truth in these islands. You gave us the true understanding of God and us as His children, set the standard, and raised us above the common man.

You were called by the prophet, and everything in you went out to us. You have finished your work in a blaze of glory, but as the old Tongans say: "When one gives his whole self to others, he becomes a part of them and a shadow of the future."

Through you we have seen the work of the Master Sculptor. We have done many things wrong, but always you have smiled, showing us that to have that precious inner burning we must love others, smile at them, and hold to the rock of truth.

Your being here has been as a beautiful dream. Like a vision of a cloud in the west that is crying. Our hearts are full and weeping as you leave. The flowers blooming about us are bare. The plentiful fish are meaningless, for you are gone.

CHORUS

Like the legend of the dove, it was here, it is gone, but it will return. There is a higher power that rules—you came to us, you must leave, but you will return. We of the islands must prepare and keep on as you have taught us, so we may be ready for your return and for His also. Only those who overcome will inherit the kingdom.

been district president for nearly a year and a half. "I should have made it," I thought. "How could God be happy with me? How could I be happy with myself? I have missed visiting one island in my charge."

I began to feel worse and worse. All the good feelings and farewells became somewhat muted, or held in abeyance, as I fretted over part of an assignment unfulfilled. I could tell that powerful forces, almost beyond my control, were working on my emotions. Why had I not gone to that last island? I prayed for forgiveness. I prayed for understanding. I knew it was no excuse, but I pleaded, *I intended to visit there, only I was cut short. Was it really my fault?* I reasoned. *Of course it was. Don't try to make up excuses; you didn't do your full duty.*

The battle between light and dark, peace and disturbance, good feelings and bad feelings, raged on. *I must have some peace,* I thought. *I can't leave feeling this way. I have felt so good up to now. Why at this last hour have I been shown my failures? Why such focus on one island? Oh, why didn't I go there?*

I poured out my soul for peace. I had tried, and I would have made it had others not made decisions over which I had no control. What should I do? I pleaded for understanding through bitter tears of remorse.

Then, quietly, a soft covering of peace began to enter my heart. It increased in clarity and intensity until suddenly, like a light turning on, a new and overpowering force took over and dispersed everything else. I felt a voice in my heart that said, "Look." I opened my eyes and looked out across the beautiful, sandy seashore, out across the vast, open expanse of magnificent, rolling ocean. I could see very clearly the outline of the one island I had not been to. I recognized it without question. That same warm feeling I had experienced a few days before returned, and the voices in my mind and the visions of my soul continued.

I watched as another island rose behind the first, then another behind it, and another, and another, each larger and grander than the one before. I found myself marveling and saying, "Islands upon islands arise."

The voice in my mind went on, "Yes. Islands upon islands arise, and more. Look."

I looked again and saw more islands and behind them grander scenes, even worlds rising in splendor. I felt the words, "Worlds upon worlds arise, and more."

I was totally caught up in the whole experience. The feelings or words of my mind continued: "The physical goal of visiting all seventeen islands is not the most important. Had you accomplished that goal, there are more beyond it. What is important is following the Spirit, obeying, loving, serving, blessing, teaching, healing, testifying, and explaining that God is over all, that He is all-powerful, all-loving, all-kind, that Jesus is the Savior of the world, that Joseph Smith is the Prophet of this last dispensation, and that living prophets and priesthood authority are on the earth today. With these things in place, it matters not the number of islands, worlds, or universes, for these truths are eternal and control all islands and worlds and more."

I was satisfied. While I know that much more will be required of all of us, I am confident one of the greatest feelings we can experience in this life is to know that God is pleased with our efforts. Nothing can compare to that. We should strive to know that our efforts are acceptable and that faith, love, testimony, and proper actions will always bring eternal blessings. What more could anyone desire?

I also learned another great lesson. I knew I could have done better and was painfully aware of my faults. But a kind Father in Heaven allowed me to leave with good memories and a feeling of approbation for the things I had accomplished rather than a feeling of self-incrimination for the things I had not accomplished. I knew I must do better and accomplish more, and I was determined to do so. But in it all I sensed a shadow of things to come in the total forgiveness and acceptance I felt. I understood that as I dealt with others, especially family and friends, I needed to give much less criticism for failures and much more praise for accomplishments. It is God's way. I knew that.

This reverie must have occupied the balance of the night because I soon found the sun was, in fact, chasing the moon away. The day of my departure had arrived. I returned to my home, gathered what few things I had, and put them on the boat. There were lots of people at the wharf—some going with us, others sending things, and many gathering to say good-bye.

I cannot describe those last hours of embraces, tears, and deep feelings—feelings of unparalleled joy, of certainty, of blessings, and of deep understanding. It is simply beyond mortal description.

The boat finally left. There were songs, tears, and waves of good-bye; heartfelt sobs; and testimonies of assurance that we would meet again sometime, somewhere, somehow. I knew it to be true. I knew that meeting our loved ones—sometime, somewhere—is inevitable for all of us. And while the time of the meeting itself is largely beyond our control, the feelings we will have at that meeting are largely within our control. If we have been faithful, it will be a glorious meeting, but if we have not been faithful, it will not be as glorious as it could be. I knew and loved those faithful Tongan people and knew that these, my brethren and sisters, were faithful and would remain so. What an incentive that is to remain true! I determined again to be faithful always. I hoped I was ready for the next step.

I knew for sure that the most important thing in life is to remain faithful to God and His cause so that when we meet our loved ones, we can experience the same type of joy I was feeling then, only in its fullness. I knew that if we remained faithful, we would have a glorious reunion and know even more surely that islands upon islands and more will arise—forever!

# 59

## *The Trip Back*

I had been awake almost constantly for the last several days and nights and was so physically and emotionally drained that shortly after leaving Pangai harbor and getting into the open ocean, I collapsed into a deep sleep. I slept for most of that day and evening and some of the next day.

Of course, I was up from time to time, especially as we had our evening and morning devotionals, but the feeling of an overpowering tiredness was hard to shake. When you are tired, night and day tend to blend together, and rest, not the hour, is what seems important.

During the night I woke several times and visited with the captain, as was my custom on long voyages. He was a good man and a skilled mariner. I never mentioned the steep price he had charged me to charter the boat but sensed he felt a little uneasy. I did not talk about it but rather asked about him, his family, and his future. When he could tell I was interested in him and not in asking for a refund, he relaxed some, and we had some good visits. We talked about God, the wind, the ocean, the currents; about families; about the price of *copra;* about gardens and boats; about the Church and priesthood authority; and many other things.

After visiting with the captain for a while, I lay down and slept until there was a sudden shift of wind, or an unexpected movement, or a heavy wave that crashed against our boat—then I got up and visited with the captain some more. Generally it was a smooth voyage, and I slept most of the time.

Years later I ran into an older man at a stake conference in Tonga.

He asked if I remembered him. He looked familiar, but I wasn't sure. He then explained that he was the captain who had charged too much for the boat from Pangai to Nuku'alofa. I remembered then. He went on to say that it always bothered him that he had taken advantage of a missionary in need. As he put it, "It especially bothered me that you didn't fuss more. But when I realized you were interested in me and in returning good for evil, I determined I would someday investigate the Church. It took me many years to do so, but eventually I did. My wife and I have been sealed in the temple. I'm now a high priest and served for some time on the high council. Thanks for not getting angry with me." The fact is, I was upset at the time but was glad I hadn't shown it or that the Spirit had prompted me not to do any more on the matter at that time.

In the early afternoon of the next day, I was awakened and told that Tongatapu was in sight and we should arrive by midafternoon, well within the time I had promised my mission president. Before we landed, I opened the bag and counted the money I had received. I checked the list of passengers and freight to make sure everyone had paid. They had. When I totaled up the money received, it came to £54-10-6, nearly £15 more than the charter price of the boat! I marveled and reflected on the feeling I had received and on the telegram I had sent to the mission president saying that he would get his money back. It may seem like a small thing, but considering the circumstances of the time, to me it was a true miracle.

As we slowly pulled into the harbor at Nuku'alofa, I could not express my gratitude sufficiently to God for the safe trip, the timely arrival, and the fulfilling of impressions. I tried again to express adequate appreciation for the incalculably precious experience of being a missionary in His service, of knowing and feeling His power and goodness, of knowing of the love and mercy of the Savior. Those deeper-than-life feelings of gratitude recurred over and over again and came from so deep within me that when we finally landed, I found myself again emotionally and physically drained and almost as weak as when we left Ha'apai.

The mission president was at a wharf to meet us as some members had spotted us coming in and informed him. Nearby the SS *Tofua* was in port also. What a gigantic ship it was compared to our tiny sailboat! *But,* I thought, *it won't get us to our destination any more safely than our solid sailboat.* I thought of the long voyages of the ancient Polynesians and realized again that they were every bit as skilled as our modern engineers, boatbuilders, or captains.

The first thing I did was give the mission president the £54-10-6 and told him that this was his £40 back, plus the Lord's increase. I told him to do what he wanted with the extra, except to not even think of giving it to me or the captain. He smiled and replied, "Are you a mindreader also?" We laughed, and he put the money in his pocket. Then we went to the mission home for a final interview.

In those days missionaries were released in the field by the mission president, so after a very special interview the mission president handed me my release certificate along with my ticket on the SS *Tofua* to New Zealand via Vava'u; Niue; Pago Pago, Samoa; Apia, Samoa; and Suva, Fiji.

I thanked him for all he had done to help me. I realized that probably the biggest help he had given me was his trust. I felt deeply that he was a good man. I loved and respected him and told him so. Feki had gone on a building assignment to another island, so I stayed that evening at the mission home.

There was a huge crowd at the wharf the next morning as I boarded the *Tofua*. I couldn't figure it out because I knew hardly anyone on Tongatapu. When I was told that Prince Tungi and Princess Mata'aho were taking the same boat, I understood. I joked with the mission president about the great send-off he had arranged. Everything seemed to be in order, and soon we were on our way.

The mission president asked me to speak at some meetings in Vava'u and Niue on the way to New Zealand. It was a pleasure to do so. I also enjoyed the company of the prince and the princess on the voyage. One evening, the sea got very rough; little by little everyone left the dining area until Prince Tungi and I were the only two left. For some reason, I was not feeling sick, nor was the prince. We talked, laughed, and even played the piano for a long time. The prince is a good piano player, and I still remembered a few numbers even though I hadn't touched a piano for nearly three years. Playing that piano, which was heavily chained down in the turbulent sea, was like trying to ride a bucking bronco. We had a fun time as we visited, laughed, and tried to hit the right notes. Eventually we also retired.

My father had sent a telegram saying he would meet me in New Zealand at the conclusion of my mission. When we arrived in Suva, Fiji, I had a cablegram from him saying he was in Nadi and would be flying from there to Auckland, New Zealand. The boat was to spend the day in Suva, so I quickly called the International Airport in Nadi, which is on the opposite side of the island. I explained my situation and wondered if there was any way my father could come to Suva and we could go together to New Zealand on the *Tofua,* or if I could go to Nadi and fly with him to New Zealand.

The Air New Zealand people were most helpful and said they would check and let me know. Later I received word from them that Dad had already flown to New Zealand the evening before. They told me, however, that if I wanted they would honor my steamship ticket, and I could fly to New Zealand that night and save two or three days' travel time. I decided to do that. I knew the airfare was more than the boat fare, but when I got on the large Air New Zealand plane and found myself the one and only passenger, I could see why they took my steamship ticket so eagerly!

I arrived in New Zealand the next morning and took a taxi to the mission home. It was winter in the southern hemisphere, and I was very cold. However, meeting my father was such a warm experience that the cold didn't seem to bother. Dad's grandparents were converted and baptized in Christchurch, New Zealand, and immigrated to the United States in the late 1870s. They were the only members of their family to join the Church, so we still had lots of relatives in New Zealand.

It was fun looking up and visiting family members, none of whom were yet members of the Church. We had some great discussions and gathered a lot of genealogical and family history information. We visited some cemeteries and made arrangements for more appropriate headstones and had many wonderful and heartwarming experiences. There is a special feeling about visiting graves of ancestors in distant lands. You feel a kinship or linkage that is hard to express.

After a while in New Zealand, we flew to Australia, and Dad proposed that we fly home through India, the Middle East, and Europe. I had enjoyed doing family history work in New Zealand, but the prospects of being a tourist or just seeing things held no special appeal for me. I was beginning to feel tired and just wanted to get home. I was also anxious to see Jean again.

I explained to Dad my appreciation for his thoughtfulness, but said that if he felt okay about it, I would like to catch the next plane straight back to the United States. I explained that I would like to go back to Idaho Falls, settle down, and just stay there and never travel anywhere ever again. He smiled knowingly and said it was a good desire, but things would probably turn out different from that. He graciously accepted my request and made the necessary arrangements. So after refueling stops on Canton Island and Hawaii, we landed in Los Angeles two days later.

# 60

## *The Next Step*

What a humming, churning place Los Angeles was! Even though I had been in New Zealand, Australia, and Hawaii for a few days each, I was still terrified by so many people, cars, and such fast movements by everyone and everything. The English language seemed strange as well, but it was mostly the pale color of people and the rapid movements and fast pace of everything that made me feel uncomfortable.

We had several relatives in the Los Angeles area and went to visit some of them. When we got to my aunt's house and had access to a phone, the first thing I did was call Jean. We had a nice conversation. I asked what she was doing that evening. She said she was going to Mutual and asked if I would like to come. "Sure," I responded, "I'll see you this evening." I thought I still remembered how to get to her house.

Dad and I visited some other people, and when the sun started to get low in the sky, I told him I had promised Jean I would meet her in North Hollywood and go to Mutual with her.

"What time is Mutual?" he asked.

"7:30 P.M. How long does it take to get there?"

"It doesn't take long, but do you know what *time* it is?"

"No. I don't have a watch, but the sun is low, so it must be around 6:00 P.M."

"We are in the northern hemisphere now," he responded. "It's nearly 9:00 P.M.!"

I could have fainted. My first promise to Jean, and I had broken it terribly! I asked if we could go to North Hollywood anyway, which we did.

By the time we arrived in North Hollywood, Mutual was long over, but Jean was waiting at her home. It was wonderful to talk to her again! Even after three years' absence, there was a comfortableness in being with Jean that felt good. Since it was late, we arranged to meet and visit the next day. I promised I would buy or borrow a watch and not miss the next appointment. I apologized to Jean for making her wait so long for me, which, as things have turned out, may have been an omen of things to come.

The next day, Dad said he had other things to do, so I could take the car and drive to North Hollywood and return when I was through. I was petrified, as I had not driven a car for three years and was scared to death to do so again, especially on those crazy Los Angeles freeways! It is hard to understand, but when you have not been around cars and have only walked, ridden horses, or been on sailboats for three years, the speed and power of cars is a very scary thing. However, my desire to see Jean eventually overcame my fear of driving, and I braved the freeways and arrived in North Hollywood safely and on time. We spent most of the day visiting, going places, walking, talking, and just enjoying being with each other. That evening when I returned to my aunt's home, Dad asked how things had gone. "Great," I said, "I've decided I will marry Jean."

"Oh, that's interesting. What does she say?"

"Well, we haven't talked about that yet, but I'm sure it will be fine with her." (How arrogant men can be at times!)

Dad told me I shouldn't take things for granted or assume things I didn't know for sure. I couldn't say much as I knew he was right. But the fact was, I did know for sure.

Dad and I left the next day for Idaho Falls, and Jean and I agreed to continue writing. We arrived home to a tumultuous reception of parents, brothers, sisters, relatives, friends, and neighbors. It was great to be home! The sacrament meeting schedule in our ward was full for several weeks, so my welcome home was put off for about a month. I enjoyed being home for a few days, but soon wanted to go back to North Hollywood. My parents agreed, so I left by train for Los Angeles.

As I rode down, I wondered what I should do. I knew that giving a diamond engagement ring was traditional, but I also knew I had no money, so I would have to think of an alternative. I couldn't come up with anything profound, so I decided the only thing to do was tell the truth. I would simply tell Jean that I loved her, that I wanted to marry her, and that I didn't have anything to give her except my love and my life.

I won't go into detail, but Jean carefully and prayerfully considered my proposal, and after receiving her own confirmation she accepted. That evening we looked into the heavens together, chose a star to reach for, and committed ourselves to each other and to the Lord for eternity.

We spent a few days working on plans and schedules and went to Anaheim and cancelled her teaching contract for that fall. Jean's father was tied up with a special aeronautical defense contract and his first open date was 6 September. The Los Angeles Temple was open then, so that was to be our place and date of marriage.

I should emphasize that this was not a spur-of-the-moment decision. Jean and I had been friends for five years. We had dated for two years at college and corresponded for another three years during my mission, so while we had not previously spoken openly about marriage, we knew each other's feelings pretty well.

We had an engagement announcement party at which I was able to meet many of Jean's friends. We did lots of visiting and planning, but mostly we just enjoyed one another's company.

I returned to Idaho Falls to work and get ready for my homecoming talk, our marriage, and school. I asked Jean to come to my homecoming meeting. I don't suppose too many missionaries introduce their fiancée to the ward at their homecoming, but I sure did.

We picked out a pair of inexpensive wedding bands (it was eleven years and six children later before I gave Jean a diamond).

Jean went through the Idaho Falls Temple, met a lot of my family and friends, then returned to North Hollywood to complete marriage preparations with her family. Not long after, I left with my parents for Los Angeles and our big day in the temple on 6 September.

I remember the day well. It was beautiful in Los Angeles. I arrived at the temple early with my folks. I noted the beauty of the temple, the trees, the grass, the flowers, and the sky. But they all paled to nothingness compared to the beauty of my Queen Jean when she drove up with her parents and stepped out of the car. We went into the temple arm in arm. I thought I was the luckiest and happiest man alive. I sensed that Jean felt good also.

The ceremony was short, sweet, and powerful. President Bowring was wonderful, and the words, promises, and meanings of that perfect ceremony were literally out of this world. There were many relatives and friends in attendance. We all had a meal together at the temple cafeteria after the ceremony. It was a wonderful time!

When we left the temple, I took Jean to her parents' car and told her I needed to run some errands and rent some clothes for the reception, so I would go with my folks and she could go with hers and I would see her that evening at the cultural hall in North Hollywood. It never dawned on me that from her point of view I was sort of abandoning her, at least temporarily, right after we were married! I don't know exactly what she thought, but she just smiled beautifully and said, "Okay. See you soon."

I picked up the rental suit, got my suitcase, borrowed some money from Dad, and asked if I could use the car for a few days. Mom and Dad were very supportive. We drove to Jean's home in North Hollywood and almost immediately went to the ward cultural hall for a reception. It was a wonderful evening of visiting with many friends and relatives. The best part, however, was being with Jean.

After the reception, we went to Jean's home to pack and change. Her father kept asking about where we were going on our honeymoon. I hadn't even thought about that. I was still not in a mode of doing too much planning ahead. I guess I was still remembering that a small change in the wind, or a slight tear in the sail, or a leak in the boat could make hours or even days of difference in arrival or departure times, so why bother about detailed schedules or specifics. They were just a dream and a waste of time.

Her father asked me again, and it finally dawned on me that it was late, I was *married* to Jean, and our suitcases were in the car, so we really should have someplace to go! I had a general plan, but no specifics. It was hard to bring these two worlds together. I finally explained that I really hadn't thought of where to go. Jean probably assumed I had everything worked out and would surprise her with the details. I finally told her father, "I guess we will just drive down the freeway and see what happens." He looked horrified. I suppose he wondered if I was kidding or just dumb or what. When I could see his concern, I asked if he had any suggestions.

When he realized I seriously had no specific plans, he asked me to "wait right there." His nonmember neighbors had a nice beach bungalow down on Lido Isle in Balboa Beach. I don't know what arrangements he made, but soon he came back with a set of keys, a map, and some directions. I was most appreciative.

We finally bade good-bye to everyone and left in the car. As we drove down the freeway towards Orange County, thoughts of all kinds went through my mind. I remembered some of the feelings of three years ago when I was a missionary in Orange County, and many of the names on the freeway signs began to look familiar. The freeways weren't so crowded at night, and in the moonlight I almost felt like I had my hand on a boat tiller and was sailing down a beautiful silver sea path with a perfect breeze behind me filling the sails—only this was better, as I had my beautiful wife beside me. I hoped we could just keep sailing forever and ever and ever. I tried to tell Jean those feelings but found the English language was inadequate to do so.

Finally Jean said, "We need to take the next exit." I was in a dream world back in my beloved islands. I didn't want to turn off the freeway, now or ever, or do anything to break the reverie. But Jean insisted we had to turn right here or we couldn't get to the bungalow. "Crazy details," I thought, "always interfering with that which is important!" I turned off and followed Jean's directions. Soon we arrived at a lovely bungalow.

Every couple's honeymoon is private and personal. All I can say is, it was wonderful. We spent some blissful days at Balboa Beach, then drove to Idaho Falls for another reception, and then back to Provo, where I was registered for school. We went to the temples in St. George, Manti, and Logan on the way coming and going. Everything was beautiful. I had Jean by my side. What else could anyone want!

Even though my focus was on Jean and on school now, I often thought of Tonga and the lessons I had learned there. I remember saying I would not take a million dollars for my experiences there, nor would I go through them again for a million dollars. I realized that Tonga, its language, its people, and missionary work was one world, and being in the United States, speaking English, attending school, being married, and working for a living was another world. I had a difficult time reconciling these two worlds but knew I must. I could see parallels all around me, and I began to realize that there were two distinct worlds right in Provo and everywhere—spiritual and temporal—forever things and not forever things. I knew you could never equate inner peace and understanding, or spiritual power and assurance, with popularity, glitz, learning, money, or anything else limited to this world. I knew that peace comes from doing right and that the only power that is real comes from obeying God, who gives the power to love, help, and serve.

I thought again of what a wonderful blessing a mission is! What an opportunity to serve, and, by serving, learn to love and come closer to God! Serving, then, is the key. What a blessing to be given a calling to serve!

I finally realized that marriage and family is a mission and thus an opportunity to love, serve, and come closer to God. It was still hard to work for money or study for position, but I knew I had to get on with my life; as long as I had the proper attitude and did the right thing, my mission would never end. That was a good thought. I felt that in reality all of life is a mission, an opportunity to love and serve God through loving and serving others. I felt I could accept that and move ahead.

I knew I would never forget Tonga, but I was determined to put myself just as fully into my marriage, family, and future opportunities to serve as I had in my mission.

I realized I was no more prepared for marriage or family than I had been for my mission. Both of them carried responsibilities far beyond my abilities. But I also knew that God had given me the strength and protection and understanding needed to see me through my mission responsibilities so I was confident He would give me the strength, protection, and understanding needed to see me through my marriage and family responsibilities.

I could tell from talking to others and listening to their comments that I was perceived as being a bit of a "plunger," one who just moved ahead without what some might perceive as proper planning. I hoped I was not jumping in too soon. I didn't feel I was. I have always related to Nephi when he said in 1 Nephi 4:6: "And I was led by the Spirit, not knowing beforehand the things which I should do."

I thought it through, and was very much at peace in my heart and mind. Along with other notations, I made the following journal entry: "I have started the next phase of missionary work. I'm sure I'll enjoy it. On September 6, 1957, I married Jean Sabin in the Los Angeles Temple and we have begun the process of living happily ever after."

The next step had begun.

# Glossary

auhangamea (the destroyer of things)
faifekau (preacher, minister, missionary)
faifono (reading of the new laws)
fakahua (tacking maneuver, shifting sails, used mainly when going
    into the wind)
fale (house)
fanga ko paluki (Pangai harbor)
fangota (fishing or digging for shellfish in the reef area)
fau ( a rope-like substance used for straining kava)
Ha'apai veu (Ha'apai in turmoil)
hala tahi (path on sea)
hala uta (path on land)
hamu (non-animal source of food)
kai tunu (cookout)
kainga (extended family)
kaitu'u (to eat while standing)
kape (big tuberous plants weighing up to eighty pounds apiece)
kava (pepper root-type drink)
kiki (animal source of food)
ko ia (that's it)
koe maama 'e (there is the light)
Kolipoki (Elder Groberg)
kumala (a tuber similar to sweet potatoes)
kuo moho 'ae toupai? (is the pudding done?)
lafa lafa (barge)

laka laka (line dancing)
loloto (deep spot)
lu (spinach-like greens)
ma pakupaku (dried biscuits)
mataka (copra board)
matapule (chief)
mili mili (rubbing or massaging)
moho (baked well)
ngoue fakafaifekau (a piece of land given either to the Church or to
    the missionaries)
oku ou'ife? (where am I?)
palangi (a white person)
pea na'e hoko o pehe (and it came to pass)
peito (separate kitchen house)
po malanga (evening cottage meeting)
pola (woven coconut leaf)
pule fakakolo (town officer)
pule fakavahe (district officer)
Punaki (most respected and talented poet, singer, choir director,
    dancer, or choreographer)
pusiaki (like adoption)
saliote (horse-drawn cart)
seilo, seilo (a boat is coming)
ta'eaonga (useless)
tahi kula (red tide)
taimi kai (time to eat)
talo (taro root)
tangi lau lau (mourning for the dead)
ta'ovola (a woven sash)
tapa (a coarse cloth made from pounded bark)
te'eki ai (not yet)
toe taha atu (a little farther from me)
toe taha mai (a little closer to me)
toupai (pudding)
tuku ia (stop it)
tupenu (large piece of cloth)
ufi (a large potato-like tuber)
umu (meal cooked in earth oven)
vala (skirt)

# HA'APAI GROUP

Ofolanga

Mo'unga'one

Hā'ano

Ha'āno

Pukotala

Kao

Faleloa

Fotua   Lotofoa

Niniva

Fanfale'ounga   Foa

Koulo

Fotuha'a

PANGAI   Lifuka

Hihifo

Tofua

Lofanga

Uoleva

'Uiha

Felemea   'Uiha

'Auhangamea

Kotu

Ha'afeva

Uonuku

Matuku

LULUNGA

Tungua   'O'ua

Nomuka

Fonoifua

Nomukaiki   Mango

Telekitonga

N

W   E

Kelefesia

S

0   5   10   15
KILOMETERS